STUDIO PAPERBACK

Philip Johnson

Peter Blake

Birkhäuser Verlag
Basel · Berlin · Boston

Diese Publikation wurde durch die Graham Foundation for
Advanced Studies in the Fine Arts, Chicago unterstützt./
This book was aided by a grant from the Graham Foundation
for Advanced Studies in the Fine Arts, Chicago.

Büro Johnson, Ritchie & Fiore/Office Johnson, Ritchie & Fiore:
Redaktion und Archiv/Co-editor and archivist:
Christian Bjone
Redaktionelle Mitarbeit/Contributing editor:
Aaron McDonald
Architekturzeichnungen/Architectural drawings:
Philip Schwarz, Ian Weisse
Assistenz/Assistant:
Franca Giammarino

Übersetzung aus dem Amerikanischen/
Translation into German:
Karin Bruckner: Projekttexte/Project texts
Nora von Mühlendahl: Einleitung und Nachwort/
Introduction and Postscript

Umschlag/Cover:
Pennzoil Place, Houston

Abbildung Seite 2/Illustration page 2:
Philip Johnson 1996 mit Modell der Skulptur «Turning Point»,
Case Western University, Cleveland
Philip Johnson 1996 with model of Turning Point Sculpture
for Case Western University, Cleveland

Library of Congress Cataloging-in-Publication Data

A CIP catalogue record for this book is available from the
Library of Congress, Washington D.C., USA.

Die Deutsche Bibliothek – CIP-Einheitsaufnahme

Blake, Peter:
Philip Johnson / Peter Blake. [Transl. into German: Karin Bruckner ;
Nora von Mühlendahl]. - Basel ; Berlin ; Boston : Birkhäuser, 1996
    (Studiopaperback)
    ISBN 3-7643-5393-7 (Basel ...)
    ISBN 0-8176-5393-7 (Boston)

© 1996 Birkhäuser – Verlag für Architektur, P.O.Box 133,
CH-4010 Basel, Switzerland
Printed on acid-free paper produced from chlorine-free pulp. TCF ∞
Layout/Page layout: Miriam Bussmann, Basel
Printed in Germany

ISBN 3-7643-5393-7
ISBN 0-8179-5393-7

9 8 7 6 5 4 3 2 1

Inhalt

ARTS

NA
737
J6 B55
1996

(handwritten)

Contents

9   Einleitung

Bauten

26   Ash Street Haus, Cambridge
29   Scheune auf der Townsend Farm, New London
30   Haus Farney, Sagaponack
32   Glashaus, New Canaan
40   Anbau Museum of Modern Art, New York
43   Rockefeller Gästehaus, New York
46   Haus Hodgson, New Canaan
48   Haus Oneto, Irvington
50   Schlumberger Verwaltungsgebäude, Ridgefield
52   Innenräume Gästehaus, New Canaan
54   Skulpturengarten des Museum of Modern Art, New York
58   Haus Wiley, New Canaan
60   Haus Davis, Wayzata
62   Haus Boissonnas, New Canaan
65   Kneses Tifereth Israel Synagoge, Port Chester
68   Haus Leonhardt, Lloyd's Neck
70   St. Thomas Universität, Houston
72   Asia House, New York
74   Four Seasons Restaurant, New York
78   Munson-Williams-Proctor-Institut, Utica
80   Nuklearforschungsreaktor, Rehovot
82   Kirche ohne Dach, New Harmony
84   Amon Carter Museum of Western Art, Fort Worth
86   Pavillon am Teich, New Canaan
88   Museum für präkolumbische Kunst, Dumbarton Oaks
92   Sheldon Memorial Kunstgalerie, Lincoln
94   Haus Boissonnas II, Cap Bénat
96   Museum of Modern Art Ostflügel, New York
98   New York State Theater am Lincoln Center, New York
101   New York State Pavillon, New York
103   Haus Beck, Dallas
105   Haus Geier, Indian Hills
106   Gemäldegalerie, New Canaan
108   Henry Moses Forschungsinstitut, Bronx
110   Kline Biologiegebäude der Yale Universität, New Haven
113   Haus Kreeger, Washington

9   Introduction

Buildings

26   Ash Street House, Cambridge
29   Townsend Farms Barn, New London
30   Farney House, Sagaponack
32   Glass House, New Canaan
40   Museum of Modern Art Annex, New York
43   Rockefeller Guest House, New York
46   Hodgson House, New Canaan
48   Oneto House, Irvington
50   Schlumberger Administration Building, Ridgefield
52   Guest House Interior, New Canaan
54   Sculpture Garden at the Museum of Modern Art, New York
58   Wiley House, New Canaan
60   Davis House, Wayzata
62   Boissonnas House, New Canaan
65   Kneses Tifereth Israel Synagogue, Port Chester
68   Leonhardt House, Lloyd's Neck
70   University of St. Thomas, Houston
72   Asia House, New York
74   Four Seasons Restaurant, New York
78   Munson-Williams-Proctor Institute, Utica
80   Research Nuclear Reactor, Rehovot
82   Roofless Church, New Harmony
84   Amon Carter Museum of Western Art, Fort Worth
86   Pavilion at Pond, New Canaan
88   Museum for Pre-Columbian Art, Dumbarton Oaks
92   Sheldon Memorial Art Gallery, Lincoln
94   Boissonnas House II, Cap Bénat
96   Museum of Modern Art East Wing, New York
98   New York State Theater at Lincoln Center, New York
101   New York State Pavilion, New York
103   Beck House, Dallas
105   Geier House, Indian Hills
106   Painting Gallery, New Canaan
108   Henry Moses Institute, Bronx
110   Kline Biology Towe at Yale University, New Haven
113   Kreeger House, Washington

114	Kunsthalle, Bielefeld		114	Art Gallery, Bielefeld
116	John F. Kennedy Gedenkstätte, Dallas		116	John F. Kennedy Memorial, Dallas
117	Skulpturengalerie, New Canaan		117	Sculpture Gallery, New Canaan
121	Albert und Vera List Kunstinstitut der Brown Universität, Providence		121	Albert and Vera List Art Building at Brown University, Providence
123	Kunstmuseum für das südliche Texas, Corpus Christi		123	Art Museum of South Texas, Corpus Christi
127	Elmer Holmes Bobst-Bibliothek der New York Universität, New York		127	Elmer Holmes Bobst Library at New York University, New York
129	Kevorkian-Studienzentrum für den Nahen Osten, New York		129	Kevorkian Center for Near Eastern Studies, New York
130	IDS Center, Minneapolis		130	IDS Center, Minneapolis
134	Stadtbibliothek, Boston		134	Boston Public Library, Boston
138	Messezentrum, Niagara Falls		138	Convention Center, Niagara Falls
140	Wassergarten, Fort Worth		140	Water Garden, Fort Worth
143	Post Oak Central, Houston		143	Post Oak Central, Houston
145	Innenausbau Avery Fisher Hall, New York		145	Avery Fisher Hall Interior, New York
147	Pennzoil Place, Houston		147	Pennzoil Place, Houston
151	Thanksgiving Square, Dallas		151	Thanksgiving Square, Dallas
154	Zentrum der Schönen Künste am Muhlenberg College, Allentown		154	Fine Arts Center at Muhlenberg College, Allentown
156	Fassade 1001 Fifth Avenue, New York		156	1001 Fifth Avenue Facade, New York
158	Fassade Marshall Field & Co., Houston		158	Marshall Field & Co. Facade, Houston
160	Kristallkathedrale, Garden Grove		160	Crystal Cathedral, Garden Grove
164	Glockenturm, Garden Grove		164	Bell Tower, Garden Grove
165	Studierklause und Bibliothek, New Canaan		165	Library Study, New Canaan
167	101 California Street, San Francisco		167	101 California Street, San Francisco
170	Transco Tower, Houston		170	Transco Tower, Houston
174	Neues Schauspielhaus, Cleveland		174	The New Cleveland Playhouse, Cleveland
176	PPG Hauptsitz, Pittsburgh		176	PPG Headquarters, Pittsburgh
180	Republic Bank Center, Houston		180	Republic Bank Center, Houston
186	53rd at Third-Lipstick Building, New York		186	53rd at Third-Lipstick Building, New York
190	Dade County Kulturzentrum, Miami		190	Dade County Cultural Center, Miami
192	AT&T Hauptsitz, New York		192	AT&T Headquarters, New York
196	580 California Street, San Francisco		196	580 California Street, San Francisco
198	Geisterhaus, New Canaan		198	Ghost House, New Canaan
200	Lincoln Kirstein Turm, New Canaan		200	Lincoln Kirstein Tower, New Canaan
202	500 Boylston Street, Boston		202	500 Boylston Street, Boston
206	Architekturfakultät, Houston		206	School of Architecture, Houston
210	190 South LaSalle Street, Chicago		210	190 South LaSalle Street, Chicago
213	One Atlantic Center, Atlanta		213	One Atlantic Center, Atlanta
216	One and Two International Place am Fort Hill Square, Boston		216	One and Two International Place at Fort Hill Square, Boston
218	191 Peachtree Tower, Atlanta		218	191 Peachtree Tower, Atlanta
220	Kanadisches Rundfunk- und Fernsehzentrum, Toronto		220	Canadian Broadcasting Center, Toronto
222	Wissenschaftsbibliothek der Ohio State Universität, Columbus		222	Ohio State University Science Library, Columbus
224	Rundfunkmuseum, New York		224	Museum of Broadcasting, New York
226	Puerta de Europa, Madrid		226	Puerta de Europa, Madrid
228	Torhaus, New Canaan		228	Gate House, New Canaan

232 Bürgerhaus, Celebration

234 Millenia Walk Einkaufszentrum, Singapur

236 Das Business Center am Checkpoint Charlie, Berlin

238 Kapelle des Heiligen Basilius an der St. Thomas Universität, Houston

241 Nachwort

246 Biographie

247 Werkverzeichnis

253 Bibliographie

254 Bildnachweis

232 Town Hall, Celebration

234 Millenia Walk, Singapore

236 Das Business Center, Berlin

238 St. Basil Chapel at University of St. Thomas, Houston

241 Postscript

246 Biography

247 List of Built Work

253 Bibliography

254 Illustration Credits

Einleitung

Introduction

Vor vielen Jahren begegnete ich einem angesehenen Philosophen, mit dessen Kindern ich befreundet war. Trotz der Tatsache, daß er deutlich älter war als wir alle, war er so lebhaft und voll von überraschenden Ideen, daß wir ihn viel interessanter fanden als die meisten unserer Altersgenossen.

Eines Tages, als ich mich von seiner Gegenwart nicht mehr eingeschüchtert fühlte, fragte ich ihn, welchen Umständen er seine erstaunliche Jugendlichkeit zuschrieb. «Ich werde dir mein Geheimnis verraten», sagte er. «Hin und wieder spiele ich so etwas wie ein Spiel – ich stelle mir vor, daß alles, wovon ich jemals überzeugt war, tatsächlich gar nicht wahr sei; daß das genaue Gegenteil wahr ist. In den meisten Fällen ist das Ergebnis natürlich absoluter Unsinn. Aber manchmal eröffnet es einige sehr interessante, neue Perspektiven.» Ab und an pflegte der alte Herr seine neuen Einsichten an uns zu testen, und wir waren – wie vorherzusehen – schockiert, begeistert, amüsiert und stets erstaunt – aber niemals gelangweilt.

Ich kenne Philip Johnson seit etwa fünfzig Jahren, und in all dieser Zeit hat er mich (wie die meisten seiner Freunde) in zunehmend häufigeren Abständen schockiert, begeistert, amüsiert und erstaunt. Aber er hat niemals einen von uns gelangweilt. Erzürnt, ja, aber niemals gelangweilt.

Johnson wurde am 8. Juli 1906 in Cleveland/Ohio in eine wohlhabende Familie geboren, deren Vorfahren etwa 250 Jahre zuvor in die Neue Welt eingewandert waren. Er studierte an der Harvard University Geschichte und Philosophie und machte nach einigen Unterbrechungen dort seinen Abschluß in Philosophie. Mit verschiedenen Freunden, unter anderen dem Architekturhistoriker Henry-Russell Hitchcock Jr., unternahm er mehrere ausgedehnte Reisen nach Westeuropa. Als Johnson in Europa war, nahm sein Interesse an der Architektur zu – nicht etwa nur an der modernen, sondern auch an der Architektur früherer Zeiten und Stätten: Er besichtigte den Parthenon, Chartres, Paris, Rom, Berlin, London, Kairo und alle sonstigen Orte, die Hitchcock und andere ihm empfahlen (und lernte fließend deutsch und französisch sprechen). In einem Aufsatz von Hitchcock las er von einem jungen, aufstrebenden modernen europäischen Architekten, dem Holländer J.J.P. Oud, und besuchte diesen, sah verschie-

A great many years ago, I met a distinguished philosopher whose children were friends of mine. Despite the fact that he was obviously a great deal older than the rest of us, he was so lively and so full of surprising ideas that all of us found him much more interesting than we found most of our contemporaries.

One day, after I had ceased being overawed by his presence, I asked him to what he ascribed his remarkable youthfulness. «I'll let you in on my secret,» he said. «Every so often, I play a kind of game – I assume that everything I have ever believed was, in fact, not true at all; that the exact opposite was true. Most of the time, of course, the result is utter nonsense. But sometimes it opens up some very interesting new perspectives.» Now and then, the old gentleman would try out his new insights on the rest of us; and we were, predictable, shocked, charmed, amused, and always amazed. And never, ever bored.

I have known Philip Johnson for about fifty years, and during that time he has shocked, charmed, amused and amazed me (and most of his other friends) at increasingly frequent intervals. And he has never, ever bored any of us. Infuriated, yes; but never bored.

Johnson was born in Cleveland, Ohio, on July 8, 1906, to a well-to-do family whose ancestors had arrived in the new world some 250 years earlier. He went to Harvard, where he studied History and Philosophy, and graduated in 1930, after several interruptions, with a degree in Philosophy. There had been a series of extended trips to Western Europe with various friends, including the architectural historian Henry-Russell Hitchcock, Jr. And while in Europe, Johnson became increasingly interested in architecture – not only modern architecture, by any means, but the architecture of many earlier times and places as well: he visited the Parthenon, Chartres, Paris, Rome, Berlin, London, Cairo and every other site recommended by Hitchcock and others. (He became fluent in German and French.) He read an essay by Hitchcock on one of the new, emerging modern European architects, the Dutchman J.J.P. Oud, and went to meet Oud, saw several of his buildings, and was greatly impressed. Unlike most of his contemporaries among young, American intellectuals, Johnson became quite «Europeanized» at an early age.

dene seiner Bauten und war tief beeindruckt. Im Gegensatz zu den meisten seiner Altersgenossen unter den jungen amerikanischen Intellektuellen wurde Johnson bereits in jungen Jahren völlig «europäisiert».

Während seiner Jahre in Harvard lernte Johnson eine Anzahl von Studenten und jungen Absolventen kennen, die eine Art Vereinigung gegründet hatten, welche sie Harvard Society for Contemporary Art nannten. Zu diesen gehörten Lincoln Kirstein und Edward Warburg – Männer, die später zu bedeutenden Förderern der Künste und Museums-Kuratoren wurden. Nach dem Besuch einer von der Vereinigung in Cambridge veranstalteten Ausstellung traf Johnson einen etwas älteren Harvard-Absolventen namens Alfred H. Barr Jr., der damals Vorlesungen über moderne Kunst am Wellesley College hielt. Barr schlug Johnson vor, sein Interesse an der modernen Architektur zu vertiefen – was dieser dann auch tat. Bis heute ist Johnson Barr dafür dankbar, daß er ihn anleitete und ermutigte, sich auf diesen speziellen Bereich zu konzentrieren.

Als Barr 1929 zum ersten Direktor des New Yorker Museum of Modern Art ernannt wurde, erhielt Johnson die Position des Leiters der Abteilung für Architektur und Design am MoMA. Zwar hatte er in Harvard seinen Universitätsabschluß in Philosophie erworben, aber keine weiteren akademischen Zeugnisse. Alles was er hatte, waren ein außergewöhnlich scharfer Blick und eine enorme Neugier gegenüber allen Fragen der bildenden Künste. Und natürlich hatte er eine Reihe von Freunden, die ihm den richtigen Weg wiesen.

Eine der ersten von Philip Johnson arrangierten Ausstellungen war eine kleine, aber radikale Veranstaltung mit dem Titel «Rejected Architects» («Abgelehnte Architekten»), die in einem Laden an der Ecke 57. Straße und der Seventh Avenue gezeigt wurde. Die Ausstellung wurde als Reaktion auf die jährliche Präsentation der Architectural League von New York veranstaltet, die, wie vorherzusehen, eine Anzahl konventioneller Bauten in modischer historischer Manier ausgewählt hatte – und fast ein Dutzend «moderner» Bauwerke von derzeit als gefährlich radikal bezeichneten Architekten abgelehnt hatte. (Die Ausstellung der Architectural League wäre etwa fünfzig Jahre später «politisch» oder «ideologisch richtig» gewesen und hätte anläßlich einer solchen Gelegenheit höchstwahrscheinlich mehrere Bauten von Philip Johnson enthalten! Aber dies waren die radikalen dreißiger Jahre, und Johnson war einer ihrer engagiertesten Verfechter ...)

Die Schau der «abgelehnten Architekten» wurde von einem Beitrag Philip Johnsons eingeführt, der kaum präziser sein konnte: «Der Internationale Stil hat wenig gemeinsam mit den kapriziösen und unlogischen Bauwer-

During his years at Harvard, Johnson came to know a number of students and recent graduates who had formed something they called the Harvard Society for Contemporary Art. Among them were Lincoln Kirstein and Edward Warburg – men who would later become important patrons and curators of the arts. After looking at an exhibition staged by this Society in Cambridge, Johnson met a somewhat older Harvard graduate called Alfred H. Barr, Jr., who was then teaching courses on modern art at Wellesley College; and Barr suggested that Johnson should pursue his interest in modern architecture – which he proceeded to do. To this day, he credits Barr with having guided and encouraged him to concentrate on this particular area.

When Barr became the New York Museum of Art's first Director, in 1929, Johnson became MoMA's Director of the Department of Architecture and Design. He had his Harvard degree in Philosophy, but no other formal, academic credentials. All he did have was an extraordinary eye or two, and an enormous curiosity about all aspects of the visual arts. And, of course, he had a couple of friends who steered him in the right directions.

One of the first exhibitions arranged by Philip Johnson was a small but radical effort entitled «Rejected Architects», and shown in a store front at the corner of 57th Street and Seventh Avenue, opposite Carnegie Hall. The exhibition was mounted in response to an annual show at the Architectural League of New York, which had selected a number of predictably conventional buildings done in a fashionable, historicist manner – and rejected close to a dozen «modern» structures by architects then considered dangerously radical. (The Architectural League's show would have been «Politically» or «Ideologically Correct» some fifty years later; and it would, in all likelihood, have contained several buildings by Philip Johnson himself on such an occasion! But these were the Radical Thirties, and Johnson was one of their most articulate advocates...)

The «Rejected Architects» show was introduced with a text by Johnson that could hardly have been more precise: «The International Style has little in common with the capricious and illogical work of the ‹modernistic› architects who have recently won such popularity in America,» the text proclaimed. «The ‹Rejected Architects›, all of them under thirty years of age, work in the International Style,» the text continued. «Some of them have worked with Mies or Le Corbusier.» It went on to define the «International Style» as follows: «Design depends primarily on function ... (it) takes advantage of new principles of construction and new materials such as concrete,

ken der ‹modernistischen› Architekten, die in letzter Zeit eine derartige Popularität in Amerika erreicht haben», erklärte der Text und fuhr fort: «Die ‹abgelehnten Architekten›, alle im Alter von unter dreißig Jahren, arbeiten im Internationalen Stil. Einige von ihnen waren bei Mies oder Le Corbusier tätig.» Im weiteren Verlauf definierte er den «Internationalen Stil» wie folgt: «Gestaltung hängt in erster Linie von der Funktion ab...,(sie) nutzt die Vorzüge neuer Konstruktionsprinzipien und neuer Materialien wie Beton, Stahl und Glas ...» Das hätte genügt, um den Philip Johnson des AT&T Building von 1979 in seiner postmodernen Manier erschauern zu lassen!

Es war für ihre Zeit eine beachtliche kleine Ausstellung, die Arbeiten von Modernisten wie Oscar Stonorov, William Muschenheim, Claus & Daub sowie anderer von der Architectural League zu Beginn der dreißiger Jahre «abgelehnter» Architekten enthielt. Während Johnson eindeutig die in dieser Schau vorgestellten Prinzipien vertrat, war er sich bestimmt der Tatsache bewußt, daß die meisten der «Abgelehnten» sich schwertaten, mit einem «Stil» identifiziert zu werden – sie waren schließlich Funktionalisten! Und er war sich auch der Tatsache bewußt, daß einige seiner eigenen Avantgardistenfreunde den Begriff «Internationaler Stil» für eine unglückliche Fehlbenennung hielten, nur geprägt zur Besänftigung der mit dem neuen MoMA verbundenen wohlhabenden Kunstförderer – denen es gefallen mochte, in Zusammenhang mit einem neuen Stil gebracht zu werden, die aber durch gewisse linkslastige, von der Bauhauslehre geprägte Begriffe verunsichert worden wären.

Auf die Ausstellung «Rejected Architects» folgte ein Jahr später die weit berühmter gewordene Ausstellung im MoMA mit dem Titel «Modern Architecture – International Exhibition». Diese Schau wurde im Hecksher Building an der Fifth Avenue und der 56. Straße eröffnet und war nur sechs Wochen an diesem Ort zu sehen. Obgleich sie damals als Wanderausstellung in mehr als ein Dutzend Städte ging und ausführlich in Publikums- wie in Fachzeitschriften besprochen wurde, scheint ihr Einfluß im Laufe der Jahre eher noch an Bedeutung zugenommen zu haben: in der Tat hat Terence´Riley, der heutige Leiter der Abteilung für Architektur und Design am MoMA, 1992 die «International Exhibition» in der Buell Hall der Columbia University sozusagen buchstäblich wiedererweckt und eine ausgezeichnete Neuauflage des Originalkatalogs veröffentlicht, ergänzt durch historische Anmerkungen. Kurz gesagt, sogar sechzig Jahre nach dem Ereignis wird die große Ausstellung von 1932 noch als Meilenstein in der Entwicklung der modernen Architektur in Amerika betrachtet.

steel and glass ...» Enough to make the Philip Johnson of 1979 AT&T Building shudder in his post-modern mode.

It was a remarkable little show for its day and contained work by such International Stylists as Oscar Stonorov, William Muschenheim, Claus & Daub, and others «rejected» by the Architectural League in the early 1930s. While Johnson clearly believed in the principles laid down in this show, he was surely aware of the fact that most of the «rejected ones» squirmed at being identified with a «style» – they were functionalists, after all! And he was aware of the fact that some of his own, fellow avant-gardists thought the term «International Style» was an unfortunate misnomer, coined to assuage the wealthy art patrons associated with the new MoMA – patrons who might be pleased to be associated with a new style, but who would have been unsettled by some of the left wing notions implied by Bauhaus dogma.

The «Rejected Architects» show was followed a year later by the much more famous exhibition, at MoMA, entitled «Modern Architecture – International Exhibition.» That show opened in the Hecksher Building, at Fifth Avenue and 56th Street, and remained on view in that location for a mere six weeks. Although it moved on to more than a dozen cities as a traveling exhibition, and was widely reviewed in popular as well as professional publications, its impact seems to have grown in significance over the years: in fact, as recently as 1992, Terence Riley, now the Director of MoMA's Department of Architecture and Design, resurrected the «International Exhibition» verbatim, as it were, at Columbia University's Buell Hall, and published an excellent new edition of the original catalogue, complete with historic annotations. In short, even sixty years after the fact, the great 1932 exhibition is considered a landmark in the development of modern architecture in America.

Those responsible for the exhibition, which was planned over a period of more than two years, certainly considered it a landmark, although no one could have predicted its enormous impact. The exact chronology of the exhibition – who said what, when first, or ever – is difficult to nail down at this late date; but the leading triumvirate clearly consisted of Alfred Barr, Henry-Russell Hitchcock and Philip Johnson, in no particular order. Lewis Mumford became significantly involved when the triumvirate was looking for someone to tackle the social and political aspects of the new movement, and nobody in the triumvirate was very passionately concerned about any of this, or especially well informed. Mumford was suggested for this task and his contributions on modern housing and city planning were essential, particularly in defusing any sugges-

Die Veranstalter dieser Ausstellung, die über einen Zeitraum von mehr als zwei Jahren geplant wurde, betrachteten sie gewiß als einen Meilenstein, obgleich niemand ihren ungeheuren Einfluß voraussehen konnte. Ihre exakte Chronologie – wer was, wann zuerst oder überhaupt sagte – ist nach diesen vielen Jahren schwer auszumachen; aber das leitende Triumvirat bestand eindeutig aus Alfred Barr, Henry-Russell Hitchcock und Philip Johnson, in keiner bestimmten Rangordnung. Lewis Mumford wurde entscheidend beteiligt, als das Triumvirat nach jemandem suchte, der die sozialen und politischen Aspekte der neuen Bewegung behandeln sollte, an denen keiner von den dreien großes Interesse zeigte oder besonders gut darüber informiert war. Mumford wurde vorgeschlagen, und seine Beiträge über modernen Wohnungsbau und Stadtplanung waren wichtig, vor allem weil sie jegliche Vorwürfe entschärften, daß die Ausstellung des MoMA lediglich eine elitäre Übung in Ästhetik darstelle.

Dennoch war der eindrucksvollste Aspekt der Ausstellung ganz offenkundig die Architektur, welche sie zur Schau stellte. Sie zollte Frank Lloyd Wright großen Tribut, dessen Frühwerk im Vergleich zu den Bauten anderer mehr als nur ein wenig altmodisch wirkte. (Es handelte sich um Bauten aus der Zeit vor Johnson Wax, vor Falling Water und vor vielem, vielem anderen.) Sie zeigte eine beeindruckende Menge Arbeiten von Le Corbusier, Gropius und Oud und vor allem von Mies – Mies' gebaute und ungebaute frühe Projekte, seinen Barcelona-Pavillon und sein Haus Tugendhat in Brünn in der Tschechoslowakei. Kein anderes Werk in der Ausstellung war so selbstsicher, so glatt, so zeitlos modern.

Außer dieser Vorstellung der Meisterwerke gab es eine etwas weniger eindrucksvolle Darstellung des Werkes von Richard Neutra, Howe & Lescaze und mehreren anderen Amerikanern, die in der Rückschau weniger avantgardistisch erscheinen, als es vermutlich im Jahre 1932 den Anschein hatte. Alles in allem wurden annähernd einhundert Fotos, Zeichnungen und Modelle in den Räumen gezeigt – die meisten von ausgeführten Bauten, aber einige auch von theoretischen Projekten (einschließlich mehrerer, die niemals realisiert wurden). Es war 1932 eine eindrucksvolle Ausstellung, die sechzig Jahre später fast noch stärker beeindruckte, derweil verschiedene modische «Ismen» ihre seltsamen Häupter außerhalb der Museumstüren erhoben. Die Ausstellung von 1992 war übrigens viel kleiner in den Ausmaßen als das Original von 1932, das aus riesigen Vergrößerungen der Fotos und Zeichnungen bestand. In der Buell Hall der Columbia University war einfach nicht genug Platz dafür...

Rückblickend läßt sich sagen, daß die Ausstellung von 1932 vermutlich für die moderne Architektur in Amerika

tions that the MoMA show was solely an elitist exercise in aesthetics.

Still, the most impressive aspect of the exhibition was, quite obviously, the architectural work it displayed. There was a massive tribute to Frank Lloyd Wright, whose early work looked more than a little old-fashioned by comparison with the work of others in the show (this was pre-Johnson Wax, pre-Falling Water, and pre-much, much more!); there was an impressive display of the work of Le Corbusier, Gropius and Oud; and then there was Mies – Mies's early projects, built as well as unbuilt, and his Barcelona Pavilion and his Tugendhat House in Brno, Czechoslovakia. Nothing in the exhibition was so self-assured, so polished, so timelessly modern.

In addition to this display of the masterpieces, there was a somewhat less impressive display of work by Richard Neutra, Howe & Lescaze, and several other Americans who seem less avant-gardist in retrospect than they probably did in 1932. All in all, there were close to one hundred photographs, drawings, and models on display in the galleries – most of them of completed buildings, and a few of theoretical projects (including several that were never realized). It was an impressive exhibition in 1932, and it was even more impressive sixty years later, while various fashionable «isms» were raising their funny heads outside the gallery's doors. The 1992 exhibit, incidentally, was much smaller in actual size than the 1932 original, which consisted of huge enlargements of photographs and drawings. There just wasn't enough room in Columbia's Buell Hall...

In retrospect, the 1932 exhibition probably did for modern architecture in America what the Armory Show of 1913 had done for modern art in the United States some twenty years earlier. Soon after the 1932 exhibition closed, American architectural education changed radically, from the traditional routines inherited from the Ecole des Beaux-Arts to something quite close to the Bauhaus in spirit. Only four years after the Modern Architecture exhibition closed at MoMA, Mies van der Rohe was invited to head the School of Architecture at Armour Institute in Chicago (later known as the Illinois Institute of Technology), and Gropius was invited to head the architecture program at Harvard. And within another ten years or so, there was hardly a single school of architecture in the United States not dominated by the ideas first advanced by the International Style architects in Europe, and first publicized in the 1932 exhibition mounted at MoMA by Philip Johnson and his friends.

Over the next several years, Johnson produced a number of smaller exhibitions at the Museum of Modern Art. Two

das gleiche bewirkt hat wie zwanzig Jahre zuvor die Armory Show von 1913 für die moderne Kunst in den Vereinigten Staaten. Bald nach der 1932er Ausstellung veränderte sich die Architekturausbildung in Nordamerika radikal, vom traditionellen, von der Ecole des Beaux Arts übernommenen Routineprogramm zu dem Geist des Bauhauses nahestehenden Auffassungen. Nur vier Jahre nach dem Ende der Ausstellung «Modern Architecture» am MoMA wurde Mies van der Rohe die Leitung der School of Architecture am Armour Institute in Chicago (dem späteren Illinois Institute of Technology) übertragen, und Gropius wurde zum Leiter der Architekturausbildung in Harvard ernannt. Und im Laufe von etwa zehn weiteren Jahren gab es kaum eine Architekturhochschule mehr in den Vereinigten Staaten, die nicht von den zuerst durch die Architekten des Internationalen Stils in Europa vorgebrachten und erstmals in der Ausstellung von Philip Johnson und seinen Freunden 1932 veröffentlichten Ideen beherrscht wurde.

In den folgenden Jahren veranstaltete Johnson eine Reihe kleinerer Ausstellungen im Museum of Modern Art, darunter zwei besonders interessante: die erste – eine sehr kleine, aber faszinierende Schau – wurde im April 1933 eröffnet und trug den Titel «Objects 1900 and Today»; die zweite hieß «Machine Art» und wurde 1934 eröffnet.

Beide Ausstellungen befaßten sich mit «gestalteten» und manchmal auch «ungestalteten» Gebrauchsgegenständen (aber nicht mit Gebäuden) und standen im Thema den Aktivitäten, die von einem modernen Museum zu erwarten wären, näher: Die erste bestand aus einer Anzahl von Gegenüberstellungen – eine herrliche Tiffany-Schale von 1900 neben einer von 1933 im Bauhaus-Stil aus der Massenproduktion einer deutschen Porzellanfabrik; oder ein wunderbarer, 1900 von Eugene Colonna in Jugendstilmanier entworfener und handgearbeiteter Stuhl neben Mies van der Rohes Sessel aus Leder und Chromstahl von 1933, der aussah wie aus der computergesteuerten Massenfabrikation, wenn es solche Geräte damals schon gegeben hätte. Die Ausstellung war eine sehr überzeugende Übung in historischen Gegenüberstellungen: Kunstwerke von Menschen, die sich von Pflanzen, Muscheln und anderen natürlichen Formen inspirieren ließen, mit Objekten von Menschen, die von der Maschine fasziniert waren.

Die Ausstellung «Machine Art» war eine präzis artikulierte Aussage der Überzeugungen Johnsons – derzeit und der kommenden Jahre. Sie war weit umfangreicher als «Objects 1900 and Today» und nahm das ganze Stadthaus ein, in dem sie gezeigt wurde. Die Zeitschrift «New Yorker» beschrieb die Schau als «von Brancusi und Fern-

of them were especially interesting: the first – a very small show, but an intriguing one – opened in April of 1933, and was entitled «Objects 1900 and Today»; the second, entitled «Machine Art», opened in 1934.

Both of them were concerned with «designed» and sometimes «undesigned» useful objects (rather than buildings), and both were closer in orientation to the sort of thing a modern museum would be expected to do: the first consisted of a number of juxtapositions – a vintage 1900 Tiffany bowl, next to a 1933 bowl in the Bauhaus manner, mass-produced in a porcelain factory in Germany; or a vintage 1900 chair, designed and hand-crafted by Eugene Colonna in the Art Nouveau manner, next to a 1933 chromium-plated steel-and-leather chaise by Mies van der Rohe, which looked as if it had been mass-produced by computer, if there had been such gadgets in 1933. The exhibition was a fascinating exercise in historic juxtaposition; with artifacts shaped by people in love with plants and seashells and other natural forms, next to objects shaped by people enamored with the machine.

«The Machine Art» exhibition was a precisely articulated statement of where Johnson stood at that time – and for some time to come. It was much larger than the «1900 and Today» exhibit, and occupied the entire townhouse in which it was held. The «New Yorker» magazine described the show as a «hardware store … run by Brancusi and Fernand Léger,» which may have been the finest compliment Johnson and Barr could have hoped for. As this comment suggests, the exhibition consisted almost exclusively of «undesigned» objects like ball bearings and light bulbs – undesigned by anyone interested in aesthetics, that is. While this may seem like a tame theme to us today, it clearly upset some of those who thought that a museum of art should concern itself with art rather than nuts and bolts. Since that exhibition opened, needless to say, this sort of argument is no longer heard – and the quaint concept of «Arts and Crafts» seems to have been replaced by our interest in what Johnson and Barr called «Machine Art» in the 1934 exhibition.

There were other, smaller exhibitions on architecture and design in the new MoMA galleries that opened a couple of years before World War II, and Philip Johnson was involved in all of them. The two exhibitions that changed virtually all perceptions held in America about the shapes of buildings and the shapes of utensils – the 1932 show on modern architecture, and the 1934 show – these were Johnson's most important efforts, even though he gave much credit to Barr and to others. Not a bad record for a young dilettante who mounted both exhibitions before he was thirty years old, and before he had any of the standard academic credentials!

and Léger geleitetes Haushaltswarengeschäft», was als höchstes Kompliment gegolten haben muß, das Johnson und Barr erhoffen konnten. Wie dieser Kommentar andeutet, bestand die Ausstellung fast ausschließlich aus «ungestalteten» Objekten wie Kugellagern und Glühbirnen – das heißt, nicht von jemandem an Ästhetik Interessierten gestalteten Objekten. Während uns das heute als harmloses Thema erscheint, erregte es damals eindeutig die Gemüter derjenigen, die meinten, ein Kunstmuseum solle sich mit Kunst befassen und nicht mit praktischem Kleinkram. Selbstredend ist seit jener Ausstellung diese Art von Argumentation verstummt – und das kuriose Konzept von «Arts and Crafts» durch unser Interesse an dem, was Johnson und Barr in ihrer Ausstellung von 1934 «Machine Art» nannten, ersetzt worden.

Es gab weitere kleinere Ausstellungen über Architektur und Design in den neuen Räumen des MoMA, die einige Jahre vor dem Zweiten Weltkrieg eröffnet wurden, und Philip Johnson war an ihnen allen beteiligt. Die beiden Ausstellungen, welche tatsächlich alle bisher in den Vereinigten Staaten vorherrschenden Auffassungen über die Form von Gebäuden und die Form von Gebrauchsgegenständen veränderten – die Ausstellung von 1932, «Modern Architecture», und die von 1934, «Machine Art» –, blieben jedoch Johnsons bedeutendste Leistungen, auch wenn er vieles davon Barr und anderen zuschrieb. Das ist kein schlechtes Zeugnis für einen jungen Dilettanten, der beide Ausstellungen organisierte, ehe er das dreißigste Lebensjahr erreicht und einen der üblichen akademischen Grade erworben hatte.

Ende der dreißiger Jahre wurde Johnsons Interesse an der Kunst und besonders an Architektur und Design durch verschiedene andere Engagements abgelenkt. Wie viele seiner Zeitgenossen in jenen Jahren befaßte er sich mit radikaler Politik und verwendete immer weniger Zeit auf die Arbeit mit Barr und anderen für die Kunst. Aber als der Krieg in Europa ausbrach, kehrte Johnson zu seiner früheren Beschäftigung zurück und begann 1940 ein Studium an der Graduate School of Design in Harvard, um anerkannter Architekt zu werden.

Zu der Zeit hatte er sich schon einen beachtlichen Namen als Kritiker und Gestalter großer Ausstellungen über Architektur und Design gemacht. Er hatte auch gezeigt, daß seine persönliche Vorliebe dem Werk Mies van der Rohes und nicht dem von Gropius galt – eine Haltung, die das Leben für ihn an der von Gropius und anderen Sympathisanten des Bauhauses und seiner Lehre beherrschten Schule nicht einfacher machte. Es half nichts, daß die Position in Harvard ursprünglich Mies angeboten worden war und man Gropius erst angesprochen hatte, nachdem

In the late 1930s, Johnson's interest in the arts, and especially, in architecture and design was sidetracked by various other involvements. Like many of his contemporaries in those years, he became preoccupied with radical politics, and he spent less and less time working with Barr and others in the arts. But once the war had started in Europe, Johnson returned to his earlier preoccupation, and in 1940 entered the Graduate School of Design at Harvard, to become a bona fide architect.

By this time he had made a very considerable name for himself as a critic and as a designer of major exhibitions on architecture and design. He had also made it quite clear that his personal preferences were for the work of Mies van der Rohe rather than Gropius – a stance that did not make life much easier for him at a school that was dominated by Gropius and by others in sympathy with the Bauhaus and its doctrines. It didn't help that the Harvard position had initially been offered to Mies, and that Gropius had only been approached after Mies had turned down the offer because of some silly misunderstanding.

Johnson's preference for Miesian and for other, purist aesthetics was clearly related to what he (and others) saw as the ideological orientation of the Bauhaus – at least in the 1920s. While most people both inside and outside the Bauhaus felt that its principal concerns had to do with social, political, technological and city planning issues – all of them perfectly reasonable at a time of rapid industrialization and population growth – Johnson and others continued to insist that architecture (including modern architecture) was primarily an art. Its shapes and forms and details might be different from those of earlier times; but it was still primarily an art, and not a social science.

At Gropius' school at Harvard, that view was probably considered somewhat elitist, and Johnson was considered something of an outsider. His devotion to Miesian perfectionism was looked upon askance; and since he was also about a dozen years older than most of his classmates (as well as wealthier, more famous and probably more notorious), his position at Harvard was not exactly that of a typical graduate student.

The times, of course, were hardly typical either. Like most of his fellow students, Johnson found himself drafted into the U.S. Army before long. He was never sent overseas, and was able to return to civilian life after 2 1/2 years in uniform. In the meantime, Harvard had granted him his degree in architecture (his thesis project was the Miesian house he had built for himself in 1942, in Cambridge), and he was now ready to practice what he had preached for so long: established in New York, he revived his association with MoMA and opened his own architectural firm, with a former Harvard classmate, Landis Gores.

The International Style
Ausstellung im Museum of Modern Art, 1932
Mit Alfred Barr und Henry-Russell Hitchcock

Im Hinblick auf ihre Einführung der Moderne in die Vereinigten Staaten kann die Bedeutung dieser Ausstellung, die den Verlauf der amerikanischen Architektur in diesem Jahrhundert entscheidend prägte, nicht überschätzt werden. Die Ausstellung, in der eine Anzahl von Projekten amerikanischer und europäischer Architekten, darunter Frühwerke von Le Corbusier, Mies und Gropius, zusammengetragen und klassifiziert war, kennzeichnete eine neue Architekturrichtung, die auf der Verwendung neuer Baumaterialien, der Betonung des Volumens anstelle der Masse, dem Weglassen des Ornaments sowie auf der Vorstellung beruhte, daß die Form eines Gebäudes seine Funktion ausdrücken solle. Die Schau, welche die Moderne als einen geschlossenen, klaren Stil präsentierte, hatte ungeheuren Einfluß auf den gesamten Berufsstand. Kritiker haben bemängelt, daß die Gestalter der Ausstellung die formalen Charakteristika der modernen Architektur auf Kosten ihrer (zumindest in ihrer europäischen Version) politischen Aussage überbetonten.

The International Style
Exhibition at the Museum of Modern Art, 1932
With Alfred Barr and Henry-Russell Hitchcock

In terms of its introduction of modernism to the United States, the importance of this show in shaping the course of American architecture this century cannot be overstated. Collecting and labelling a group of projects by American and European architects, including early work by Le Corbusier, Mies, and Gropius, the exhibit described a new architectural movement based on the use of new building materials, the emphasis on volume rather than mass, lack of ornament, and the idea of a building's form reflecting its function. Presenting Modernism as a coherent, clear style the show had enormous influence on the profession. Critics have noted that the curators emphasized the formal characteristics of modern architecture at the expense of its (at least in its European form) political agenda.

Mies das Angebot aufgrund eines törichten Mißverständnisses abgelehnt hatte.

Johnsons Vorliebe für die Ästhetik von Mies und anderen Puristen war eindeutig gegen das gerichtet, was er (und andere) als die ideologische Ausrichtung des Bauhauses betrachtete – zumindest in den zwanziger Jahren. Während die meisten Menschen innerhalb und außerhalb des Bauhauses meinten, daß dessen Hauptanliegen soziale, politische, technologische und stadtplanerische Aspekte betrafen – was in jener Zeit der rapiden Industrialisierung und des rasanten Bevölkerungswachstums durchaus einleuchtete –, bestanden Johnson und andere weiterhin darauf, daß Architektur (einschließlich der modernen) in erster Linie eine Kunst sei. Ihre Gestalten und Formen mochten von denen früherer Zeiten abweichen, aber sie wäre immer noch vorwiegend eine Kunst und keine Sozialwissenschaft.

An Gropius' Schule in Harvard wurde diese Ansicht vermutlich als ziemlich elitär und Johnson als Außenseiter betrachtet. Wegen seiner Vorliebe zum Perfektionismus von Mies wurde er schief angesehen, und da er etwa ein Dutzend Jahre älter war als die meisten seiner Kommilitonen (und dazu wohlhabender, berühmter und wahrscheinlich bekannter), entsprach seine Position in Harvard nicht der eines normalen Studenten.

Die Zeiten waren natürlich auch nicht normal. Wie die meisten seiner Kommilitonen wurde Johnson nach kurzer Zeit in die US-Armee eingezogen. Er wurde aber nicht nach Europa geschickt und konnte nach 2 1/2 Jahren in Uniform ins Zivilleben zurückkehren. In der Zwischenzeit hatte er in Harvard sein Architekturstudium abgeschlossen (Thema seiner Abschlußarbeit war das Haus im Mies-Stil, das er für sich selbst im Jahre 1942 in Cambridge erbaut hatte), und er war nun bereit zu praktizieren, was er so lange gepredigt hatte: Wieder in New York etabliert, erneuerte er seine Verbindung zum MoMA und gründete ein eigenes Architekturbüro zusammen mit Landis Gores, einem früheren Semesterkollegen aus Harvard.

Zu der Zeit war Philip Johnson den meisten Architekten und Kritikern als ein begeisterter Anhänger von Mies bekannt, und es überraschte niemanden, daß eines der ersten Projekte nach seiner Rückkehr zum MoMA eine große, dem Werk von Mies gewidmete Ausstellung war. Sie fand 1947 in den großzügigen neuen Räumen des MoMA statt und war von Mies selbst gestaltet worden. Johnsons wesentlicher Beitrag war ein umfassendes und ansprechendes Buch über das Werk von Mies – die erste bis dahin erschienene Publikation und noch heute eine der besten Übersichten über die frühen Projekte und Bauten dieses Architekten.

By this time, Philip Johnson was known to most architects and critics as an utterly devoted Mies disciple; and it surprised no one that one of his first projects upon returning to MoMA was a major exhibition devoted to Mies van der Rohe's work. The exhibition was held in the spacious new MoMA galleries in 1947, and it was designed by Mies himself. Johnson's principal contribution was a comprehensive and handsome book on Mies' work – the first such book published up to that point, and still one of the best surveys of the architect's earlier projects and buildings.

Although Johnson continued to be involved in many of MoMA's exhibitions that dealt with architecture or design, he turned over most of those responsibilities to Arthur Drexler, who was appointed Director of the Department of Architecture and Design in 1950. And Johnson was deeply involved in all of MoMA's other activities, both as Alfred Barr's close friend and as MoMA's architect for significant new, post-war additions, all of which are documented and discussed elsewhere in this book. The most important of these, the Sculpture Garden designed by Johnson in 1953, survives more or less intact – one of the finest urban spaces in Manhattan.

Johnson's work in the 1950s continued much in the tradition of Mies van der Rohe, although some Miesian rigorists thought that Johnson's buildings were frequently a little more playful than the disciplinarian Mies would have tolerated. In the mid-1950s, when Mies was working on the Seagram Building on Manhattan's Park Avenue, Johnson was asked to design the Four Seasons Restaurant on the main floor of the structure; and while it was Miesian in all its essentials, it also contained some details and some works of art that Mies probably considered a trifle frivolous. And once the Seagram Building and the Four Seasons were opened, Johnson cut his architectural ties to Mies and began to explore new directions – directions at variance with just about everything he had ever professed to believe in.

Like that aforementioned philosopher, Philip Johnson seems to have decided to look at architecture from the other end of the telescope, and assume, for a moment, that much of what he had believed and practiced until then was, in fact, not necessarily valid at all.

The result was a series of buildings from about 1960 to the present that explore various directions quite far removed from Johnson's earlier, Miesian work: there were several museums and other cultural institutions that seem almost neo-classical in composition and in their modernized facades; there were other institutional buildings dominated by applied arches and other traditional forms – and massively symmetrical in composition – that recalled earlier

Deconstructivist Architecture
Ausstellung im Museum of Modern Art, 1988
Mit Mark Wigley

Diese Ausstellung vereinte das Werk von sieben Architekten, die in einem Stil arbeiten, der unter der Bezeich-
nung «Dekonstruktion» bekannt geworden ist. Die Architekten Frank Gehry, Rem Koolhaas, Peter Eisenman,
Bernard Tschumi, Zaha Hadid, Daniel Libeskind und die
Gruppe Coop Himmelblau zeigten Projekte, deren formale Kollisionen und aus dem Gleichgewicht geratene
Ordnung Johnson und Wigley mit der Malerei der russischen Konstruktivisten in Verbindung setzten. Bilder von
Malewitsch, Rodschenko und El Lissitzky wurden in
einem angrenzenden Raum gezeigt. Die kritische Diskussion über diese Ausstellung erhitzte sich an Argu-
menten, die sich um die subversive Wirkung und die
möglicherweise elitäre Haltung der vorgestellten Werke
drehten.

Deconstructivist Architecture
Exhibition at the Museum of Modern Art, 1988
With Mark Wigley

This exhibition tied together the work of seven architects
practicing in a style which has become known as «De-
construction.» Architects Frank Gehry, Rem Koolhaas,
Peter Eisenman, Bernard Tschumi, Zaha Hadid, Daniel
Libeskind, and the firm Coop Himmelblau presented projects whose formal collisions and balanced disorder
Johnson and Wigley linked to the paintings of the Russian
Constructivists. Paintings by Malevich, Rodchenko, and El
Lissitzky were also displayed in an adjacent room. Critical
debate over the show was heated, with arguments re-
volving around the work's sense of subversion and also
its alleged elitist stances.

Obgleich Johnson nach wie vor an vielen Ausstellungen des MoMA beteiligt war, die sich mit Architektur oder Design befaßten, übertrug er den Großteil der Verantwortung Arthur Drexler, der 1950 zum Leiter der Abteilung für Architektur und Design ernannt wurde. Johnson war auch stark in alle anderen Aktivitäten des MoMA involviert, sowohl als enger Freund von Alfred Barr als auch als Architekt des Museums für die wichtigen neuen Erweiterungen der Nachkriegszeit, die alle an anderer Stelle in diesem Buch dokumentiert und kommentiert sind. Die bedeutendste von ihnen, der 1953 von Johnson gestaltete Skulpturengarten – einer der schönsten urbanen Räume in Manhattan – ist mehr oder weniger intakt erhalten.

Johnsons Werk der fünfziger Jahre setzte die Tradition Mies van der Rohes fort, obgleich einige rigorose Mies-Anhänger meinten, daß Johnsons Bauten häufig ein wenig verspielter seien, als der strenge Lehrer es tolerieren würde. Mitte der fünfziger Jahre, als Mies am Seagram Building an Manhattans Park Avenue arbeitete, wurde Johnson beauftragt, das Restaurant «Four Seasons» im Hauptgeschoß des Gebäudes zu planen; wenn es auch in allen entscheidenden Aspekten im Mies-Stil gehalten war, so enthielt es doch auch einige Details und einige Kunstwerke, die Mies vermutlich für etwas frivol hielt. Und nachdem das Seagram Building und das Restaurant eröffnet worden waren, brach Johnson seine architektonische Bindung an Mies van der Rohe ab und begann neue Richtungen zu erforschen – Richtungen, die im Widerspruch zu buchstäblich allem standen, was er stets zu glauben beteuert hatte.

Wie jener zuvor erwähnte Philosoph erschien Philip Johnson entschlossen, die Architektur vom anderen Ende des Teleskops zu betrachten und für einen Moment anzunehmen, daß vieles von dem, was er bis dahin geglaubt und praktiziert hatte, gar nicht unbedingt überhaupt gültig war.

Das Ergebnis war eine Reihe Bauten von etwa 1960 bis heute, die verschiedene Richtungen ausprobierten und sich weit von Johnsons früherem, an Mies orientiertem Werk entfernten: Dazu gehören mehrere Museen und andere kulturelle Einrichtungen, die in der Komposition und mit ihren modernisierten Fassaden beinahe neoklassizistisch wirken. Andere öffentliche Gebäude Johnsons sind von aufgesetzten Bogen und anderen traditionellen Formen beherrscht sowie in der Komposition vollkommen symmetrisch und rufen frühere architektonische und politische Ordnungen wach. Und es gibt die zunehmend häufigere Verwendung edler Materialien wie Marmor und Bronze, die an aristokratische Architektur der Vergangenheit erinnern.

architectural and political orders; and there were increasingly frequent uses of noble materials like marble and bronze reminiscent of an aristocratic architecture of the past.

Some of these buildings irritated Johnson's contemporaries, many of whom were wedded to a more populist architectural language, and who saw in Johnson's neo-classical work a trace or two of undemocratic preferences. Still, several of his new buildings raised questions that had not been raised previously by him or by any of his «modern» predecessors or contemporaries. Johnson's 1974 addition to McKim, Mead & White's Boston Public Library, for example, seems today to have been a remarkably interesting (and innovative) effort to relate an entirely modern structure to an impressively neo-classical work of the past century – without compromising the latter or the former.

And Johnson's increasing preoccupation with such esoteric aspects of architecture as light and shade, space and form, color and texture and other concerns of the art of architecture tended to confuse those of his contemporaries who believed that the primary concerns of modernism should be social, technological, political, and functional – issues like housing, urban as well as regional planning, environmental control, and so on. These, it seemed, were matters that should and did concern an egalitarian society; but they were not matters of very great priority to Philip Johnson. His concerns, it was said, were essentially «elitist,» even anti-modern!

Chances are that much of this was true. But nobody else – certainly no one in the Modern Movement – was talking very much about the art of architecture, or about some of its more esoteric manifestations. Even great artists like Le Corbusier and Mies van der Rohe and Alvar Aalto rarely talked about their buildings in other than functional or political terms. Only Philip Johnson, a member of the third generation of modern architects, seemed to talk about his work as if it were a continuation of that of Schinkel, or Ledoux, and of others of their ilk.

Many, if not most of Johnson's contemporaries, schooled (as he was) at Gropius' and Breuer's school at Harvard or at Mies van der Rohe's school at I.T.T., or at the Bauhaus in the years before Hitler, had very little knowledge of the history of architecture, or of the artistic concerns manifested in great works of the past. Most of Johnson's contemporaries claimed to be primarily concerned with the social and political problems raised by a mass society, and stressed those aspects of architecture that seemed to address those issues to the virtual exclusion of art.

Marcel Breuer, for example, who had been one of Johnson's studio critics at Harvard, liked to define his own

Einige dieser Bauwerke irritierten Johnsons Zeitgenossen, von denen viele einer populistischeren Architektursprache verbunden waren und in Johnsons neoklassizistischen Bauten Spuren undemokratischer Neigungen erkannten. Dennoch warfen manche seiner neuen Gebäude Fragen auf, die bisher weder von ihm selbst noch von einem seiner «modernen» Vorläufer oder Zeitgenossen gestellt worden waren. Johnsons Erweiterung aus dem Jahre 1974 der Bostoner Stadtbibliothek von McKim, Mead & White zum Beispiel erscheint heute als bemerkenswert interessanter (und innovativer) Versuch, ein völlig neues Gebäude in Beziehung zu einem eindrucksvollen neoklassizistischen Bauwerk des vorigen Jahrhunderts zu setzen, ohne beim ersteren oder letzteren faule Kompromisse zu schließen.

Und Johnsons zunehmende Beschäftigung mit solch abstrakten Aspekten der Architektur wie Licht und Schatten, Raum und Form, Farbe und Textur sowie anderen Belangen der Kunst der Architektur begann jene seiner Zeitgenossen zu verwirren, die glaubten, daß die wichtigsten Anliegen der Moderne sozialer, technischer, politischer und funktionaler Natur seien – Aufgaben wie Wohnungsbau, Stadt- und Regionalplanung, Umweltschutz usw. Dies, so schien es, waren Fragen, die eine egalitäre Gesellschaft angehen sollten und angingen; aber für Philip Johnson waren das keine Fragen höherer Priorität. Seine Anliegen seien, so sagte man, im wesentlichen «elitär», ja sogar antimodern!

Vermutlich traf vieles von dem zu. Aber niemand anderes, bestimmt kein Vertreter der modernen Architektur, redete viel von der Kunst der Architektur oder über ihre abstrakteren Manifestationen. Selbst große Künstler wie Le Corbusier, Mies van der Rohe und Alvar Aalto sprachen selten über ihre Bauten außer in funktionalen oder politischen Begriffen. Nur Philip Johnson, Vertreter der dritten Generation moderner Architekten, redete über seine Projekte, als handle es sich um eine Fortführung des Werkes von Schinkel, Ledoux oder ähnlichen Größen.

Viele, wenn nicht sogar die meisten von Johnsons Zeitgenossen, die (wie er) an der Schule von Gropius und Breuer in Harvard, der von Mies am Illinois Institute of Technology oder in den Jahren vor Hitlers Machtübernahme am Bauhaus studiert hatten, wußten nur wenig über die Geschichte der Architektur oder von den künstlerischen Anliegen, die sich in den großen Werken der Vergangenheit manifestierten. Die meisten Kollegen Johnsons behaupteten, sich vorwiegend mit den aus einer Massengesellschaft resultierenden sozialen und politischen Problemen zu befassen, und betonten jene Aspekte der Architektur, die solche Fragen beinahe bis zum tatsächlichen Ausschluß künstlerischer ansprachen.

work as being the product of a number of concerns like technological innovation, functional investigation, and so on – «plus that one percent, which is art.» One percent? He was exceedingly modest so far as his own work was concerned; but his analysis was not very different from that advanced by «modernists» everywhere in the years between the two world wars.

But in the second half of this century, much of the talk and action in modern architecture began again to focus on philosophical and aesthetic issues, some of them more pressing and convincing than others; and Johnson's voice was heard more and more frequently, and listened to more and more attentively.

One reason was that Philip Johnson was and is exceedingly eloquent, articulate and amusing. His comments on his own work and that of others were and are more interesting (and often more devastating) than those of most critics of our time; and his easy access to various platforms – not only at MoMA, but at other institutions as well for which he had designed buildings or to whose well-being he had otherwise contributed – certainly helped.

In any event, Johnson's critical intervention in the architectural debates in the second half of our century did a great deal to advance the often controversial work of others. He clearly contributed to the success of architects like Robert Venturi, Michael Graves, Peter Eisenman, Robert Stern, and Frank Gehry – all of them very far removed from the Miesian dogma that Johnson had espoused in the earlier years of the century. He helped publicize the work of neo-constructivists, deconstructivists, technocrats, and God only knows what else – not necessarily in his own work, which tended to remain somewhat conservative, at least until he experienced an infusion of youthfulness in the 1990s, but certainly through his words and his influence. And the result was, and continues to be, a lively debate among practitioners of a great range of concerns – some more valid than others. Much of this debate was sparked by Johnson's words, and some of it by his own works.

In fact, it is difficult to imagine the past fifty years or so in architectural dialogue, in the United States and elsewhere, without Philip Johnson's initial spark.

While Johnson's architectural practice took up more and more of his time, he did involve himself in several major exhibitions in MoMA's galleries: the most important of these was the «Deconstructivist Architecture» show mounted there in the spring and summer of 1988. As the name of the exhibition suggests, the new architectural di-

Marcel Breuer zum Beispiel, der einer von Johnsons Entwurfslehrern in Harvard gewesen war, pflegte seine eigenen Arbeiten als Produkte einer Reihe von Anliegen wie technische Innovation, funktionale Untersuchungen usw. zu definieren «plus jenes eine Prozent, das Kunst ist». Ein Prozent? Er war zwar äußerst bescheiden im Hinblick auf sein eigenes Werk, aber seine Auffassung unterschied sich nicht wesentlich von derjenigen, welche die «Modernisten» überall in den Jahren zwischen den beiden Weltkriegen vertraten.

In der zweiten Hälfte dieses Jahrhunderts begannen sich Diskussionen und Aktionen der modernen Architektur wieder auf theoretische und ästhetische Fragen zu konzentrieren, von denen einige besonders drängend und berechtigt waren; Johnsons Stimme war dabei immer häufiger zu hören und wurde auch immer aufmerksamer gehört.

Ein Grund dafür ist, daß Philip Johnson stets eloquent und amüsant gewesen ist und sich gut artikulieren kann. Die Kommentare über seine eigenen Bauten und die anderer waren und sind interessanter (und häufig vernichtender) als die der meisten Kritiker unserer Zeit; und sein leichter Zugang zu verschiedenen Ebenen – nicht nur zum MoMA, sondern auch zu anderen Institutionen, für die er Gebäude geplant oder zu deren Nutzen er in anderer Form beigetragen hat – trug sicher dazu bei.

Auf jeden Fall hat Johnsons kritische Beteiligung an den Architekturdiskussionen in der zweiten Hälfte unseres Jahrhunderts einen wichtigen Beitrag zur Förderung der vielfach kontroversen Arbeit anderer Architekten geleistet. Er hat eindeutig zum Erfolg von Architekten wie Robert Venturi, Michael Graves, Peter Eisenman, Robert Stern und Frank Gehry beigetragen, die sich alle weit vom Dogma Mies van der Rohes entfernten, dem Johnson sich doch in den früheren Jahren des Jahrhunderts verschrieben hatte. Er unterstützte die Publikation der Arbeiten von Neo-Konstruktivisten, Dekonstruktivisten, Technokraten und Gott weiß was noch – nicht unbedingt durch sein eigenes Werk, das immer etwas konservativ blieb, zumindest bevor er in den neunziger Jahren einen jugendlichen Schub erlebte, aber sicherlich aufgrund seiner Fürsprache und seines Einflusses. Das Ergebnis dessen war und ist noch heute eine lebhafte Diskussion unter den Praktikern mit einer breiten Palette von Anliegen von unterschiedlicher Bedeutung! Ein Großteil dieser Debatten entzündete sich an Johnsons Worten und einige auch an seinen Bauwerken.

In der Tat ist es schwierig, sich den Architekturdialog der vergangenen fünfzig Jahre in den USA und anderswo ohne Philip Johnsons zündenden Funken vorzustellen.

rection or movement that was its subject owed a good deal to Russian Constructivist ideas advanced in the second and third decades of the century – especially but unintentionally in such areas as unbuildability, uninhabitability, and unintelligibility. As in other exhibitions mounted at MoMA, there seemed little concern with architecture as habitat, and a great deal of concern with architecture as double-talk. A remarkable and heavily illustrated catalogue to the show was published by Johnson and Professor Mark Wigley of Princeton, who was associated with Johnson in curating the show. The exhibition and the catalogue were especially interesting, to some observers, in that they seemed to represent a final act in MoMA's divorce, architecturally speaking, from reality – and in MoMA's divorce from the rational principles laid down in Johnson's own «International Style» show of 1932. Of the dozen or so Decon projects illustrated in the catalogue, virtually none was ever built, nor could they have been. The exhibition was dedicated, exclusively, to aesthetic fantasies, and it treated such matters as function and structural integrity with open contempt. In short, it had little to do with architecture in the real world. It may have had something to do with virtual architecture in the virtual world.

Johnson's enthusiastic support of such fantasies was not unexpected. His concerns were always primarily aesthetic, and much of the time this produced some very interesting ideas and some very handsome buildings. Moreover, unlike most theorists who would have advanced and pursued ideas that seemed, on the face of it, absurd, Johnson had the courage to build what he preached; and if he could not find a client to go along with his fantasies, he would realize them for himself. Not many people in our time have shown such daring, or had such resources.

Although the buildings Johnson has designed and built over the past fifty years or so have not been uniformly first- – or even second-rate, he designed and built a very considerable amount of structures of very high quality – many more, in fact, than can be claimed for a similar period by architects of greater critical renown or public acclaim. This book documents close to half of the some two hundred projects designed and built over the past fifty years by Johnson and several associates. Christian Bjone of Mr. Johnson's office made major contributions to this part of the text, keeping the record straight by assembling important drawings and photographs to document the work further. Others in Mr. Johnson's office assisted in significant ways. Some two dozen buildings designed by Philip Johnson have been documented in some detail, because they seemed especially significant for a variety of reasons.

Peter Blake und Philip Johnson 1996

Peter Blake and Philip Johnson 1996

Während Johnson praktische Architekturtätigkeit immer mehr von seiner Zeit in Anspruch nahm, beteiligte er sich dennoch an mehreren großen Ausstellungen des MoMA: Die wichtigste von diesen war «Deconstructivist Architecture», die im Frühling und Sommer 1988 gezeigt wurde. Wie der Name der Ausstellung andeutet, war die neue Richtung oder Bewegung, die sie zum Thema hatte, sehr den Ideen verpflichtet, welche die russischen Konstruktivisten im zweiten und dritten Jahrzehnt dieses Jahrhunderts entwickelt hatten – vor allem, wenn auch unbeabsichtigt, im Hinblick auf Unbaubarkeit, Unbewohnbarkeit und Unverständlichkeit. Wie auch andere vom MoMA veranstaltete Ausstellungen schien sie sich wenig mit Architektur als Habitat und viel mit Gerede über Architektur zu befassen. Ein beachtlicher und reich bebilderter Katalog wurde von Johnson und Professor Mark Wigley von der Princeton University, die gemeinsam die Ausstellung erarbeitet hatten, veröffentlicht. Ausstellung und Katalog waren für manche Beobachter besonders interessant, weil sie architektonisch betrachtet offenbar einen Schlußakt in der Abwendung des MoMA von der Realität wie von den rationalen Prinzipien darstellten, die Johnson in seiner Ausstellung «International Style» von 1932 vertreten hatte. Von dem etwa einen Dutzend im

One of these outstanding structures, needless to say, is Johnson's own Glass House in New Canaan, completed in 1949, plus several surrounding structures he built for himself in the years since. In addition to the Glass House, Johnson designed and built at least half a dozen houses of superior quality for various clients (during a time when Mies van der Rohe built just one splendid house, the one for Dr. Edith Farnsworth). Johnson also designed and built the garden and surrounding structures for Manhattan's Museum of Modern Art, the Crystal Cathedral in Garden Grove, California, the IDS Building in the center of Minneapolis, the Pennzoil towers in Houston, the Water Garden in Forth Worth, and at least a dozen structures that were equal or superior to the work of contemporaries who were being lavishly praised by critics the world over during those same years.

Johnson continues to live and function, at full blast, well beyond the age that few architects, past and present, have reached (he is almost 90 years old, as of this writing); and he has used his years well. Admittedly, his inherited wealth and his connections have made it easier for him to build for himself and to reach wealthy clients less accessible to others. But he lives and works for architecture, and his built accomplishments over the years

Katalog abgebildeten dekonstruktivistischen Projekten wurde keines ausgeführt und konnte auch keines ausgeführt werden. Die Ausstellung war exklusiv ästhetischen Phantasievorstellungen gewidmet und behandelte Fragen wie Funktion und konstruktive Integrität mit offener Verachtung.

Kurz, sie hatte wenig mit Architektur in der realen Welt zu tun. Aber möglicherweise hatte sie etwas mit virtueller Architektur in einer virtuellen Welt zu tun.

Johnsons enthusiastische Unterstützung derartiger Phantasien kam nicht von ungefähr. Seine Anliegen waren stets in erster Linie ästhetischer Natur gewesen, und dadurch produzierte er überwiegend sehr interessante Ideen und einige sehr schöne Bauwerke. Darüber hinaus hatte Johnson im Gegensatz zu den meisten Theoretikern, die auf den ersten Blick absurd erscheinende Ideen vertraten und verfolgten, den Mut, auch zu bauen, was er verkündete. Und wenn er keinen Bauherrn finden konnte, um seine Phantasien umzusetzen, so pflegte er sie für sich selbst zu realisieren. Nur wenige Menschen in unserer Zeit haben soviel Mut gezeigt oder die Mittel dazu gehabt!

Obgleich die von Johnson in den vergangenen etwa fünfzig Jahren geplanten und ausgeführten Bauten nicht durchweg erst- oder auch nur zweitklassig waren, hat er doch eine beachtliche Anzahl von Bauwerken sehr hoher Qualität entworfen und gebaut – in der Tat erheblich mehr, als für den gleichen Zeitraum von anderen Architekten behauptet werden kann, die von Kritikern hoch gelobt und vom Publikum gepriesen wurden. Das vorliegende Buch enthält fast die Hälfte von ungefähr zweihundert Projekten, die von Johnson und mehreren Partnern in den letzten fünfzig Jahren geplant und ausgeführt wurden. Johnsons Mitarbeiter im Büro, Christian Bjone, lieferte ausführliche Beiträge zu diesem Teil des Textes und stellte wichtige Zeichnungen und Fotos zusammen, um das Werk besser zu dokumentieren. Auch andere Kollegen aus dem Büro unterstützten die Arbeit wirksam. Etwa zwei Dutzend von Philip Johnsons Bauten sind detaillierter beschrieben, weil sie aus verschiedenen Gründen als besonders signifikant erscheinen.

Eines der herausragenden Bauwerke ist selbstredend Johnsons eigenes, 1949 fertiggestelltes Glass House in New Canaan mit den umgebenden Bauten, die er für sich in den folgenden Jahren errichtete. Außer dem Glass House plante und baute Johnson mindestens ein halbes Dutzend Wohnhäuser von höchster Qualität für verschiedene Bauherren (während einer Zeit, in der Mies van der Rohe nur ein einziges großartiges Wohnhaus baute: dasjenige für Dr. Edith Farnsworth). Und Johnson entwarf und realisierte den Garten (und angrenzende Bauten) für das

are of impressive quality, and often outshine those of most of his contemporaries. One reason is that they are extremely well built; and so they will continue to stand up and impress long after some more famous 20th century works have crumbled.

The discussions on these major projects are based in part on recorded conversations held over the years between Mr. Johnson and the author of this monograph. In addition, there are quotations from various comments by critics that appeared in print at the time when these projects were constructed or published – and some of the more amusing comments are from Mr. Johnson himself. It would have been a pity if his voice had been drowned out – a pity, and out of character as well.

Peter Blake

Museum of Modern Art in Manhattan, die Crystal Cathedral in Garden Grove/California, das IDS Building im Zentrum von Minneapolis, die Pennzoil-Hochhäuser in Houston, den Wassergarten in Fort Worth und mindestens ein weiteres Dutzend von Gebäuden, die gleichbedeutend oder besser sind als das Werk von Zeitgenossen, welche im gleichen Zeitraum von der internationalen Kritik hoch gelobt wurden.

Johnson, weit jenseits eines Alters, das nur wenige Architekten in Vergangenheit und Gegenwart erreicht haben (als dieser Text geschrieben wurde, war er schon fast neunzig Jahre alt), lebt und arbeitet weiterhin mit voller Kraft, und er hat seine Jahre gut genutzt. Zugegebenermaßen haben sein ererbter Wohlstand und seine Verbindungen es ihm erleichtert, für sich selbst zu bauen und reiche Bauherren zu gewinnen, die für andere schwerer zu erreichen waren. Aber er lebt und arbeitet für die Architektur, seine in all den Jahren ausgeführten Werke sind von beeindruckender Qualität und überragen oft die seiner Zeitgenossen. Ein Grund dafür ist, daß sie extrem gut gebaut sind; daher werden sie Bestand haben und noch lange beeindrucken, wenn einige der berühmter gewordenen Bauten des 20. Jahrhunderts längst verfallen sein werden.

Die Kommentare zu diesen großen Projekten basieren zum Teil auf Aufzeichnungen von Gesprächen des Autors dieser Monographie mit Johnson aus mehreren Jahren. Darüber hinaus sind Zitate von Kritikern aus verschiedenen Rezensionen verwendet, die während oder nach Fertigstellung der betreffenden Projekte veröffentlicht wurden, und einige eher erheiternde Kommentare stammen von Philip Johnson selbst. Es wäre schade gewesen, seine Stimme zu übertönen – schade, und auch nicht angemessen.

Peter Blake

Bauten   Buildings

Ash Street Haus

Philip Johnson
1942
Cambridge, Massachusetts
Assoziierter Architekt: S. Clements Horsley

Zum Abschluß seines Architekturstudiums in Harvard wählte Philip Johnson als Thema für die Diplomarbeit den Entwurf eines Hofhauses für ein Grundstück in Cambridge, Massachusetts – und baute es anschließend für sich selbst. Man schrieb das Jahr 1942, und die finanziellen Mittel, seinen Entwurf umzusetzen und das Haus nach dessen Fertigstellung zu beziehen, standen ihm zur Verfügung. Er besaß außerdem etliche Hofhaus-Prototypen, die Mies van der Rohe in den dreißiger Jahren entwickelt hatte und die ihm als Anregung dienen konnten.

Das Gebäude, das daraus hervorging, nimmt im Grundriß ein Rechteck von etwa 15,20 m x 18,30 m ein und ist von einer 3,65 m hohen Mauer umgeben. An einer Seite des Rechtecks bedeckt ein Flachdach das eigentliche Haus von 6,10 m x 18,30 m; eine raumhohe Glaswand, 18,30 m lang und 3,65 m hoch, trennt den Innenraum vom gepflasterten Gartenhof. Innen befinden sich Schlafzimmer, Bad, Nebenräume, Küche und Wohnzimmer. Alles in allem ein geschmackvolles Haus für einen Junggesellen, mit Mies van der Rohes Barcelona-Möbeln eingerichtet. Vorgefertigte Sperrholzpaneele bildeten die Wände, möglicherweise als Zugeständnis an das ideologische Anliegen von Gropius. Das Tragwerk besteht zum größten Teil aus schichtverleimtem Holz, da an Stahl während des Zweiten Weltkriegs nur schwer heranzukommen war.

Das Haus bleibt ein Diagramm, aber ein schönes – es entsteht der Eindruck, daß sich das Innere des Hauses bis in den schönen, von einer Mauer umschlossenen Garten ausdehnt. Der (wirkliche wie scheinbare) Wohnbereich wird dadurch räumlich großzügig, hell belichtet und dennoch privat. Dieses Hofhaus stellt, ähnlich dem Rockefeller-Stadthaus, das Johnson etwa 10 Jahre später für ein typisches Grundstück in Manhattan entwirft, ein sehr gutes Modell für eine Standardsituation dar – in diesem Fall ein Grundstück in einer amerikanischen Vorstadt der Art, wie sie nach dem Zweiten Weltkrieg auf oftmals verschwenderische und absurde Weise auf Millionen von Hektar entstanden. Dieser Entwurf war wohl kein Versuch Johnsons zur Lösung des Massenwohnproblems, das den USA in nur wenigen Jahren bevorstehen würde, aber dennoch hätte die Arbeit gegen Ende der vierziger Jahre einen bedeutenden Beitrag zur Vorstadtplanung leisten können – falls sich jemand dafür interessiert hätte.

Aber auch so wurden, vor allem in Kalifornien, Ende der fünfziger Jahre und in den sechziger Jahren so manche

Ash Street House

Philip Johnson
1942
Cambridge, Massachusetts
Associate Architect: S. Clements Horsley

When Philip Johnson was asked to pick a project for a design thesis that would qualify him for a graduate degree in architecture from Harvard, he decided to draw up a court house for a site in Cambridge, Massachusetts – and then to build the house for his own private use. The year was 1942, and he had the financial resources to realize his design and to move into the house when it was built. He also had a number of prototypes for court houses drawn up by Mies van der Rohe in the 1930s to suggest some of the directions in which he might go.

The resulting house is a rectangle in plan, measuring 50 feet by 60 feet, surrounded by a 12 foot high wall. A flat roof covers one 20 foot by 60 foot end of the rectangle; and a floor-to-ceiling glass wall, 60 feet wide and 12 foot high, separates the interior from a paved garden court. The interior contains a bedroom, bathroom, utilities, kitchen and living room. It is a very neat bachelor pad, elegantly furnished with Mies van der Rohe's Barcelona furniture. Possibly as a concession to Gropius' ideological concerns, the walls were prefabricated plywood panels. The structural frame is largely of laminated wood, since steel framing was hard to come by during the World War II years.

The house is a diagram, but a beautiful one: the enclosed areas of the house extend, visually, into a lovely walled garden, and so the living areas, real and apparent, are very spacious, brightly lit, and yet private. Like the Rockefeller Town House which Johnson would design about ten years later for a typical urban site in Manhattan, this court house is an excellent prototype for a typical site – in this case, an American suburban site of the kind developed, often wastefully and absurdly, on millions of acres after World War II. Although Johnson probably did not attempt, in this design, to solve any problems of mass-housing of the sort that would face the United States in a very few years, he did, in fact, produce a design that might have made a significant contribution to suburban planning in the late 1940s and in the decades after that – if anyone had paid attention.

As it was, several «patio houses» were designed by architects and built by developers, especially in California, in the late 1950s and in the 1960s; and these were undoubtedly influenced by Philip Johnson's little court house done as a thesis project before he was drafted into the US Army. Alas, by that time vast suburban areas throughout

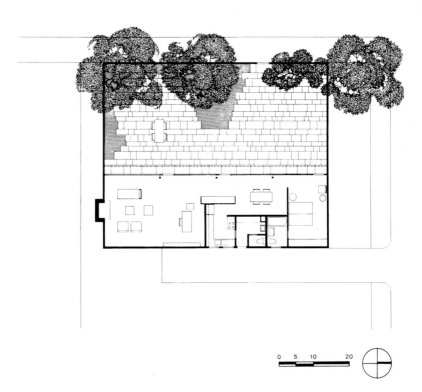

Grundriß Erdgeschoß, 1:300
Außenansicht bei Nacht

Ground floor plan, 1:300
Exterior night view

Innenraum bei Tag

Interior day view

«Patiohäuser» entworfen und gebaut, die zweifelsohne von Philip Johnsons kleinem Hofhaus beeinflußt waren, also seiner Diplomarbeit, bevor er zur Armee eingezogen wurde. Leider waren zu diesem Zeitpunkt schon ausgedehnte Vorstadtgebiete unter schäbigem Billigwohnungsbau von ganz anderem Charakter begraben worden, und es war einfach zu spät, um dieser Entwicklung Einhalt zu gebieten.

Wie sehr Philip Johnson auch dazu neigen mochte, die funktionalen und sozialen Anliegen eines Gropius und anderer Gleichgesinnter zu verspotten, bemerkenswert ist doch, daß einige dieser Belange sein eigenes Werk von Anfang an auf nicht unbedeutende Weise mitformten und daß er in diesem Bereich wichtige Beiträge geleistet hat. Einer davon war das kleine Haus an der Ash Street mit seinem geräumigen ummauerten Garten. Als Johnson in die Armee eintrat, wurde das Haus von einem Harvard-Professor gekauft, er selbst richtete sich nach Kriegsende in New York und New Canaan ein. Unter seinen Kommilitonen gab es nicht viele, die mit ihrer ersten Arbeit einen so sorgfältig ausgearbeiteten und überzeugenden Beitrag zur amerikanischen Architektur geleistet hatten.

the country had been laid waste with ticky-tacky developments of a very different sort, and it was clearly too late to reverse the trend.

It is interesting to see that, however much Philip Johnson tended to deride the functionalist and social concerns of Gropius and others, his own work from the earliest years was significantly shaped by some of those concerns as well, and he made important contributions in those areas. The little Ash Street House, with its spacious walled garden, was one of those. It was bought by a Harvard faculty member when Johnson went into the army; and he moved to New York and New Canaan after the war was over. Not many of his fellow students at Harvard made such a neat and convincing contribution to American architecture with one of their very first works.

Cambridge Sun, April 23, 1942
Architectural Forum, 1942

Scheune auf der Townsend Farm
Philip Johnson
1944
New London, Ohio

Townsend Farms Barn
Philip Johnson
1944
New London, Ohio

Dieser Werkzeugschuppen entstand auf der Familienfarm der Johnsons in Ohio. Die Außenwände bestehen aus unbehandelten Formsteinen, der obere Abschluß ist ein Oberlichtband. Bemerkenswert ist die Verwendung Mies' scher Elemente, wie sie Johnson auch später noch einsetzte. Das Dach sitzt auf ausgesteiften Holzträgern, die von der Betonsteinwand abgelöst sind. Das Gebäude ist heute ungenutzt und verfallen.

This tool shed, with blank block walls topped by clerestory windows, was built on the Johnson family farm in Ohio. It is notable for its use of Miesian elements Johnson utilized further in his career. The roof was built on a wood-framed truss independent of the concrete block walls. The building has been abandoned and fallen into ruin.

«Philip Johnson» – A+U 1979

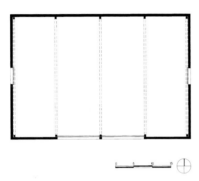

Grundriß Erdgeschoß, 1:300
Gegenwärtiger Zustand
Außenansicht

Ground floor plan, 1:300
Current state
Exterior view

Haus Farney
Philip Johnson
1947
Sagaponack, New York
Partner: Landis Gores
Assoziierter Architekt: S. Clements Horsley

Dieses Strandhaus steht auf einem Höhenkamm mit Blick auf den Atlantik. Funktional ist der Grundriß in drei voneinander getrennte Bereiche unterteilt – den zentral gelegenen Wohn- und Eßbereich, die drei Schlafzimmer am einen und die Nebenräume am anderen Ende. Die Organisation entspricht einem Entwurf von Mies van der Rohe für ein Einfamilienhaus in Jackson Hole, Wyoming aus dem Jahre 1938 (nicht ausgeführt), mit dem Johnson und andere sich immer wieder auseinandersetzten. Den Mittelteil bildet ein verglaster Rücksprung um einen kleinen Eingangshof.

Farney House
Philip Johnson
1947
Sagaponack, New York
Partner: Landis Gores
Associate Architect: S. Clements Horsley

This beach house sits atop a ridge overlooking the Atlantic. Its plan is split functionally into three separate areas: a central living room and dining space; three bedrooms at one end, and service quarters at the other end. This organizational arrangement derives from a Mies project for a house in Jackson Hole, Wyoming, designed in 1938 (unbuilt), and it is a scheme which Johnson and others continued to explore. The midsection is glazed and recessed, and forms a small entry court as well.

«Philip Johnson», John Jacobus, 1962

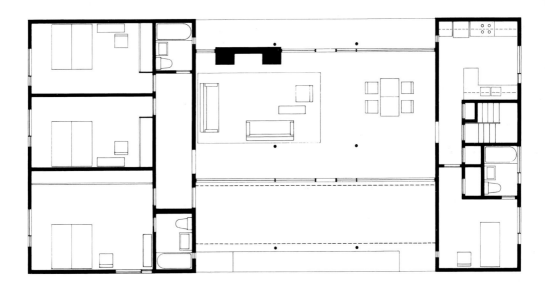

Grundriß Erdgeschoß
Außenansicht

Ground floor plan
Exterior view

Glashaus

Philip Johnson
1949
New Canaan, Connecticut
Statik: Eipel Engineering Co.
Lichttechnik: Richard Kelly

Das Glashaus, das Philip Johnson Ende der vierziger Jahre in New Canaan, Connecticut für sich bauen ließ, zählt heute wohl zu den weltweit bekanntesten Bauten der Moderne (und wurde 1996 unter Denkmalschutz gestellt). Es war in allen Fachzeitschriften veröffentlicht und ebenso in vielen an das breite Publikum gerichteten Illustrierten. Es erhielt zahlreiche Auszeichnungen, darunter die Ehrenmedaille in Silber der Architectural League of New York 1950. Es gibt ein ausführliches und schönes Buch darüber, das seinen Vorläufern sowie der Formensprache, dem Raum und den Details gewidmet ist, es war Gegenstand von Doktorarbeiten und wissenschaftlichen Studien und wurde von Tausenden geladener und ungeladener Besucher auf seinem Grundstück besichtigt. Kurz, es gibt nur weniges zu diesem Thema, das nicht schon – und wahrscheinlich weitaus besser – gesagt oder geschrieben worden wäre.

Dennoch gibt es einige Aspekte am Glashaus, die selbst jetzt, fast fünfzig Jahre nach seiner Errichtung, genauerer Betrachtung wert sind.

Zunächst handelt es sich nicht eigentlich um ein alleinstehendes Haus. Es ist das Herzstück einer von Johnson entworfenen Gesamtanlage und ist gewissermaßen immer noch im Bau bzw. wird, während diese Zeilen geschrieben werden, erweitert. Bei seiner ersten «Fertigstellung» bestand das Gebäude nicht nur aus einem, sondern aus zwei Bauwerken, das eine fast nur Glas, das andere fast nur Ziegel. Der Raum zwischen ihnen (ca. 25 m) und wie man sich darauf zubewegte, war beinahe so wichtig wie die Bauwerke selbst.

Johnson hat seither noch etliche Bauwerke auf seinem 45 ha großen Grundstück entworfen und gebaut: eine Galerie für seine Gemälde- und eine für seine Skulpturensammlung; einen wie eine Etüde in Bogen, Säulen und Eckgestaltung anmutenden Pavillon ähnlich seiner größeren Kunstgalerie Sheldon in Nebraska (1972); einen quasi leeren Turm, der seinem kürzlich verstorbenen alten Freund Lincoln Kirstein skulptural Tribut zollt; einen Pavillon als Studierzimmer und Klause (1980) sowie ein Torhaus (1995), von dem verschiedentlich als «Monsta», «Stealth Bomber» oder auch «Liebe und Tod» die Rede war und das nach Johnsons Tod, wenn das Anwesen dem National Trust zufällt, als eine Art Checkpoint Verwendung finden wird.

Glass House

Philip Johnson
1949
New Canaan, Connecticut
Structural Engineer: Eipel Engineering Co.
Lighting: Richard Kelly

The Glass House which Philip Johnson built for himself in New Canaan, Connecticut, in the late 1940s, may be one of the best known modern houses in the world today. It has been published in every professional magazine printed for architects anywhere, and in many popular magazines published for architecture buffs as well. It has won numerous awards, including the 1950 Silver Medal of Honor of the Architectural League of New York. It has one complete and beautiful book devoted to its forms, spaces, details and antecedents; it has been the subject of scholarly and doctoral theses; and it has probably been seen by thousands of invited as well as uninvited visitors to the site. In short, there is very little that can be said about it that hasn't already been said and written, and probably much better.

Still, there are some aspects to the Glass House that seem worth exploring even at this late date – almost 50 years after the fact.

To begin with, it is not really a single house; it is the center piece of a complex designed by Johnson and still, in a sense, under construction and/or expansion as this is written. When the house was first «completed», it consisted of not one but two structures – one virtually all glass, the other virtually all brick. The space between the two, and the approaches to that space (and to the two buildings set some 90 feet apart), seemed almost as important as the structures themselves.

Since that time, Johnson has designed and built several other structures on the 45-acre property: a gallery for his collection of paintings, and a gallery for his collection of sculptures; a pavilion that was an exercise in arches, columns, and corners of the sort that Johnson employed at a much larger scale in his Sheldon Art Gallery Building done in Nebraska in 1972; a tower that is a sculptural tribute to his old friend, the late Lincoln Kirstein, and contains virtually nothing; a pavilion that is Johnson's study and retreat, and was completed in 1980; and a gatehouse, completed in 1995 that has been variously referred to as «Monsta» or «Stealth Bomber» or «Love and Death», and that will serve as a kind of Checkpoint when the estate is turned over to the National Trust after Johnson's death.

In short, the «Glass House» is really a kind of Living Museum of Modern Architecture: it contains first-rate examples of everything from Schinkel Revival to Miesian

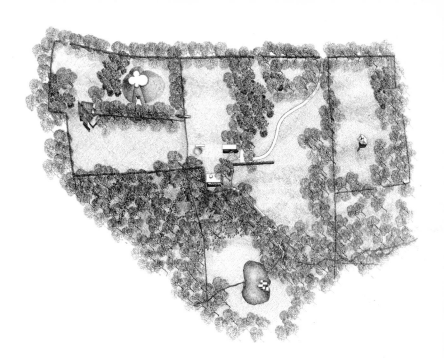

Kurz, das Glashaus ist eigentlich eine Art «Lebendes Museum» moderner Architektur: Man findet erstrangige Exemplare aller Art, von Neo-Schinkel über Mies'sche Perfektion bis zu Paul Rudolphs konstruktivistischen Etüden in Betonwerkstein. Und wenn man sieht, wie energiegeladen Johnson seit eh und je seine Ziele verfolgte und verfolgt, dann mag das noch lange nicht alles sein.

Das Anwesen in New Canaan ist in mehrfacher Hinsicht bemerkenswert: Zusammengetragen von einem hochgebildeten Historiker und Sammler mit unvergleichlicher Kenntnis, ist es eine erstaunliche Ansammlung von Verweisen auf das Werk von zwei oder drei Architektengenerationen, die im Laufe der Jahre die Moderne bestimmten. Johnsons Sammlung verweist auf einige der gelungensten Arbeiten Mies van der Rohes, auf eine der interessantesten Finsterlin-Fantasien, auf Vantongerloos Arbeiten, perfekter als alles, was der De Stijl-Künstler jemals ausgeführt hat, sowie auf andere Fantasien der frühen Moderne, die das Licht der Welt nicht erblickten – bis Johnson sie baute.

Die Sammlung ist deswegen bemerkenswert, weil die Stücke nicht von den Pionieren, die sie ursprünglich erdachten, sondern natürlich von Philip Johnson selbst entworfen und gebaut wurden – ein erstaunlicher Umstand, insbesondere wenn man die Sammlung Johnsons mit dem Nachlaß vergleicht, den uns andere Architekten, wie zum Beispiel Frank Lloyd Wright – wo alles, bis zum kleinsten Kerzenständer oder Türknauf typisch «Wright» ist – hinterlassen haben oder, wie ihn Le Corbusier oder Mies van der Rohe hinterlassen haben könnten (es aber nicht taten) und was selbstredend genauso reiner Mies oder Le Corbusier gewesen wäre. In der Johnson-Sammlung gibt es so gut wie nichts, das reiner Johnson wäre, es handelt sich um eine wunderbare Beispielsammlung einer Schaffensperiode, die Johnson wie kein anderer kannte und aufs peinlichste genau verzeichnete – in seinem Kopf.

Kurz, sie gleicht viel eher Bernard Berensons Villa I Tatti als Frank Lloyd Wrights Taliesins. Wie I Tatti stellt sie mehr das kreative Schaffen eines ungeheuer beschlagenen Historikers und Sammlers dar als das eines zielstrebigen Architekten.

Der Landsitz in New Canaan ist noch in anderer Hinsicht bemerkenswert – wegen der Art und Weise, wie die sorgfältig plazierten Elemente von der Lehre der Moderne abweichen und was dies über Philip Johnson als Architekten aussagt. In den Jahren vor Entwurf und Bau des Glashauses und seines Pendants in Ziegel galt Asymmetrie als Teil des Credos eines jeden Architekten wahrhaft moderner Bauten. Es war schlichtweg nicht möglich, nach klassischer Manier symmetrisch zu bauen, und die wenigen

perfection to Paul Rudolph's exercises in concrete-block constructivism. And judging by Johnson's energetic pursuits in recent years as before, this may not be the whole story by a long shot.

The New Canaan estate is remarkable in several respects: it is an amazing accumulation of mementos assembled by a highly sophisticated historian and collector – some of the best references to work produced by two or three generations of architects who have shaped the modern movement during the years that Philip Johnson has recorded more knowledgeably than most. The Johnson collection contains references to some of Mies van der Rohe's most accomplished works, to one of Finsterlin's most interesting fantasies, to work by Vantongerloo that is more accomplished than anything the Dutch DeStijlist ever built, and to exercises in other, early modern fantasies that never saw the light of day – until Johnson constructed them.

What makes this collection so specially remarkable is that all the mementos were, of course, designed and built not by the pioneers who originally inspired them, but by Philip Johnson himself – a truly astonishing fact, especially when one compares the Johnson Collection with such estates as those left to us by architects like Frank Lloyd Wright (in which every piece, down to the tiniest candlestick or doorknob was totally Wrightian), or the kinds of estates that might have been left to us by Le Corbusier or Mies van der Rohe (but were not) – all of which would, of course, have been Miesian or Corbusian. There is, in the Johnson Collection, virtually nothing that is exclusively Johnsonian: it is a collection of wonderful examples of work from a period that no one other than Philip Johnson knew so well or recorded so meticulously – in his head.

In short, it is much more like Bernard Berenson's Villa I Tatti than Frank Lloyd Wright's Taliesins. And, like I Tatti, it is the creative work of an enormously knowledgeable historian and collector, rather than that of a single-minded architect.

But the New Canaan estate is remarkable in another respect as well: it is remarkable and revealing in the way its careful elements depart from modern dogma and what these departures say about Philip Johnson as an architect. In the years prior to the design and construction of the Glass House and its brick companion, it was considered an act of faith for any architect, from Wright to Le Corbusier, that a truly modern building had to be asymmetrical. It was simply unacceptable to design and build symmetrical structures in the classical manner; and the few buildings by Gropius, Wright, Mies and Le Corbusier that violated this axiom seemed distinctly unconvincing to architects of the modern faith.

Außenansicht

Exterior view

Bauten von Gropius, Wright, Mies und Le Corbusier, die sich über dieses Axiom hinwegsetzten, wurden von Architekten der modernen Konfession ganz entschieden nicht für überzeugend gehalten.

Diese Regel hat Johnson hier ohne Zögern gebrochen: beide Bauwerke sind geradeso symmetrisch wie Versailles und ebenso streng wie all die anderen Schloßanlagen, die, wie Sanssouci, diesem Muster folgten. Für die meisten Architekten kam dies einem Verrat an den Prinzipien gleich, einem Abfall vom Glauben, einer Rückkehr zum aristokratischen Formalismus. Obwohl rückblickend die Argumentationsweise hinter sogearteter Kritik leicht absurd erscheint – schließlich ist es normalerweise hilfreich, wenn man sofort instinktiv weiß, wo die Eingangstür eines Gebäudes zu suchen ist, sei es eines Schuppens oder einer Kathedrale –, beunruhigte dieser Aspekt die meisten seiner modernen Zeitgenossen. Lediglich der Umstand, daß sowohl der Innenbereich des Glashauses als auch die Fußwegerschließung beider Gebäude eindeutig asymmetrisch waren, versicherte Johnsons Freunde, daß er nicht zur Gegenseite übergelaufen war. Die der Architektur innewohnenden Widersprüche ließen ahnen, daß es sich bei Philip Johnson in Wirklichkeit ganz und gar nicht um einen Architekten der Moderne handelte.

Zu der Zeit, als Johnson seine Freunde erstmals im Glashaus willkommen hieß, war nur wenigen unter ihnen klar,

Yet here, in his own house and in the brick guest house, Johnson broke that rule without hesitation: both of these structures are as symmetrical as Versailles, and as formal as all those other palaces, like Sans Souci, that followed the guidelines. To most modernists, this seemed almost a betrayal of basic principles, a breach of faith, a return to aristocratic formalism. Although the rationale underlying such criticism seems slightly absurd in retrospect – after all, it usually helps to know, instinctively and instantly, where to look for the front door in any building, from outhouse to cathedral – this aspect of Johnson's Glass House complex was disturbing to most of his modern contemporaries. Only the fact that the interior of the Glass House, and the pedestrian approach to the two buildings, were distinctly asymmetrical reassured Johnson's friends that he had not joined the opposition. But even these inherent architectural contradictions suggested that Philip Johnson was not really a modern architect at all.

Few of his friends, in the days when Johnson first welcomed them to the Glass House, realized how right they were. In fact, in the years after Johnson broke his architectural ties to Mies van der Rohe – roughly after Mies and Johnson had completed their collaboration on the (symmetrical) Seagram Building – virtually all of Johnson's major buildings became symmetrical, except for some smaller, free-standing structures which he tended to treat

Innenansichten

Interior views

wie recht sie mit ihrer Ahnung hatten. Nachdem Johnson seine architektonische Bindung zu Mies van der Rohe gelöst hatte – mehr oder weniger kurz nach dem Abschluß ihrer Zusammenarbeit am (symmetrischen) Seagram Building –, nahmen nahezu alle seiner wichtigen Bauten symmetrische Gestalt an, mit Ausnahme einiger kleinerer Gebäude, die Johnson ohnedies eher als Skulpturen denn als Nutzbauten behandelte. Mehr noch, zum Teil machte Johnson neben ein, zwei anderen die Symmetrie wieder salonfähig – ein Richtungswechsel, von dem die Moderne als Bewegung kaum Notiz nahm. Man kann sagen, daß er einer der ersten war, der Regeln brach, die schon bei ihrer Entstehung nicht allzu viel Sinn ergaben.

Laut Johnson beruhte der Entwurf des Glashauses in Tat und Wahrheit auf einem früher entstandenen Stahl- und Glashausentwurf Mies van der Rohes für Dr. Edith Farnsworth – ein schöner Pavillon, der erst etliche Jahre, nachdem Johnson seinen Wohnsitz bezogen hatte, fertiggestellt wurde. Johnson bestand darauf, daß der ursprüngliche Entwurf Mies' Verdienst gewesen sei, was aber doch

as works of sculpture rather than works of shelter. Moreover, in part because Johnson and one or two others made symmetry respectable again, this change in direction in the modern movement was barely noticed; and it is fair to say that Johnson was one of the first to break the rules that never made much sense when first formulated. The design of the Glass House, according to Johnson, was really based on Mies van der Rohe's earlier design for a steel and glass house for Dr. Edith Farnsworth – a beautiful pavilion that was not completed until a couple of years after Johnson had moved into his New Canaan residence. Johnson insisted on giving Mies credit for having initiated the design, but this was overly generous on Johnson's part. Although the two structures are superficially similar, they differ in essential respects: the Farnsworth House is asymmetrical, inside and out, while Johnson's is symmetrical outside (and asymmetrical within). The Farnsworth House is raised off the ground on steel columns, while Johnson's sits firmly on a flat and grassy plain. The Farnsworth House stands alone in the landscape, while Johnson's was, from the start, part of a

zu großmütig war. Die beiden Bauten weisen zwar oberflächliche Ähnlichkeiten auf, unterscheiden sich aber in entscheidener Hinsicht: Das Haus Farnsworth ist im Innen- und Außenbereich asymmetrisch angelegt, Johnsons Bau dagegen von außen symmetrisch (und von innen asymmetrisch). Stahlstützen heben es vom Boden ab, während Johnsons Haus unverrückbar auf der flachen, grasbewachsenen Erde aufsitzt. Das Haus Farnsworth steht allein für sich in der Landschaft, Johnsons Haus hingegen war von Anfang an Teil einer formalen Gesamtanlage, die vom Gästehaus sowie den verbindenden Fußwegen bestimmt wird, und die Stahlkonstruktion des Hauses Farnsworth trägt einen weißen Anstrich, während Johnsons dunkelgrau ist.

Weiter: das Haus Farnsworth kragt zu beiden Seiten der Stahlrahmenkonstruktion aus, so daß es den Anschein hat, als seien die Eckbereiche aus auf Gehrung geschnittenem Glas gebildet, wodurch das ganze Gebäude über der Landschaft zu schweben scheint. Bei Johnsons Haus dagegen, fest mit dem Boden verwurzelt, bestehen die Eckbereiche aus massiven Stahlstützen. Die Stahlrahmen-

formal composition, shaped by the brick Guest House and the pedestrian walkways approaching and connecting the two; and the Farnsworth House was framed in steel painted white, whereas Johnson's was framed in steel painted dark gray.

There were other significant differences: for example, the Farnsworth House is cantilevered from the steel frame at its two ends and its corners almost seem formed by mitered glass, so that the whole structure looks as if it were afloat in the landscape; whereas the Johnson House is firmly planted on the ground, its corners formed by massive steel columns. Moreover, the detailing of the steel frame in the two houses is very different: whereas the detailing of the columns and beams in the Farnsworth House is quite spare and minimal – so tightly reduced that it looks almost as if the steel were connected by little more than magnetic force – the detailing in the Johnson Glass House is rather massive. The corner columns (which, in fact, carry less of a load than the columns at the center) look twice as bulky in cross section as those at the center – an overstatement that Johnson

konstruktion ist sehr unterschiedlich ausgeprägt: während die Träger und Stützen im Haus Farnsworth minimiert sind – sogar so weit, daß ihre Verbindungen kaum mehr als magnetisch gehalten scheinen –, fallen die Details in Johnsons Glashaus recht massiv aus. Die Eckstützen (die in Tat und Wahrheit weniger Lasten als die Mittelstützen aufnehmen) sind im Querschnitt doppelt so dick als in der Mitte; Johnson übertrieb hier, um das klassische Erscheinungsbild des Gebäudes zu unterstreichen. Wie bei den symmetrischen Fassaden wurde auch hier Johnsons Aspekt seinen Zeitgenossen in der Architekturbranche, die gelernt hatten, an teuren Materialien wie Stahl zu sparen, leicht unwohl.

Es gibt noch andere Widersprüche, nicht alle so augenscheinlich. Während das Haus Farnsworth durchgängig eine Stahlkonstruktion aufweist, findet Stahl in Johnsons Glashaus nur dort Verwendung, wo man ihn auch sieht. Die Dachnebenträger zwischen den artikulierten Stahlhauptträgern sind aus Holz – ein Umstand, der Mies van der Rohe bei einem Wochenendbesuch derartig aus der Fassung brachte, daß er sich weigerte, die Nacht unter einem so «unehrlichen» Dach zuzubringen. Darüber hinaus ist die Stahlkonstruktion von Johnsons Glashaus entgegen ihrem Anschein nicht besonders steif ausgebildet: vor Einbringung der ca. 65 mm dicken Flachglasscheiben schwankte die Deckenplatte beunruhigend hin und her, wenn man aufs Dach kletterte, um die Aussicht zu genießen; tatsächlich war die Rahmenkonstruktion erst stabil, nachdem die gesamte Verglasung zur Aussteifung eingebracht worden war. Es gab zu der Zeit nicht einen eingeschworenen Architekten der Moderne, der einen derart «unehrlichen» Ausdruck der Konstruktion hingenommen hätte – obwohl selbst Mies van der Rohe selten davor zurückschreckte, das Tragwerk seiner Wolkenkratzer dadurch zu artikulieren, daß er die eigentliche Tragstruktur mit davorliegenden Stützen versah, die fast so wirkten, als seien sie ihm nachträglich eingefallen.

Für Philip Johnson ist das alles nie ein Thema gewesen. Ihn interessiert nur, wie seine Bauten aussehen, wie sie sich anfühlen und anhören – vor allem auch in der ihnen eigenen Umgebung. Das Gästehaus und das Glashaus mit all den verschiedenen skulpturalen Pavillons, die sie umgeben, sind eine ausgesprochen gelungene Übung in der Kunst, Raum zu schaffen.

Wenn man Gelegenheit hatte, das Glashaus über die Jahre hinweg immer wieder, bei jedem Wetter und unterschiedlichsten Lichtverhältnissen, zu besuchen, sind es nicht die Bauten selbst, die einen am meisten beeindrucken, sondern die Art und Weise, in der sie die umgebende Landschaft gliedern und einrahmen. Das Glashaus ist im Grunde eine Serie von gerahmten Blicken auf na-

sought quite deliberately to emphasize the building's classical presence.

Johnson's contemporaries in architecture, who had been taught to minimalize the expenditure of costly materials like steel, felt a bit uncomfortable about that aspect of the house – just as they did about its symmetrical facades.

There are other contradictions, some of them less visible. While the Farnsworth House is steel-framed throughout, the Johnson Glass House is steel-framed only where the steel is visible; the secondary framing joists in the roof, between the «expressed» steel girders, are of wood – a fact that deeply disturbed Johnson's weekend visitor Mies van der Rohe, who refused to spend the night under so «dishonest» a structure. Moreover the steel frame of Johnson's Glass House, despite its apparent strength, is not especially rigid: during construction, before the 1/4" thick plate glass had been put in place, the roof deck tended to sway sideways rather disconcertingly when one climbed onto it to enjoy the views of the landscape; the frame of the house did not, in fact, become rigid until the glass framing was in place and braced the structure. No bona-fide modern architect of that time could accept so «dishonest» a structural expression – although Mies van der Rohe himself, in his own work, rarely hesitated to «express» the structural frame of one of his skyscrapers by decorating the actual structure with columns that would be applied to the exterior almost as an afterthought!

To Philip Johnson, such issues have never been especially compelling. He is interested only in the way his buildings look and feel and sound – and in the way they look and feel and sound in their settings. The Glass House and its Guest House, and the various sculptural pavilions surrounding it, are a hugely successful exercise in the art of making space.

After a good many years of visiting the Glass House in all sorts of light and in all sorts of weather, the most vivid impressions are not of the buildings themselves as they appear in photographs, but of the way they frame and articulate the landscape around them. The Glass House is really a series of frames that define the views of nearby trees and lawns, of stone walls, of lakes and pools, of distant hills on far horizons. At night, the lighting of the nearby landscape spills over into the house itself, and endows it with an intimate glow; in the fall and in the winter, curtains of raindrops or snowflakes may engulf the house and turn the views of the landscape into dream-like mysteries. The reflections within (and without) double the visions of the surroundings and add to the magic. It is an almost impossible place to photograph – it is all impressions superimposed upon fleeting images that change almost every minute.

hegelegene Bäume und Wiesen, Steinmauern, Seen, Wasserbecken und ferne Hügel am weiten Horizont. Nachts umspült die Beleuchtung in der unmittelbaren Umgebung des Gebäudes das Haus selbst und verleiht ihm ein intimes Licht, im Herbst und im Winter verhüllt ein Schleier aus Regentropfen oder Schneeflocken mitunter das ganze Haus und verwandelt den Ausblick auf die Landschaft in eine geheimnisvolle Traumwelt. Die Spiegelungen innen (wie auch außen) lassen einen die Umgebung doppelt sehen und verstärken den Zauber. Hier ist ein Ort, der sich nicht auf Fotos bannen läßt – man hat es nur mit Eindrücken zu tun, die flüchtige, sich stetig ändernde Bilder überlagern.

Obwohl vorher die Rede vom Glashaus als Johnsons I Tatti war – nicht nur mit Kunstwerken ausgestattet, die Johnson selbst geschaffen hat, sondern auch mit einer Wechselausstellung von Werken der Bildhauerei von Lipchitz über Kiesler und Donald Judd zu Ellsworth Kelly und anderen –, so ist es doch eigentlich viel mehr als das. Es ist eine atemberaubend anschauliche Darstellung davon, wie ein erstklassiger Architekt den unvorhersehbaren Reichtum der Natur – Licht und Dunkel, Sonne und Schatten, Wolken und Nebel, Regen und Schnee und vor allem Bäume und Blumen, Stein und Gras – zu bändigen und in ein beständig wechselndes Spiel der Formen und des Raums zu verwandeln weiß, angeregt vom Licht, so wie Le Corbusier einst Architektur beschrieb. Daß Johnson all dies so gut gelang, gereicht ihm als Baumeister zur Ehre; was das Glashaus aber zu einem bleibenden Werk der Kunst und Architektur erhebt, ist der Zauber, den das Erlebnis birgt.

Although the Glass House, as suggested earlier, is Johnson's I Tatti – endowed with a remarkable collection not only of Johnson-made works of art, but with constantly changing works of sculpture by everyone from Lipchitz to Kiesler to Donald Judd to Ellsworth Kelly and beyond – it is really much more that. It is a stunning demonstration of the way a first-rate architect can harness the unpredictable resources of nature – light and shade, sun and shadow, clouds and mists, rain and snow, and, above all, trees and flowers and stone and grass – and turn them into a constantly changing play of forms and spaces animated by light, as Le Corbusier once described architecture. The fact that all this was accomplished so meticulously well is a tribute to Johnson's competence as a builder; but it is the magic of the experience that makes the Glass House a lasting work of architecture and of art.

Awards: Silver Medal of Honor, Architectural League of New York, 1950
Twenty-Five Year Award, AIA, 1975
National Historic Landmark, 1996

«Philip Johnson: The Glass House», David Whitney 1993
«Philip Johnson: Processes», Catalogue 9, IAUS, 1978

Anbau Museum of Modern Art
Philip Johnson
1950
New York, New York
Statik: Eipel Engineering Co.

Im Jahre 1950 beschloß das Whitney Museum of American Art seinen bisherigen Standort von Greenwich Village in die Mitte Manhattans zu verlagern und erwarb das Grundstück neben und hinter dem ursprünglichen Museum of Modern Art. Die Ostfassade des neuen Whitney sollte auf den Garten des MoMA ausgerichtet werden, der zu diesem Zeitpunkt von Philip Johnson neu gestaltet wurde. Johnsons Fassade nimmt die Gebäudehöhe des alten MoMA-Gebäudes von 1939 von Stone & Goodwin auf. Die neue Fassade besteht aus einem Stahlrahmen mit Glas- und Ziegelausfachung in der Art der Bauten, die Mies van der Rohe auf dem IIT-Campus in Chicago errichtete.
Als das Whitney seinen neuen Hauptsitz an der Madison Avenue und 75. Straße, den Marcel Breuer entworfen hatte, bezog, wurde das temporäre Whitney-Gebäude mit der Fassade von Johnson der Gesamtanlage des MoMA angeschlossen, die dadurch zusätzliche Ausstellungsflächen und eine auf den neuen Museumsgarten ausgerichtete Cafeteria gewann. 1981 mußte die Fassade an der 53. Straße einer Museumserweiterung nach Osten und dem dazugehörigen Wohnhochhaus weichen.

Museum of Modern Art Annex
Philip Johnson
1950
New York, New York
Structural Engineer: Eipel Engineering Co.

In 1950, the Whitney Museum of American Art, which was then located in Greenwich Village, decided to move uptown, and acquired a property adjacent to and behind the original MoMA building. The east facade of this new Whitney would face the MoMA garden being redesigned by Philip Johnson, and so he was asked to design that side of the new Whitney. The Johnson facade matches the height of the original 1939 MoMA building by Stone & Goodwin; and this new facade is of glass and brick framed in steel, very much in the manner established by Mies van der Rohe on the IIT campus in Chicago.
When the Whitney moved to its permanent headquarters on Madison Avenue at East 75th Street designed by Marcel Breuer, the temporary Whitney building was incorporated in the MoMA complex and provided additional gallery space and a cafeteria that opens to the new Museum Garden. The 53rd Street Johnson facade was destroyed in 1981 for the eastward expansion of the Museum and the residential tower.

«Philip Johnson», John Jacobus, 1962
Architectural Forum, May 1955

Grundriß Erdgeschoß
Außenansicht

Ground floor plan
Exterior view

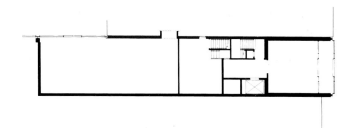

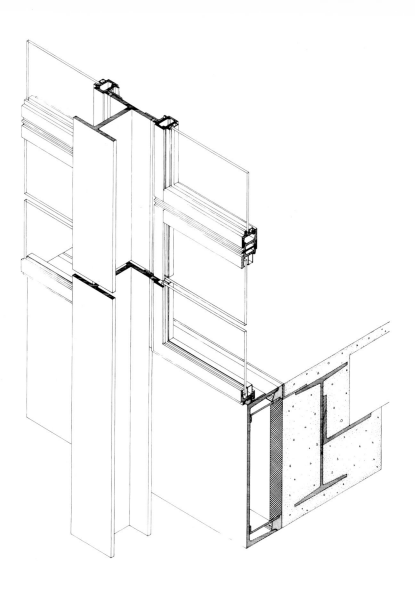

0   1   2   3

Schnitt durch die Fassade, 1:10

Facade section, 1:10

Rockefeller Gästehaus

Philip Johnson
1950
New York, New York
Partner: Landis Gores
Statik: Eipel Engineering Co.
Lichttechnik: Richard Kelly
Textilien: Anni Albers

1950 erhielt Johnson, der gerade sein Architekturbüro in New York eingerichtet hatte, von einem Mitglied der Rockefeller-Familie den Auftrag für ein kleines Gästehaus auf der Ostseite Manhattans. Das Haus sollte der Unterbringung von Gästen der Familie dienen, Freunde oder offizielle Besucher, die mit den zahlreichen Aktivitäten der Rockefellers in Verbindung standen. (Die Rockefellers selbst besaßen bereits einige Straßenblöcke weiter einen Wohnsitz am East River).

Johnson entwarf dann dieses kleine Stadthaus für die Gäste. Johnsons Bauherren erwarben zur Errichtung des Hauses eine bestehende Remise auf einem Grundstück von etwa 7,60 m x 30,50 m. Obwohl es sich bei diesem Stadthaus letztendlich um ein neues Gebäude handelt, gelang es Johnson, die Baupläne bei der zuständigen Behörde als «Umbau» genehmigen zu lassen – das hieß, er war in der Lage, Grundstücksteile zu nutzen, auf denen ein Neubebauung normalerweise untersagt gewesen wäre. Durch dieses Umgehen der Vorschriften konnte Johnson das Grundstück auf einfallsreiche und neue Weise nutzen. Die verschiedenen Räume in dem – im wesentlichen neuen – Gebäude mußten für die Bürokratie als umgenutzte Teile der ursprünglichen Remise bezeichnet werden – so firmiert zum Beispiel ein prachtvoll-luxuriöses Schlafzimmer auf der Südseite des Grundstücks in den Unterlagen des Bauamts offiziell als «umgebauter Stall».

Das Haus ist zwar kein bedeutendes Werk, ist aber dennoch so sorgfältig und gut geplant und detailliert, daß man es als eine Art Prototyp eines Stadthauses gelten lassen kann, der sich erheblich von den Stadthäusern unterscheidet, wie sie im Laufe der letzten hundert Jahre und noch länger in amerikanischen Städten routinemäßig gebaut wurden. Dieses Haus hat seinen Garten in der Grundstücksmitte, und nicht, wie die Wohnhäuser mit Treppenerschließung sonst, einen Hof im rückwärtigen Bereich – in diesem Fall besteht der Garten aus einem Wasserbecken mit Trittsteinen. Auf der anderen Seite dieses Beckens liegt der umgenutzte «Stall».

Die Stadthausfassade ist, nach Mies'scher Manier, symmetrisch ausgelegt und zweigeschossig. Dieser Teil des kleinen Hauses ist am wenigsten gelungen und kann mit

Rockefeller Guest House

Philip Johnson
1950
New York, New York
Partner: Landis Gores
Structural Engineer: Eipel Engineering Co.
Lighting: Richard Kelly
Textiles: Anni Albers

In 1950, when Johnson was establishing his architectural practice in New York, a member of the Rockefeller family asked him to design a small guest house on Manhattan's east side. The house would enable the family to put up visiting friends and dignitaries connected with one of the Rockefeller's favorite institutions. (The Rockefellers themselves already owned a residence on the East River a few blocks away.)

This small townhouse is what Johnson designed for their guests. To build the house, Johnson's clients acquired an existing carriage house on a lot measuring about 25 feet in width and 100 feet in depth. Although the townhouse is in effect, an entirely new structure, Johnson managed to get its plan approved by the local Building Department as an «alteration» – which meant that he could design it to occupy portions of the site normally off limits to new construction. This enabled Johnson to use the site in new and innovative ways normally outlawed by building codes and zoning regulations. To get the new plans approved by the bureaucrats, the various rooms in the substantially new structure had to be labeled as converted elements of the original carriage house – so that, for example, a splendid and luxurious bedroom suite at the south end of the property is now officially listed in the Building Department's records as a «remodeled stable.»

The house as a whole, while not a major work, is so neatly laid out and so well detailed that it serves as a prototype for a kind of urban townhouse very different from the ones that have been routinely constructed in American cities over the past century and more. Instead of containing a backyard in the rear of a walk-up residence, this house has its garden in the middle of the property – the garden, in this case, being a pool bridged by stepping stones. And at the far end of the pool is the converted «stable.»

The facade of the townhouse is symmetrical in the Miesian manner, and two tall stories high. It is the least successful aspect of this little house, and somewhat out of keeping with the open spaces of the interior. Certainly, a one-story building would have seemed completely out of scale and place on this urban street; and so there is an upper floor containing guest rooms. Theoretically, this end

Grundriß Erdgeschoß, 1:250

Ground floor plan, 1:250

dem fließenden Innenraum nicht mithalten. Ein einge-schossiger Bau wäre mit Sicherheit im städtischen Straßenkontext völlig fehl am Platze gewesen, und des-halb gibt es ein Obergeschoß mit Gästezimmern. Theore-tisch hätte die Fassade auf dieser Seite auch vier- oder fünfgeschossig ausfallen können, vergleichbar anderen Stadthäusern in der Gegend, jedes Geschoß hätte eine nach Süden ausgerichteten Terrasse mit Aussicht auf den Innenhof haben können. Ein asymmetrisch angeordneter Eingang hätte auch einen besseren Bezug zu so einem Grundriß geschaffen. Wie es auch sei, jede einzelne die-ser Variationen findet sich im Entwurf angedeutet. Die Verwirklichung der Hofhaus-/Stadthausidee auf einem ty-pischen Grundstück in Manhattan ist Johnsons eigentli-che, auch heute noch bedeutsame und innovative Lei-stung.

Die Hauptebene des Stadthauses weist im gebauten Zu-stand einen ausgesprochen großzügigen Wohnraum auf, der auf den Innenhof mit dem spiegelnden Wasserbecken blickt. Die Küche, eine verdeckte Reihe geschlossener Schränke, befindet sich im Eingangsbereich.

Es handelt sich hierbei ganz offensichtlich nicht um einen minimalen Lösungsvorschlag zur Wohnungsnot der mitt-leren und unteren Einkommensgruppen. Die Raumhöhe der beiden Geschosse beträgt, eindeutig auf die obere Gesellschaftsschicht zugeschnitten, ca. 3,65 m – eine großzügige Abmessung, die nicht Gefahr läuft, zum Stan-dard im Wohnungsbau zu werden. Das Haus ist zwar lu-xuriös, zeigt aber dennoch, wie es einem ingeniösen Ar-chitekten trotz schwierigster Vorgaben gelingen kann, be-achtliche städtische Typen zu schaffen. Das Ergebnis ist in diesem Fall eines der reizvollsten privaten Wohnhäuser New Yorks.

of the property could have been four or five stories in height, as most of the old townhouses in the area were; and each of those stories could have had a terrace over-looking the interior court and facing south. And an asym-metrical entrance might have related better to such a plan. In any case, all of these variations are implied in the scheme. What Johnson did accomplish – the idea of a courthouse/townhouse on a typical Manhattan lot – was immensely significant and innovative.

The main floor of the townhouse, as actually built, con-tains a very spacious living area that overlooks the inte-rior court with its reflecting pool. A kitchen is located in the entry area as a hidden set of closed off cabinets.

Obviously, this is no minimal solution to a middle- or low-income urban housing problem. The ceiling heights are a distinctly upper-class 12 feet – a sure way of establishing a very luxurious scale unlikely to be sanctioned by the Federal Housing Administration. But though the house is luxurious, it demonstrates how an imaginative architect can create some remarkable urban prototpyes, however tight the constraints. In this house, the result is one of New York's most delightful private houses.

House and Home, August 1954
«Philip Johnson», H.R. Hitchcock, 1965

Straßenfassade
Innenansicht mit Hof im Hintergrund

Street facade
Interior view with court beyond

Haus Hodgson
Philip Johnson
1951
New Canaan, Connecticut
Partner: Landis Gores

Die kompakten, gegeneinander versetzten Baukörper des Haus Hodgson bilden sich in der dreiteiligen Fassade aus Glas und Ziegel mit einem Dachabschluß aus Stahl ab. Somit ist das Haus eindeutig Mies van der Rohe verpflichtet. Der Grundriß erinnert aber auch an Grundrisse pompeiischer Villen. Das Eingangsfoyer öffnet sich mittelachsig auf einen verglasten Innenhof, der von tagsüber genutzten Wohnräumen umgeben ist, nebenachsig angeordnet liegt ein Pavillon, der die Schlafzimmer aufnimmt. Beim Bau des Hauses wurde ein blaugrauer, kobaltgefleckter Ziegel verwendet.

Hodgson House
Philip Johnson
1951
New Canaan, Connecticut
Partner: Landis Gores

The compact, offset volumes of the Hodgson house are expressed in a tripartite elevation of brick and glass, topped by a steel cornice. So the house clearly owes a debt to Mies. But its plan also echoes those of Pompeian villas. The entry foyer of the house opens on axis to a glass enclosed courtyard surrounded by day time living areas, with a secondary axis leading to the bedroom pavilion. The brick used in construction of the house is a blue-gray cobalt spot.

Award: AIA Honor Award 1956

Architectural Record, March 1953
«Philip Johnson», John Jacobus, 1962

Grundriß Erdgeschoß, 1:500
Außenansicht

Ground floor plan, 1:500
Exterior view

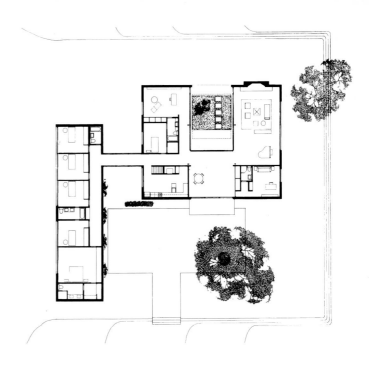

Haus Oneto

Philip Johnson
1951
Irvington, New York
Partner: Landis Gores
Assoziierter Architekt: Marios A. Kantopoulos
Statik: Wolff Engineering Inc.
Haustechnik: Sears & Kopf

Philip Johnson entwarf das Haus Oneto 1951, als er noch sehr stark unter dem Einfluß von Mies van der Rohe stand. Es gehört zu einer Reihe von Einfamilienhäusern, die demselben grundlegenden Muster folgen: ein rechteckiger Grundriß mit einem mittig angeordneten Wohnraum, raumhoher Verglasung auf der Eingangs- und auf der gegenüberliegenden Gartenseite, beidseitig angeordneten Schlafzimmern, Bädern, einer Küche und weiteren Nebenräumen; Fenster gewähren Ausblick an den Stirnseiten des Rechtecks. Der Grundriß ist ordentlich und ausgesprochen gut nutzbar, gezeichnet (aber nie gebaut) wurde er von Mies als Feriendomizil für Mr. und Mrs. Stanley Resor auf einem Grundstück in Jackson Hole, Wyoming.

Johnson verwendete den Grundriß ziemlich unverändert 1946 für ein Haus in Sagaponack, Long Island sowie in einigen anderen Wohnhäusern, die kurz nach Ende des Zweiten Weltkriegs entstanden. Das Haus Oneto, errichtet auf einem Grundstück mit Blick auf den Hudson nördlich von New York City, ist womöglich das beste von allen. Ähnlich mehreren anderen Häusern, die Johnson in den fünfziger Jahren und danach baute, ist das Haus Oneto in der Ansicht symmetrisch, im Grundriß jedoch asymmetrisch. Das Haus ist weniger transparent als Johnsons eigenes Haus in New Canaan, deshalb fällt diese Unstimmigkeit nicht besonders auf.

Der Grundentwurf funktioniert so gut, daß er, seitdem Johnson ihn der Allgemeinheit zugänglich gemacht hat, immer wieder kopiert wird. Aber seine Varianten zum Thema sind fast ausnahmslos ein bißchen eleganter, ein bißchen heiterer als die Kopien; die Raumhöhe beträgt in der Regel um die 3,00 m, die Ziegel sind im allgemeinen präzise verlegt (zu der Zeit bevorzugte er graue, eisenfarbig gefleckte Ziegel), und die Umgebung der Häuser entspricht der Mies'schen Formensprache – Stützmauern und Sichtschutzwände im gleichen Ziegel gehalten, Terrassen mit Bruchsteinplatten belegt, der Baumbestand von Buschwerk und Unterholz befreit, um hohen Wuchs und ausladende Kronen zur Geltung zu bringen; die Landschaftsgestaltung zumeist auf ordentlich geschnittene Rasenflächen und Blumenbeete beschränkt.

Man sieht an diesem wie auch an anderen Projekten ziemlich deutlich, was Johnson für ein Einfühlungsvermö-

Oneto House

Philip Johnson
1951
Irvington, New York
Partner: Landis Gores
Associate Architect: Marios A. Kantopoulos
Structural Engineer: Wolff Engineering Inc.
Mechanical Engineer: Sears & Kopf

The Oneto House, which Philip Johnson designed in 1951 while he was still very much under the influence of Mies van der Rohe, is one of several residences done by him on the same basic pattern: a rectangular plan, with the living area in its center (and glazed, floor to ceiling, on the entrance side and equally on the opposite garden side); and with each end containing bedrooms, bathrooms, kitchen, and other secondary spaces, with windows facing out of the two short ends of the rectangle. It is a neat and eminently workable plan, and it was drawn up by Mies (but never built) as a vacation house for Mr. and Mrs. Stanley Resor, for a site near Jackson Hole, Wyoming.

Johnson used much the same plan in his 1946 House in Sagaponack, Long Island, and in other houses done shortly after the end of World War II. The Oneto House, built on a site overlooking the Hudson River to the north of New York City, may be the best of these.

Like other houses done by Johnson in the 1950s and later, the Oneto House is symmetrical in its elevations, but asymmetrical in plan. But since the house is not as transparent as Johnson's own Glass House in New Canaan, this conflict is not especially apparent.

The basic scheme works so well that others have copied it ever since Johnson popularized the plan. But his versions of the scheme are almost invariably a little more elegant, a little more serene than the copies; the ceiling height is usually about 10 feet; the brick is usually precise (he preferred gray iron spot brick in those days); and the landscaping around the house is in the Miesian idiom – retaining or screen walls of the same brick, terraces paved with flagstone, existing trees liberated from bushes and undergrowth, to show their full height and spread; and landscaping usually limited to neatly trimmed lawns and beds of flowers.

In this house, as in other projects, Johnson's understanding of the landscape and of the part it plays in the glass-walled buildings is quite evident: the outward views in several directions are integral parts of the design, and the manner in which the existing elements of the landscape have been preserved and related to the new building – these are handled with a sensitivity not often found in recent years except in the work of Frank Lloyd Wright. Even

Außenansicht
Grundriß Erdgeschoß, 1:300

Exterior view
Ground floor plan, 1:300

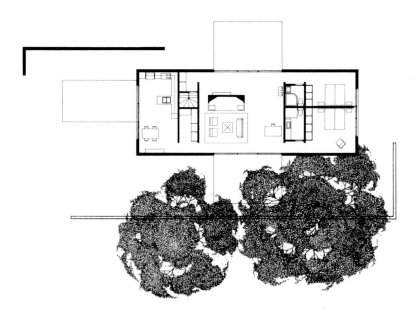

gen in die Landschaft und ihre Rolle im Verhältnis zu den verglasten Bauten hat: die Blickbeziehungen von innen nach außen in die verschiedensten Richtungen sind ein integraler Bestandteil des Entwurfs ebenso wie die Art und Weise, in der bestehende Landschaftselemente erhalten und in den Entwurf eingebunden werden – all das mit einer Sensibilität für die Bezüge zwischen Gebäude und Umgebung, wie man sie kaum noch findet, außer im Werk eines Frank Lloyd Wright. Nicht einmal Mies van der Rohe bewies diese Einfühlung, die das gute Dutzend Häuser auszeichnet, das Johnson in der Nachkriegszeit baute.

Mies van der Rohe did not show as much sensitivity toward the relationship of a building to its landscape as Johnson did in the dozen or so houses he designed and built in the years after the end of World War II.

Award: Architectural Record House of 1957

«Philip Johnson», John Jacobus, 1962
Perspecta 1, Summer 1952

Schlumberger Verwaltungsgebäude

Philip Johnson
1952
Ridgefield, Connecticut
Statik: Eipel Engineering Co.
Lichttechnik: Richard Kelly
Inneneinrichtung: Florence Knoll

Dieses kleine Bürogebäude von ca. 670 m² wurde in der Höhe eingeschossig angelegt, um es seinem Standort, einem Wohnviertel, besser anzupassen. Der asymmetrische Grundriß hat einen ausgesprochen rationalen, Mies'schen Charakter. Die außenliegenden Standardbüros gewähren Aussicht in die Landschaft, der großangelegte Konferenzbereich und Aufenthaltsraum überblickt einen innenliegenden, verglasten Gartenhof. Die Tragstruktur des Gebäudes besteht aus schwarzgestrichenem Stahl mit Ziegel- und Glasausfachung. Das Mauerwerk aus glasiertem, eisenfarbig geflecktem Ziegel wurde sowohl im Innen- als auch im Außenbereich als Sichtmauerwerk ausgeführt. Das konstruktive Grundraster ist ca. 6,10 m x 6,10 m mit einer durchschnittlichen Bürobreite von 3,05 m.

Schlumberger Administration Building

Philip Johnson
1952
Ridgefield, Connecticut
Structural Engineer: Eipel Engineering Co.
Lighting: Richard Kelly
Interior Designer: Florence Knoll

This small (7,200 square feet) office building is only one story tall, to make it more compatible with the residential neighborhood in which it is located. The asymmetric plan is extremely rational and Miesian in character, with routine offices on the perimeter facing the landscape, and a large conference area and lounge facing a glazed, interior garden courtyard. The building is steel-framed painted black, with brick and glass infill. The masonry is glazed iron-spot brick, exposed on the inside and the exterior. The basic structural bays measure 20 feet by 20 feet, and most of the perimeter offices are 10 feet wide.

Award: Grand Festival Award, Boston, 1955

Architectural Forum, September 1953
«Philip Johnson», John Jacobus, 1962
Architectural Record, April 1964

Grundriß Erdgeschoß, 1:500
Außenansicht mit dem Eingangsbereich

Ground floor plan, 1:500
Exterior view with entry

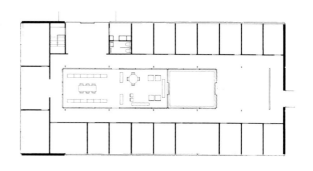

Innenräume Gästehaus
Philip Johnson
1953
New Canaan, Connecticut
Lichttechnik: Richard Kelly
Skulptur: Iboram Lassaw

Guest House Interior
Philip Johnson
1953
New Canaan, Connecticut
Lighting: Richard Kelly
Sculpture: Iboram Lassaw

Zur gleichen Zeit wie das Glashaus entstand das Ziegelhaus als Unterkunft für Johnsons Gäste. Ähnlich dem ihm gegenüberliegenden Glashaus besteht es aus einem einfachen, rechteckigen Kubus, dessen Ziegelwände den Kontrast zur Transparenz des Hauptgebäudes bilden. In der Gesamtanlage ergänzt das Ziegelhaus das Glashaus und rahmt dessen Zugang. Ursprünglich wurde das Ziegelhaus als Gästepavillon mit drei Schlafzimmern erbaut, 1953 erfolgte der Umbau zu einer luxuriösen Wohnung. Der eine Schlafraum wird nunmehr von einer in Gips ausgeführten Kuppel überdeckt, die an die Innenräume John Soanes erinnert; die Wände sind mit Fortuny-Stoff in Rosa-, Gold- und Silbertönen bezogen.

The Brick House was built at the same time as the Glass House, to accommodate Johnson's guests. Like the Glass House which it faces, its exterior is a simple rectangular prism, and its brick walls contrast with the transparency of the main building. The Brick House complements the Glass House's siting, and frames the approach to the latter. Originally constructed as a 3-bedroom guest pavilion, the Brick House was remodeled in 1953, and turned into a luxurious apartment. A domed plaster ceiling reminiscent of John Soane's interior now covers the single bedroom, and the interior wall surfaces are finished in a Fortuny fabric that is pink, gold and silver.

Interiors, July 1954
«Philip Johnson – The Glass House», David Whitney, 1993

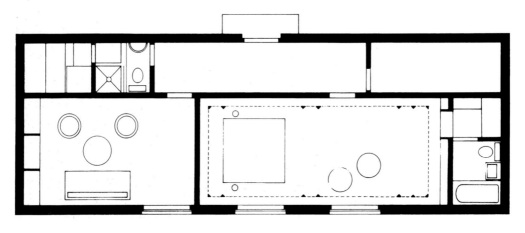

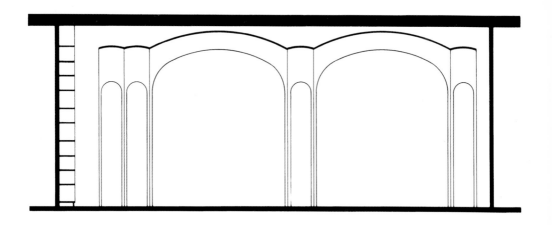

Grundriß
Schnitt
Innenansicht

Floor plan
Section
Interior view

Abby Aldrich Rockefeller Skulpturengarten des Museum of Modern Art

Philip Johnson
1953
New York, New York
Landschaftsplanung: James Fanning (1953);
Zion & Breen (1964)

Ende der dreißiger Jahre, als das New Yorker Museum of Modern Art seinen neuen Anbau erhielt, entwarfen der Kurator der Architekturabteilung, John McAndrew, und der Direktor, Alfred J. Barr Jr., einen Skulpturengarten zwischen dem Museum und der 54. Straße im Norden. Der in freier Form angelegte Garten war in Windeseile entworfen und erbaut worden, und hätte, obschon nicht einfallslos, sorgfältiger durchdacht sein können. Beispielsweise blieben die Flächen zu wenig definiert und zu formlos für die ausgestellten Skulpturen. Schließlich trat MoMA 1953 an Philip Johnson mit der Bitte heran, dem Garten eine neue und bleibende Gestalt zu verleihen.

Der von ihm erschaffene Skulpturengarten erfuhr im Laufe der Jahre einige Änderungen, dennoch entspricht der heutige Zustand im wesentlichen Johnsons Entwurf. Selbst vierzig Jahre nach der Verwirklichung des Originalentwurfs bleibt er der schönste öffentliche Garten der Moderne, den die Stadt New York vorzuweisen hat.

Johnson konzipierte ihn als Abfolge von vier oder fünf großen Bereichen, die er durch Wasserbecken und Pflanzenbeete, freistehende Ziegelmauern und Baumgruppen – europäische Buchen und Trauerbirken sowie japanische Andromedasträucher und lombardische Pappeln – voneinander trennte. Die geradlinig gegeneinander verschobenen Flächen waren dem Barcelona-Pavillon von Mies van der Rohe – seinem wahrscheinlich besten Bauwerk – aus dem Jahre 1929 entlehnt, das Johnson seit jeher außerordentlich bewunderte.

Es handelt sich beim Skulpturengarten um einen ummauerten Garten, ähnlich dem seines ersten Hauses in Cambridge, Massachusetts aus dem Jahre 1942. Die Nordseite des Skulpturengartens wird von einer ca. 4,30 m hohen freistehenden Mauer begrenzt, und die bestehenden, größtenteils ebenfalls von Johnson entworfenen MoMA-Bauten bilden die Begrenzungen nach Westen, Süden und Osten. Das Grundstück von 61 m Länge und 24 m Breite ist somit im Umriß klar definiert und wird dann durch geradlinige Elemente unterteilt.

Der ursprünglich von McAndrew und Barr entworfene Skulpturengarten war im Grundriß kurvenförmig angelegt und von dem brasilianischen Landschaftsarchitekten Roberto Burle Marx, der mit Le Corbusier und Oscar Niemeyer zusammengearbeitet hatte, beeinflußt. Dieser in

The Abby Aldrich Rockefeller Sculpture Garden at the Museum of Modern Art

Philip Johnson
1953
New York, New York
Landscape Architect: James Fanning (1953);
Zion & Breen (1964)

When the new building for New York's Museum of Modern Art was constructed in the late 1930s, John McAndrew (the Museum's Curator of Architecture) and Alfred J. Barr, Jr., MoMA's Director, laid out a free-form sculpture garden for the space between the new museum and West 54th Street to the north. The garden was designed and built in a hurry, and while it was innovative in a number of ways, it was not as carefully thought out as it might have been. (For one thing, the defined spaces within it were often too loose and too formless for the pieces of sculpture displayed in them.) And so, in 1953, MoMA asked Philip Johnson to redesign the garden and give it a more permanent form.

The Sculpture Garden created by Philip Johnson has undergone a number of changes since that time; but it is today essentially as he designed it. And some forty years after the original design was put in place, it is still the finest public garden done in a modern idiom in the City of New York.

Johnson saw it as a series of four or five large rooms, separated from each other by pools, planting beds, free-standing walls of iron-spot brick, and clusters of trees – European weeping beeches, European birches, Japanese andromedas and Lombardy poplars. These divisions were arranged in roughly the same linear sliding planes as those that shaped Mies van der Rohe's Barcelona Pavilion of 1929 – probably the best building done by Mies, and greatly admired by Johnson ever since he saw it.

The Sculpture Garden is a «walled garden» not unlike the one Johnson built on his own property in Cambridge, Massachusetts, when he constructed his first house in 1942. There is a 14 foot high, free-standing wall on the Sculpture Garden's north edge, along West 54th Street; and there are walls formed by various MoMA structures (most of them designed by Johnson also) along the west, south and east borders of the garden. So the entire plot – it measures about 200 feet in depth, and 80 feet in width – is clearly defined along its perimeter, and then subdivided by the linear landscaping devices.

The original sculpture garden by McAndrew and Barr was curvilinear in plan and somewhat influenced by the work of Roberto Burle Marx, the Brasilian landscape architect who had worked with Le Corbusier and Oscar Niemeyer.

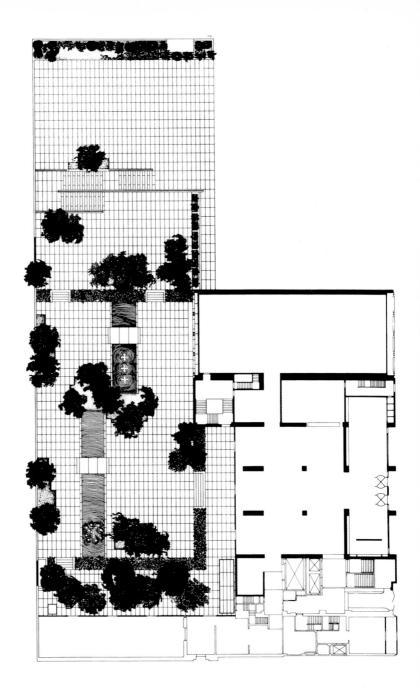

seiner Formensprache organisch geprägte Garten war für die Skulpturen des MoMA nicht besonders geeignet – in der Tat schienen die skulpturalen und organischen Formen miteinander zu konkurrieren. Johnson arbeitete seine Ausstellungsflächen daher so geradlinig und neutral wie möglich aus, um den ständig wechselnden Ausstellungsinhalten – einmal figurativer, dann wieder abstrakter Natur – einen schlichten Hintergrund zu verschaffen.

Die Hauptebene des Skulpturengartens ist mit grauem Marmor ausgelegt und liegt etwa 80 cm unterhalb der Eingangsebene des Museums. Somit hat man einen Überblick über den gesamten Gartenraum mit seinen gepflasterten Bereichen und seinen plattenartigen Brücken aus Marmor, noch ehe man ihn betritt. Der kleine Höhenunterschied erleichtert dem Besucher die räumliche Orientierung. Alles in allem ist es eine feinsinnige, klare Anordnung voller überraschender Aus- und Durchblicke.

1960 wurde auf der Ostseite des Gartens ein hoher Unterbau hinzugefügt, der dem neuen, vom Erdgeschoß des Museums aus zugänglichen Restaurant als Überdachung dienen sollte. Diese Erweiterung wurde nicht von Philip Johnson entworfen. Durch sie entsteht ein getrennter, vom Garten in seiner ursprünglichen Form abgeschnittener Ausstellungsbereich. Vom Dach des Anbaus jedoch hat man einen ähnlich eindrucksvollen Ausblick in den Garten wie von den zahlreichen Galerien und Büroräumen in den Obergeschossen des Museums, die auf den Garten ausgerichtet sind. Der vormalige Whitneybau auf der Westseite des Gartens erhielt eine Cafeteria mit Terrasse im Freien, die diesem Teil des Gartens den angenehmen Flair eines Straßencafés verleiht.

Anfang der achtziger Jahre entschloß man sich, das Hauptgebäude des Museums erheblich umzubauen, um mehr Platz für die Ausstellungen sowie eine großzügigere Innenerschließung zu schaffen. Dies sollte durch den Einbau einer Rolltreppenanlage auf der Haupteingangsebene im Erdgeschoß erreicht werden, wodurch wohl eine gartenseitige Erweiterung notwendig wurde, der Johnsons Gartenterrasse teilweise zum Opfer fiel.

Das Ergebnis war eher unglücklich und stand im eindeutigen Mißverhältnis zur eindrucksvollen Abfolge des ursprünglichen Entwurfs, von der Eingangslobby über die Terrassen bis in den tiefergelegenen Garten. MoMA-Besucher, die Johnsons Originalentwurf kannten, waren zwar enttäuscht, der Skulpturengarten hat aber immer noch seine alte ruhige Eleganz und den klaren Grundriß, was ihn wahrscheinlich den gewaltsamen Eingriff überstehen läßt. «Es heißt, daß ich im Grunde ein viel besserer Landschaftsplaner als Architekt bin», vertraute Johnson einem Besucher an. «Das stört mich gar nicht – es ist alles Teil derselben Kunst.» Es gibt jedoch nur we-

The «organic» forms of the original garden did not seem to function very well as a backdrop for MoMA's sculpture – in fact, the sculptured forms tended to compete with the organic forms of the garden. So Johnson made his backdrops as neutral and linear as possible, to form plain backdrops for the unpredictably changing display of figurative and abstract sculpture.

The «main» floor of the sculpture garden is finished in gray marble, and located about 3 feet below that of the Museum's entrance level, so that you see the entire garden room from above before you step down into it. This small change in level enables visitors to orient themselves, giving them an overview of the garden from the very start, and helping them find their way through it, over paved areas and slab-like marble bridges. It is a very subtle arrangement, full of surprising views and vistas, yet never confusing in its layout.

The high platform at the east end of the garden was added in the 1960s, to roof over a new restaurant accessible from the Museum's main floor. This extension was not designed by Philip Johnson; it creates a separate exhibition area, somewhat divorced from the original garden. However, the view of the garden from the roof platform is impressive, as are the views from various upperfloor Museum galleries and offices that face it. A cafeteria was inserted into the former Whitney building along the western border of the garden, and a terrace outside the cafeteria accommodates a pleasant «sidewalk cafe» at this edge of the garden.

In the early 1980s, MoMA decided to remodel its original building quite drastically, to provide better gallery spaces and more generous circulation. To achieve all this, it was decided to construct a bank of escalators in the main floor entrance areas of the original building, and this, in turn, made it necessary – or so it seemed – to expand that floor at the expense of some of Johnson's garden terrace. The result has been unfortunate, and clearly interfered with the impressive progression from the lobby to the terraces, and down into the sunken garden itself as originally designed. While MoMA visitors who remembered the original Johnson plans were disappointed, the Sculpture Garden retains a calm elegance and clean layout that can probably survive a rather insensitive innovation of its spaces. «People say that I am really a better landscape architect than I am an architect,» Philip Johnson once told a visitor. «I don't mind that at all – it is all the same art.» But not many landscape architects have produced a work of art that matches this one.

The secret may very well be that the Sculpture Garden was conceived as a series of «rooms» – with clearly defined entrances, clearly defined floor levels, clearly defined

Blick in den Garten

View of the garden

nige Landschaftsarchitekten, die ein vergleichbares Kunstwerk hervorgebracht haben.

Das Geheimnis hinter dem Skulpturengarten ist das Konzept der Raumabfolge – die eindeutig festgelegten Eingangsbereiche und Ebenen sowie die eindeutig definierten Begrenzungen, deren obere Ränder den Himmel als Zimmerdecke erscheinen lassen. Der Skulpturengarten ist und bleibt ein Ausstellungsraum im besten Sinne, was man von anderen Außenräumen und selbst Museumsräumen nicht immer behaupten kann.

perimeter walls, and a «ceiling» clearly defined by the top edges of those surrounding walls.

Award: City Club of New York Honor Award, 1961
The Bard Award for Excelling in Architecture and Urban Design, 1966

New Yorker, «Outdoor Room», April 25, 1953
New York Herald Tribune, September 6, 1964

Haus Wiley
Philip Johnson
1953
New Canaan, Connecticut
Partner: Landis Gores
Statik: Eipel Engineering Co.
Lichttechnik: Richard Kelly

Ein Glaskubus sitzt auf einem Säulenunterbau aus Feld-steinen. Die Tragstruktur des Obergeschosses besteht aus schichtverleimtem Holz. Die Fensterrahmen aus Kiefern-holz sind dunkel gebeizt. Im Obergeschoß befinden sich Tagesaufenthaltsräume mit einer Deckenhöhe von ca. 4,60 m. Alle Schlaf- und Technikräume liegen im steiner-nen Sockelgeschoß. Das Flachdach ist zugleich eine mit Schieferplatten ausgelegte Terrasse als Erweiterung der darunterliegenden Wohnräume.

Wiley House
Philip Johnson
1953
New Canaan, Connecticut
Partner: Landis Gores
Structural Engineer: Eipel Engineering Co.
Lighting: Richard Kelly

This house is, in effect, a glass prism atop a fieldstone sty-lobate. The upper floor is structured of laminated timber, with window frames of dark-stained white pine. This level contains the day-time living areas and has a ceiling height of 15 feet. The lower floor, within the stone walled base, contains all the bedrooms and mechanical rooms. Its flat roof forms a paved slate terrace that extends the upstairs living areas.

Architectural Record, June 1955
Perspecta 3, 1955
«Philip Johnson», by John Jacobus, 1962
Architectural Record, April 1964
«Complexity and Contradiction in Architecture»,
Robert Venturi, 1977

Grundrisse untere und
obere Ebene, 1:250
Außenansicht

Floor plans of lower and
upper level, 1:250
Exterior view

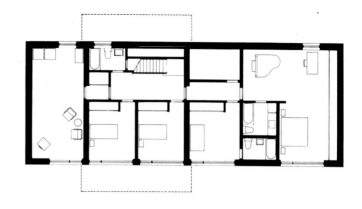

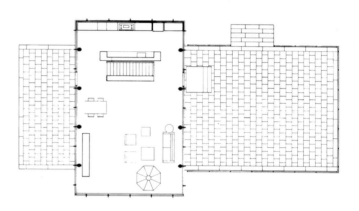

Haus Davis

Philip Johnson
1954
Wayzata, Minnesota
Bauleitung: Magney, Tusler and Setter
Statik: Eipel Engineering Co.
Haustechnik: John Dillon
Lichttechnik: Richard Kelly

Das Haus wurde für den bekannten Kunstsammler Richard S. Davis und seine Sammlung errichtet. Es ist in zwei Volumina in Form von Ziegelkuben gegliedert, eine durchaus angemessene Entwurfsidee eingedenk der extremen Klimaschwankungen und des Bedarfs an Wandfläche für die Ausstellungszwecke des Bauherren. Ein verglaster Verbindungsgang zwischen den Pavillons verknüpft die beiden Baukörper miteinander, erhält jedoch ihre Trennung im Erscheinungsbild aufrecht. Der größere der beiden Pavillons beherbergt einen ebenfalls verglasten Innengarten mit einer gläsernen Zwischendecke unter einem Dachoberlicht. Die Gemälde werden auf teakholzverkleideten Trennwänden ausgestellt. 1987 entwarfen Frank O. Gehry & Associates einen getrennten Gästepavillon.

Davis House

Philip Johnson
1954
Wayzata, Minnesota
Supervising Architects: Magney, Tusler, and Setter
Structural Engineer: Eipel Engineering Co.
Mechanical Engineer: John Dillon
Lighting: Richard Kelly

This house was built for Richard S. Davis, a prominent art collector, and it houses his collection. The two volumes of the house are brick boxes – an appropriate scheme for the extremes of the climate and the need for wallspace to display the owner's artwork. However, glass encloses the walkway between the two pavilions linking the two volumes but still maintaining their visual separation. The larger pavilion contains a garden atrium, also enclosed in glass, with a glass ceiling under a skylit roof. The paintings are displayed on teak-finished partitions. In 1987 a separate guest pavilion was designed by Frank O. Gehry & Associates.

Interiors, July 1954
House & Home, August 1954

Innenansicht
Grundriß Erdgeschoß

Interior view
Ground floor plan

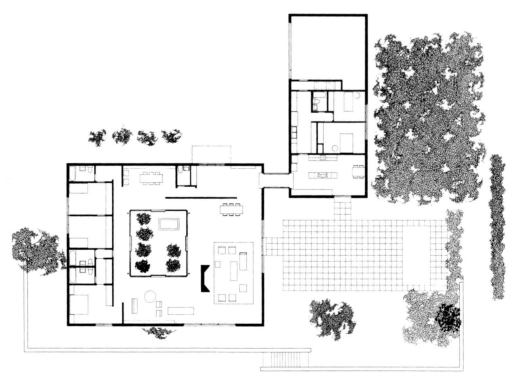

Haus Boissonnas

Philip Johnson
1956
New Canaan, Connecticut
Statik: Eipel Engineering Co.

Von Johnsons Bauten aus den fünfziger Jahren läßt das Haus Boissonnas als erstes einen Bruch mit dem Entwurfsvokabular Mies van der Rohes erkennen. Anders als bei späteren Kehrtwendungen in seiner Formensprache ließ Johnson Mies hier noch nicht völlig hinter sich, sondern kehrte zu dessen «Ursprüngen» zurück. In klassischer Kompositionsweise sind massive Ziegelstützen auf einem quadratisch ausgelegten Raster von ca. 4,90 m angeordnet. Sie sind in schachbrettartiger Abfolge offen als Pergolas oder verglast – ähnlich den Villen in Potsdam, die Karl Friedrich Schinkel 150 Jahre früher entwarf und die ihrerseits Mies in seinem Frühwerk erheblich beeinflußten.

Das Haus wirkt erhaben, der Zugang zu dem majestätisch anmutenden Grundstück ist stattlich. Das ca. 4,90 m x 4,90 m große Raster mißt in der Höhe durchgängig 3 m, mit Ausnahme des mittig gelegenen, doppelt so hohen Wohnraums. Alle Nebenräume – die Schlaf-, Studier- und Eßzimmer, die Küche usw. – passen sich dem Raster gut und überzeugend ein. Ziegelpfeiler (ca. 40 cm x 80 cm im Grundriß) rahmen den Blick in die Landschaft sowie die Pergolen und Terrassen rund um das Haus ein – eine überzeugende Komposition.

Für das Haus David Lloyd Kreeger in Washington, D.C. schuf Johnson zehn Jahre später einen sehr ähnlichen Entwurf. Der Grundriß des Hauses Kreeger – nunmehr ein kleines, elegantes Museum für moderne Kunst – ist in Ausarbeitung und Modulordnung dem des Hauses Boissonnas sehr ähnlich, jedoch im Detail und in der Komposition noch stärker klassisch, die Stützen und Bogen mit Travertin anstatt mit Ziegel verkleidet.

Alle in Europa und den USA entworfenen Wohnhäuser der Moderne haben gewisse Merkmale, mit Hilfe derer sie sich zeitlich leicht einordnen lassen – zum Beispiel Le Corbusiers Häuser aus den zwanziger und dreißiger Jahren, die Bauten von Gropius und Breuer aus den folgenden Jahren und alle Häuser von Frank Lloyd Wright bis zu seinem Tod im Jahre 1959. Das Haus Boissonnas, dessen Ursprung bei Schinkel, dessen Detail und Maßstab bei Johnson zu suchen sind, ist nur schwer einzuordnen. Es wirkt in Raum und Zeit heute so selbstbewußt wie 1956, als es gebaut wurde.

Die meisten modernen Wohnhäuser von Zeitgenossen aus den fünfziger Jahren waren in Dimension und Maßstab kleiner als die Villen für wohlhabende Bauherren,

Boissonnas House

Philip Johnson
1956
New Canaan, Connecticut
Structural Engineer: Eipel Engineering Co.

Of all the houses Johnson designed and built in the 1950s, the Boissonnas House may be the first one to reveal a break with Mies van der Rohe's steel, glass and brick vocabulary. But unlike later «breaks» in Johnson's vocabulary, this house does not go beyond Mies, but represents instead a return to Mies van der Rohe's «roots». It is a classical composition of massive brick columns placed in 16 foot squares, and forming a checkerboard of glass enclosures and open pergolas not unlike Karl Friedrich Schinkel's Potsdam villas of 150 years earlier – villas which, in turn, had greatly influenced Mies in his early work.

It is a very grand house, with a stately approach to its almost majestic site. The 16 foot by 16 foot grid is 10 feet high except for the central living room, which is twice that height; and the grid serves all the supporting spaces extremely well – bedrooms, study, dining room, kitchen, and so on all fit into the grid in a highly convincing manner. And the brick piers (16 inches by 32 inches in plan) frame the views of the landscape, and frame the pergolas and terraces around the perimeter of the house. It is a very convincing composition.

Johnson completed another structure very similar in composition to this one when he built the David Lloyd Kreeger House in Washington, D.C., some ten years later. The Kreeger House – now an elegant little Museum of Modern Art – has a plan very similar to the Boissonnas House in articulation and in modular organization; but it is rather more classical in detail and composition, constructed with travertine-finished columns and arches rather than brick.

There is a certain quality in modern houses done by various architects in Europe and in the US that can be dated very easily – Le Corbusier's houses of the 1920s and 1930s, Gropius' and Breuer's houses after that, and Frank Lloyd Wright's houses of the various decades prior to his death in 1959. The Boissonnas House, with its roots in Schinkel, and with its detail and scale supplied by Philip Johnson, is very difficult to place. It seems as self-assured as to time and place today as it did when it was first built, in 1956.

Most of the modern houses designed by Johnson's contemporaries in the 1950s were smaller in scale and size than the villas Johnson was able to build for wealthier clients. Those typical modern houses of the years after

Grundriß Erdgeschoß, 1:500

Ground floor plan, 1:500

die Johnson bauen durfte. Die typischen Häuser der Moderne aus jener Zeit waren Wohnhäuser für «Otto Normalverbraucher» (und seine Familie); Johnsons Häuser waren alles andere als das. Vielen seiner Zeitgenossen war bei dieser ungewöhnlichen Architektur unwohl – auch wenn einige gleichzeitig enge Freunde waren und zum Teil sogar in New Canaan lebten. Dieser Stil war bereits nicht «politisch korrekt», lange bevor der Ausdruck in aller Munde war.

Das Haus Boissonnas und das Haus David Lloyd Kreeger waren besonders ungewöhnlich. Beide strahlten ein weitaus größeres Selbstbewußtsein aus als alle anderen Bauten Johnsons oder anderer Architekten aus den fünfziger Jahren.

World War II tended to be houses for the «Common Man» (and his family); while many of Johnson's houses were hardly that. Although many of his contemporaries were close friends (and several of them lived in New Canaan), they seemed to feel somewhat uneasy about this «uncommon» architecture – a style that was hardly «politically correct» long before that term came into vogue.

The Boissonnas House and the David Lloyd Kreeger House were especially «uncommon». But those houses, almost more than anything else Johnson built in the 1950s, exuded a degree of self-assurance that set them apart from most of the work done by others during those years.

«Philip Johnson», John Jacobus, 1962

63

Außenansicht von der Hofseite
Außenansicht von der Gartenseite

Exterior view from patio
Exterior view from garden

Kneses Tifereth Israel Synagoge
Philip Johnson
1954–1956
Port Chester, New York
Statik: Eipel Engineering Co.
Lichttechnik: Richard Kelly
Buntglas: John Johansen

Auch in diesem Projekt beschäftigte sich Johnson mit der sichtbaren Stahlkonstruktion. Der Entwurf weicht jedoch erheblich vom Mies'schen Muster ab. Schmale Buntglasstreifen stehen in rhythmischer Abfolge zwischen den Betonpaneelen, die den Stahlrahmen ausfachen. Der Eingangsbereich sitzt abgelöst vor – und im Kontrast zu – dem rechteckigen Kubus des Hauptgebäudes als elliptischer, kuppelbedachter Pavillon. Das Hauptgebäude besteht aus einem einzigen, 11,30 m hohen Raum mit einer Gewölbedecke. Hierzu Johnson: «Die Segel aus Gips habe ich entworfen, um der Architektur die Spiritualität zurückzugeben, die den kalten, 'modern' genannten Bauten abgeht. Sie fassen den Raum und dienen der Streuung des Lichts.»

Kneses Tifereth Israel Synagogue
Philip Johnson
1954–1956
Port Chester, New York
Structural Engineer: Eipel Engineering Co.
Lighting: Richard Kelly
Stained Glass: John Johansen

The synagogue continues Johnson's exploration of the exposed steel skeleton, but has important variations from the standard Miesian practice. The infill for the steel are concrete slabs separated by narrow strips of stained glass. The building has a domed, curvilinear entrance room, set forward from the rectilinear bar of the main building as a contrasting pavilion. The main building is one large room 37 feet high, with a vaulted ceiling. Says Johnson, «in order too introduce the more spiritual feeling into what has been the rather cold style of architecture which we call modern, I have designed 'sails' of plaster that give a sense of containment to the space, and act as light baffles.»

Architectural Record, December 1956
«Recent American Synagogue Architecture», Richard Meier, The Jewish Museum, 1976

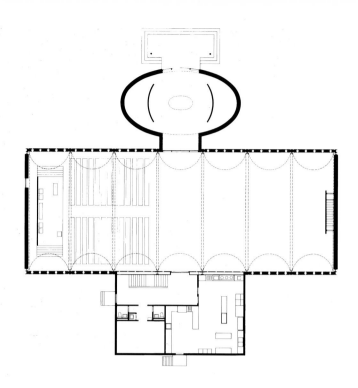

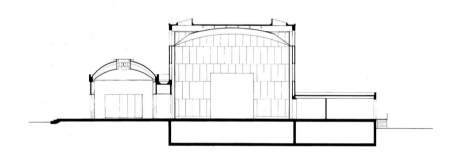

Grundriß Erdgeschoß, 1:500
Schnitt, 1:500
Außenansicht bei Nacht
Innenansicht

Ground floor plan, 1:500
Building section, 1:500
Exterior view at night
Interior view

Haus Leonhardt
Philip Johnson
1956
Lloyd's Neck, Long Island, New York
Statik: Eipel Engineering Co.
Haustechnik: Fred S. Dubin

Zwei gegeneinander versetzte Pavillons, von denen einer über den Rand einer Klippe auskragt, geben diesem Haus seine Form. Der auskragende Pavillon ist ein Wohnraum in Stahl und Glas, der in die Bucht von Long Island hineinragt. Ein von Ziegelwänden umschlossener, zweigeschossiger Schlafraum bestimmt die Gestalt des zweiten Pavillons. Beide Bauten werden durch die tiefergelegenen Nebenräume miteinander verbunden. Die Entwurfsidee für den verglasten und auskragenden Pavillon geht auf eine Skizze von Mies van der Rohe aus dem Jahre 1934 zurück.

Leonhardt House
Philip Johnson
1956
Lloyd's Neck, Long Island, New York
Structural Engineer: Eipel Engineering Co.
Mechanical Engineer: Fred S. Dubin

This house consists of two offset pavilions, one cantilevered over the edge of a cliff. The cantilevered pavilion is a steel-and-glass living area that projects out toward the Long Island Sound. The other pavilion is a brick-walled, two-story bedroom wing. The service areas are in the lower story, which connects both buildings. The basic scheme of a cantilevered, glass-walled pavilion is an elaboration of a 1934 sketch by Mies van der Rohe.

«Philip Johnson», John Jacobus, 1962
Architectural Record, May 1962
«Philip Johnson Architecture 1949–1965»,
Henry Russell Hitchcock, 1965

Grundrisse Erd- und Obergeschoß, 1:500
Außenansicht

Plans of ground and upper level floor, 1:500
Exterior view

St. Thomas Universität
Philip Johnson
1957
Houston, Texas
Bauleitung: Bolton and Barnstone
Statik: Severud-Elstad-Krueger
Haustechnik: Fred S. Dubin

Der Lageplan der St. Thomas Universität hat seinen Ursprung in Thomas Jeffersons Entwurf für den Campus der Universität von Virginia. Jeffersons Entwurf verbindet die kleinteilig angelegten Gebäude zu einem größeren Ganzen mit Hilfe eines umlaufenden Portikus. Johnson griff diese Idee auf. Die Gebäude variieren im Grundriß, haben jedoch dieselbe Traufhöhe. Die umlaufenden Kolonnaden verwandeln die Bereiche zwischen den Gebäuden in kleine Höfe und rahmen einen großen, rechteckigen Innenhof. An dessen Stirnseite wird demnächst als eine Art Schlußstein die ebenfalls von Philip Johnson entworfene Kapelle eingefügt.

University of St. Thomas
Philip Johnson
1957
Houston, Texas
Supervising Architects: Bolton and Barnstone
Structural Engineer: Severud-Elstad-Krueger
Mechanical Engineer: Fred S. Dubin

The site plan of the University of St. Thomas is based on that of the original campus of the University of Virginia, designed by Thomas Jefferson. Jefferson's organization has a running colonnade, linking smaller buildings into a larger whole. Johnson continued that idea with buildings of varying shape, but with uniform cornice heights. The continuous colonnade also forms courts between the buildings and a large, rectangular quadrangle, which will soon be transformed with the addition of a chapel also designed by Philip Johnson.

Architectural Record, September 1959

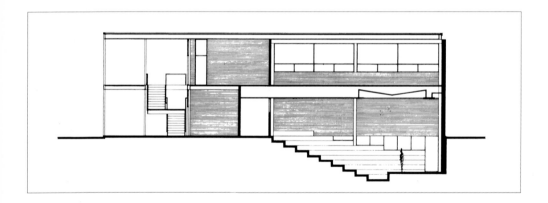

Schnitt durch das Auditorium
Außenansichten
Lageplan, 1:500

Section at auditorium
Exterior views
Site plan, 1:500

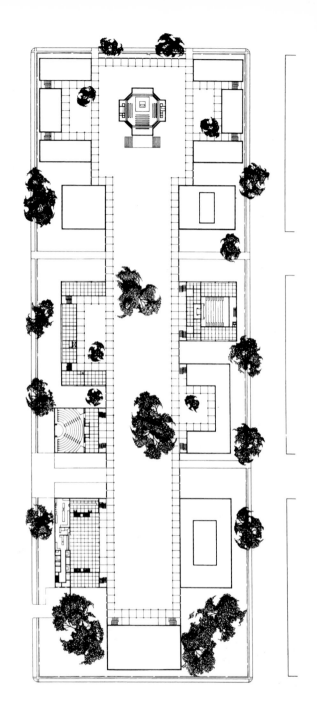

Asia House (Russell Sage Stiftung)
Philip Johnson
1958–1960
New York, New York
Statik: Eipel Engineering Co.
Haustechnik: Fred Sutton

Das sieben Geschosse zählende Kunstmuseum erstreckt
sich über zwei typische New Yorker Parzellen. Ein klein-
teiliges Fassadenraster aus Stahl und Glas im Achsabstand von 1,22 m mit aufgedoppelten Brüstungspaneelen
prägt das Erscheinungsbild und wirkt wie ein dekoratives
Muster, das den Bau im Maßstab dem niedrigeren, eklek-
tizistischen Nachbargebäude anpaßt.
Auf der Südseite des Grundstücks wurde ein offener, be-
grünter Innenhof angelegt, auf den die Ausstellungsbe-
reiche im Erdgeschoß und ersten Obergeschoß ausgerichtet sind.

Asia House (Russell Sage Foundation)
Philip Johnson
1958–1960
New York, New York
Structural Engineer: Eipel Engineering Co.
Mechanical Engineer: Fred Sutton

This 7-story building on two typical New York townhouse
lots houses an art museum. The steel and glass facade is
articulated with double spandrel panels in a grid of a small
4 foot window module. The effect is a decorative grid pattern that breaks down the scale of the building to be sym-
pathetic to the smaller adjacent eclectic townhouses.
Exhibition spaces were located on ground and first floor
with an exterior landscaped court developed at the south
of the site.

Architectural Review, February 1961
Asia Society Letter, December 1959

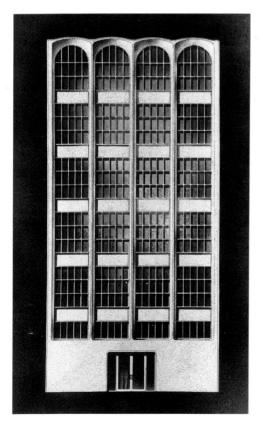

Fassade im frühen Entwurfsstadium
Außenansicht
Grundriß Erdgeschoß mit Innenhof

Preliminary facade study
Exterior view
Ground floor plan with exterior court

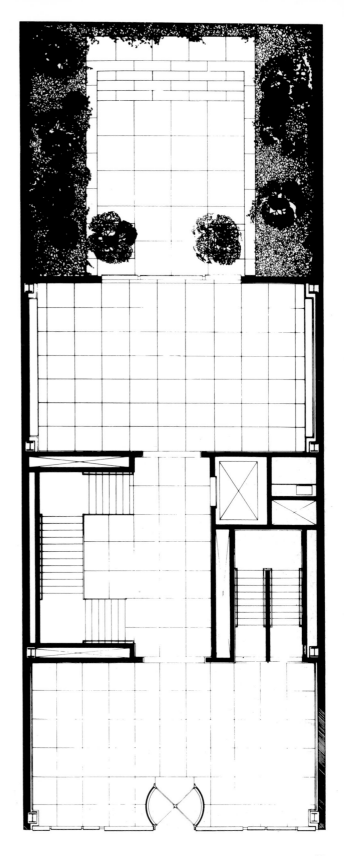

Four Seasons Restaurant

Philip Johnson
1959
New York, New York
Assoziierter Innenarchitekt: William Pahlmann
Grünplanung: Karl Linn
Lichttechnik: Richard Kelly
Skulptur: Richard Lippold
Tafelgeschirr: Ada Louise und Garth Huxtable

Während der Arbeit am Seagram Gebäude an der Park Avenue betraute Mies van der Rohe Philip Johnson mit der Gestaltung des Restaurants, das den größeren Teil des Erdgeschosses einnahm. Daraus entstand das Four Seasons Restaurant.

Die Erdgeschoßfläche eines Hochhauses wurde damals – wie oft heute noch – zumeist an Banken teuer vermietet. Das erwies sich häufig als Fehler. Banken waren in der Regel an fünf Tagen in der Woche für jeweils sechs Stunden geöffnet – mit anderen Worten, das Erdgeschoß vieler Bürobauten war meist menschenleer und wenig einladend. Mit der Entscheidung, beim Seagram Gebäude von diesem Schema abzuweichen sowie das Gebäude, auf den Vorschlag von Mies hin, durch einen großräumigen Platz von der Park Avenue zurückzusetzen, blieb der Stadtmitte Manhattans eine weitere tote Fassade erspart. Johnsons Four Seasons Restaurant erwies sich nicht nur als Belebung des städtischen Umfelds, sondern wurde seit seiner Eröffnung im Jahre 1959 auch zu einem der elegantesten und beliebtesten New Yorker Restaurants. Dies gründet größtenteils in seiner Gestaltung und in der sorgsamen Pflege dieses hohen Standards.

Der symmetrische Grundriß des Seagram Gebäudes nimmt die Gesamtlänge des Grundstücks von etwa 61 m an der Park Avenue ein. Die beiden großen Räume des Restaurants sind symmetrisch um die aufwendig ausgestattete Küche in der Mitte angeordnet. Im einen Raum befindet sich der «Bar & Grill», im anderen der «Dining Room», beide mit ihrem eigenen Ausdruck.

Der «Bar & Grill»-Teil ist zwangloser gehalten; die Tische sind unterschiedlich angeordnet über den Raum verteilt, während die quadratische Bar wie eine Insel in der Ecke liegt. Im formaler angelegten «Dining Room», dem eigentlichen Restaurant, stehen die Tische um ein quadratisches Wasserbecken in der Mitte. Auf der Ostseite weisen beide Räume ein höhergelegenes Zwischengeschoß auf, wo Gäste zurückgezogener speisen können und das den Blick auf die beiden tiefergelegenen allgemeinzugänglichen Bereiche erlaubt. Durch die ungewöhnliche Raumhöhe von 6,10 m, die hochgewachsenen Bäume an den vier Ecken des Wasserbeckens sowie die länglichen

Four Seasons Restaurant

Philip Johnson
1959
New York, New York
Associate Interior Architect: William Pahlmann
Landscape Architect: Karl Linn
Lighting: Richard Kelly
Sculpture: Richard Lippold
Tableware: Ada Louise and Garth Huxtable

In the 1950s, when Mies van der Rohe was working on the Seagram Building, he asked Philip Johnson to design the restaurant that would occupy much of the ground floor of the Park Avenue skyscraper. The Four Seasons Restaurant was the result.

In those years, and in most of the decades since, office skyscrapers invariably set aside most rentable ground floor space for occupancy by banks. That was often a mistake, since most banks were open only about six hours a day, five days a week – which meant that most office buildings at ground floor level presented a blank and uninviting face to the street, much of the time. The decision to depart from this in the case of the Seagram, together with Mies' decision to create a very large plaza in front of the building and facing Park Avenue, saved the neighborhood from one more deadly facade in Midtown Manhattan.

Johnson's Four Seasons Restaurant is a great deal more than a public amenity designed to enliven the neighborhood. It has been, from its start in 1959, one of the most elegant and popular restaurants in New York. This has been due, in large part, to the way in which it was designed, and to the sensitive way that quality has been maintained over the years.

The ground floor of the Seagram Building is symmetrical in plan, and occupies the full width of the Park Avenue block – some 200 feet. So the restaurant is more or less symmetrical in layout as well, with two large public spaces grouped around an elaborate, central kitchen. One of the two public spaces is a combination «Bar & Grill»; the other is a «Dining Room». Each space has its own distinct character.

The «Bar & Grill» is a more informal space with a square, island-shaped bar in one corner, and groups of dining tables, in different configurations, occupying the rest. The more formal «Dining Room» has a square reflecting pool at its center, and groupings of tables around the perimeter. Both rooms have raised mezzanines at their east ends, and these contain more private dining areas that overlook the two public spaces below. Because the ceiling height is close to 20 feet, these public spaces do not feel like

Grundriß, 1:500, «Bar & Grill» im Süden
Innenansicht «Bar & Grill»

Floor plan, 1:500, «Bar & Grill» south
«Bar & Grill» interior

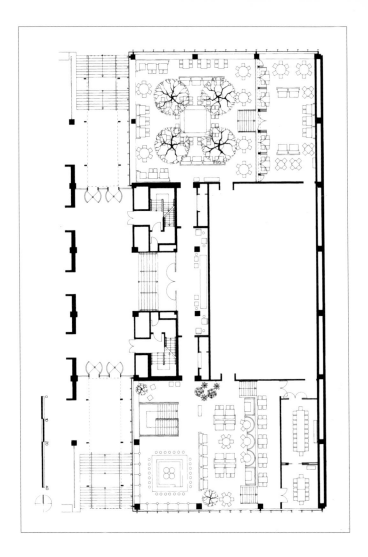

Pflanztröge im Raum und an den Fenstern wirken die Restaurants eher wie innenliegende Gärten.

Die fein abgestimmte, natürliche und künstliche Beleuchtung der beiden großen «Höfe», die Johnson in Zusammenarbeit mit seinen Fachplanern entwickelte, zieht wohlhabende New Yorker an. Die Glasfassade erhielt zur Straße und zum Platz hin Vorhänge in Form goldeloxierter Kettenglieder aus Aluminium, die sich durch die von der Heizung aufsteigende Warmluft sanft bewegen und die regelmäßig ersetzt oder neu gestaltet werden. Dazu gehörte auch ein Bühnenvorhang von Picasso aus dem Jahr 1919, der mittlerweile im Eingangsbereich hängt, von der Seagram Lobby aus sichtbar.

Wie beim Skulpturengarten des Museum of Modern Art läßt sich der gesamte Bereich vom Zwischengeschoß aus überblicken. In der Tat ist das Four Seasons Restaurant eigentlich ein Garten. Die beiden «Innenhöfe» des Four Seasons sind ein Vergnügen in einem Stadtviertel, das wenig freie Räume zu bieten hat.

Johnson konnte bei der Fertigstellung der Innenräume auf Experten jeglicher Provenienz vertrauen: den Bildhauer Richard Lippold, der mit seinen wolkenartigen Gebilden aus Bronzestangen sein – womöglich bis heute – bestes Werk schuf, den Lichttechniker Richard Kelly, den Landschaftsplaner Karl Linn sowie einen Stab aus Graphikern und Designern, die von der Streichholzschachtel und der Speisekarte über die Arbeitskleidung der Kellner bis hin zu den Gläsern, dem Geschirr und dem Edelstahlbesteck alles rigoros durchgestalteten. Kurz, im Four Seasons ist nicht nur das Essen, sondern auch das elegante Ambiente und die künstlerische Ausstattung vom Feinsten, das New York zu bieten hat.

conventional «rooms»; they are really indoor gardens, enhanced with four very grand trees at the corners of the reflecting pool, and with smaller plants in long planting boxes and in window boxes throughout the restaurant. What makes these two large «courts» so irresistible to well-to-do New Yorkers is the subtle lighting, both natural and artificial, that Johnson and his consultants designed. The glass walls facing the streetscape and the Plaza are draped with gold-anodized curtains of aluminum chains that ripple as the warm air rises from below; these are replaced and rearranged periodically. Among the permanent ones is a stage curtain painted in 1919 by Picasso, and now installed in the entrance area that faces the Seagram lobby.

Like Johnson's design for the Museum of Modern Art garden, these public spaces can be seen from above, and they «read» especially well when seen from the mezzanines. In fact, the Four Seasons Restaurant is really a garden. In a neighborhood that offers little in the way of landscape, the two «courts» of the Four Seasons are a delight. Johnson was able to call upon several experts from different areas of design to complete those spaces: Not only the sculptor Richard Lippold, whose clouds of bronze rods may be the best piece he has completed to date, the Lighting Designer Richard Kelly, the landscape architect Karl Linn, and several graphic and industrial designers who created everything from matchbook covers and menus, to waiters' uniforms, glasses, dishes, and stainless steel tableware. In short, the Four Seasons offers not only some of the best food in New York, but also the most elegant ambiance and the most sophisticated taste in the visual arts.

Award: New York City Landmark 1989

Progressive Architecture, December 1959
Architectural Record, November 1959
Interiors, December 1959

Innenansicht Restaurant mit Wasserbecken

«Dining Room» with pool

Munson-Williams-Proctor-Institut
Philip Johnson
1957–1960
Utica, New York
Statik: Lev Zetlin Associates, Inc.
Haustechnik: Fred S. Dubin Associates
Assoziierte Architekten: Bice & Baird Architects

Riesige Querträger aus Bronze tragen diesen granitver-kleideten Kubus ohne Fenster, der ein Kunstmuseum be-herbergt. Die verglaste, zurückspringende Erdgeschoßzone wird von einem umlaufenden Graben verdeckt. Man betritt das Gebäude durch einen überdimensionierten Eingang, der den Maßstab der symmetrisch angelegten Fassade noch mehr verzerrt. Im Inneren gelangt man in eine mo-numentale, zweigeschossige Halle, in der sich eine sym-metrische Treppenanlage mit elegantem, feinem Geländer befindet. Beide Geschosse sind jeweils von einer umlau-fenden Galerie gesäumt. Hierzu hat Mies mit seinen zahl-reichen Entwurfsstudien zum stützenfreien Raum der 1956 entstandenen Crown Hall am IIT das Vorbild geliefert.

Munson-Williams-Proctor Institute
Philip Johnson
1957–1960
Utica, New York
Structural Engineer: Lev Zetlin Associates, Inc.
Mechanical Engineer: Fred S. Dubin Associates
Associate Architect: Bice & Baird Architects

This windowless granite-clad cube supported by monu-mental bronze crossing girders houses an art museum. The ground level is recessed, glazed and hidden in a sur-rounding moat. The entry is through a large cut out open-ing that further distorts the scale of the symmetrical fa-cade. Within a monumental central room, two stories tall, is contained a symmetric staircase with thin, elegant balustrades. The galleries surround this central space on both levels. The inspiration is the many studies of Mies for single span structures as the 1956 Crown Hall at IIT.

«Philip Johnson», Henry-Russell Hitchcock, 1965

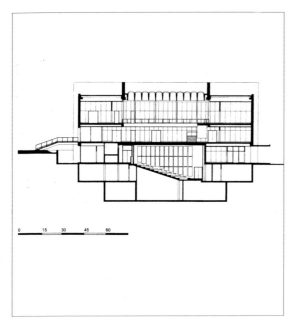

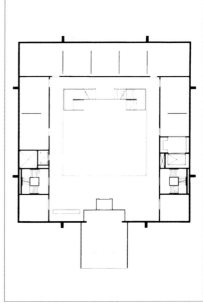

Schnitt, 1:750
Grundriß Eingangsgeschoß
mit Galerien, 1:750
Außenansicht
Innenansicht der Halle

Building section, 1:750
Entry floor plan with galleries,
1:750
Exterior view
Interior view of central court

Nuklearforschungsreaktor

Philip Johnson
1960
Rehovot, Israel
Assoziierter Architekt: Gideon Ziv
Statik: Lev Zetlin
Haustechnik: Guy B. Panero

Der Nuklearreaktor in Rehovot aus dem Jahre 1960 ist einer der am wenigsten bekannten Bauten Philip Johnsons – aus offensichtlichen Gründen. Die Sicherheitsgründe erforderten völlige Geheimhaltung. Eigentlich ist er nur den wenigen dort arbeitenden Wissenschaftlern sowie Reisenden bekannt, die das in der Wüste von Nahal Soreq, unweit der Mittelmeerküste gelegene Gelände zufällig passieren.

Dem Gebäude liegt ein wunderbar geordnetes Diagramm zugrunde. In Anordnung und Textur scheint es fast zeitlos – es könnte ebensogut in einer mesopotamischen Stadt wie einer mittelalterlichen Klosteranlage stehen. Das konisch zulaufende «Grabmal» aus Beton (ca. 20.10 m hoch), in dem der Reaktor untergebracht ist, sitzt auf einem massiven, abgeschrägten Betonsockel mit 76 m Länge und 36,50 m Breite. Dieser Sockel beherbergt die Forschungslaboratorien, die um einen großzügig angelegten Innenhof mit Arkadengang liegen – ähnlich dem Kreuzgang eines mittelalterlichen Klosters.

Das Bauwerk erinnert an Johnsons Entwurf einer «Kirche ohne Dach» in New Harmony, Indiana, der ungefähr zur selben Zeit entstand. Der Reaktor und die Kirche haben eine bemerkenswert mystisch-religiöse Ausstrahlung gemein – wobei der Reaktor noch mehr zeitlos und für die Ewigkeit gebaut scheint. Das Bauwerk ist leicht mit einer verlassenen Moschee zu verwechseln, ein Eindruck, der den auf Sicherheit bedachten israelischen Behörden sicher nicht ungelegen kam. In jedem Fall gehört es zu Johnsons eindrucksvollsten Monumentalbauten.

Research Nuclear Reactor

Philip Johnson
1960
Rehovot, Israel
Associate Architect: Gideon Ziv
Structural Engineer: Lev Zetlin
Mechanical Engineer: Guy B. Panero

One of the least known buildings designed by Philip Johnson is his 1960 nuclear reactor in Rehovot, Israel. The reasons are obvious: security requirements have kept the building under wraps, and the few people who really know it are the handful of scientists who work there, and the few who pass its site in the desert, of Nahal Soreq, not far from the Mediterranean coastline.

It is a beautifully composed diagram, a building that seems almost timeless in its composition and its texture: as much at home in the cities of Mesopotamia as it would be among the monasteries of the Middle Ages. It consists of a 250 feet long and 120 feet wide, tapered almost solid concrete base and a similarly tapered concrete «tomb» (66 feet high) that, in fact, contains the nuclear reactor. The base for this massive «tomb» contains the research laboratories, which are grouped around a spacious internal court, arcaded in the manner of a medieval monastery.

The building is, of course, reminiscent of Johnson's Roofless Church in New Harmony, Indiana, which was designed at about the same time. It is interesting that both the Reactor and the Church convey a curiously «religious» sense of mystery – but the Reactor seems even more «timeless» than the Church, and more permanently constructed. It could easily be mistaken for an abandoned mosque, which may have been the undeclared intention of the security-conscious Israeli authorities. In any event, it is one of Johnson's most impressive monuments.

Award: AIA Honor Award 1961

Architectural Forum, April 1961
«The Nahal Soreq Research Reactor IRR-I»,
Israel Atomic Energy Comm., 1960

Grundriß Erdgeschoß, 1:750
Außenansicht

Ground floor plan, 1:750
Exterior view

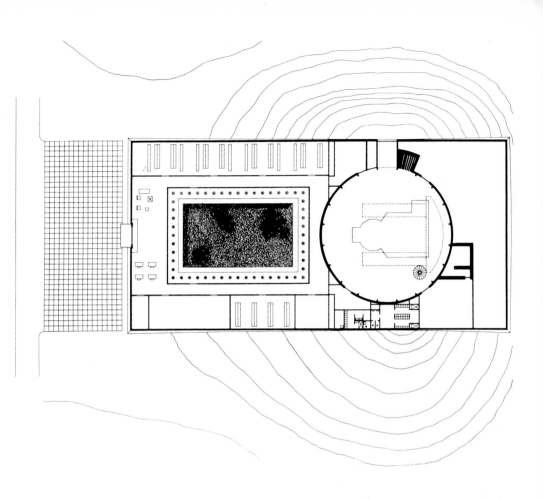

Kirche ohne Dach

Philip Johnson
1960
New Harmony, Indiana
Statik: Wilcox and Erickson
Lichttechnik: Richard Kelly

Die «Kirche ohne Dach» in New Harmony ist eine Etüde der Versinnbildlichung eines geheiligten Ortes. Die Anlage ist von einer 3,65 m hohen Mauer umschlossen. Jacques Lipchitz entwarf die ornamentierten Eingangstore, durch die man den dicht bepflanzten Vorhof betritt.
Ein gepflasterter Hof umfängt die 15,20 m hohe geschwungene und mit Zedernholzschindeln gedeckte Kuppel, die sich über der Skulptur «Herabkommen des Heiligen Geists» von Jacques Lipchitz erhebt. Die Umgebungsmauer ist auf einer Seite von einem Balkon durchbrochen, der den Blick auf das Wabashtal freigibt.

Roofless Church

Philip Johnson
1960
New Harmony, Indiana
Structural Engineer: Wilcox and Erickson
Lighting: Richard Kelly

The New Harmony Roofless Church is an exercise in defining a sacred space. The assembly is surrounded by a twelve foot wall. The entry is through decorative gates by Jacques Lipchitz into a forecourt of dense planting.
A paved court defines a so foot high lobed dome, covered with cedar shingles, which then covers the statue «Descent of the Holy Spirit» by Jacques Lipchitz. A balcony at the side looks out over the valley of the Wabash River.

Award: First Honor Award AIA, 1974

Art in America, No. 4, 1959
«Philip Johnson Architects 1949–1965»,
H.R. Hitchcock, 1965

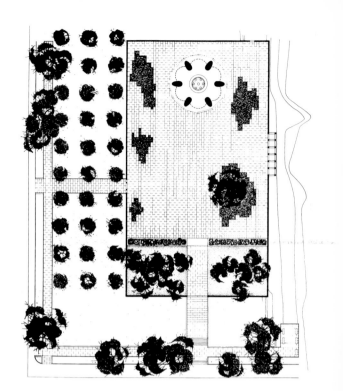

Amon Carter Museum of Western Art
Philip Johnson
1958–1961
Fort Worth, Texas
Statik: Lev Zetlin
Haustechnik: Jaros, Baum & Bolles

Das Museum beherbergt eine Sammlung von Kunst des amerikanischen Westens. Eine Abfolge weit ausgreifender, abgestufter Terrassen führt zum Gebäude hin und gewährt Blick auf die Stadt.
Die Außenhaut des zweigeschossigen Gebäudes besteht aus texanischem Muschelkalk. Die 37,80 m lange Vorhalle in Form eines Arkadengangs mit sanft geschwungenen Bögen wird von konisch zulaufenden Stützen getragen. Die Eingangsfassade aus getöntem Glas und Fassadenprofilen aus Bronze liegt hinter der Vorhalle und trennt sie räumlich von der zweigeschossigen großen Halle. Die ursprünglich fünf Galerien sind wiederum hinter dieser Halle angeordnet. Im rückwärtigen Bereich des Gebäudes wurde 1975 eine Erweiterung hinzugefügt, die vom Büro Johnson/Burgee entworfen wurde.

Amon Carter Museum of Western Art
Philip Johnson
1958–1961
Fort Worth, Texas
Structural Engineer: Lev Zetlin
Mechanical Engineer: Jaros, Baum & Bolles

This museum houses a collection of American Western art. The building stands at the end of a series of broad stepped terraces that overlook the skyline of the city.
Texas shellstone covers the exterior of the two story building. The gently arched arcaded porch, is 124 feet long and supported by tapered columns. Behind the porch is an entry facade of bronze mullions and tinted glass, which separates the porch from a two story great hall. The five original galleries are behind this hall. The firm of Johnson/Burgee designed an addition behind the building in 1975.

«Museum of Art Opens for Preview in New York.» New York Times, January 22, 1961
«Philip Johnson Architect – 1949–1965», Henry Russell Hitchcock, 1965

Lageplan, 1:1500
Ansicht von der Außentreppe

Site plan, 1:1500
View from entry stairs

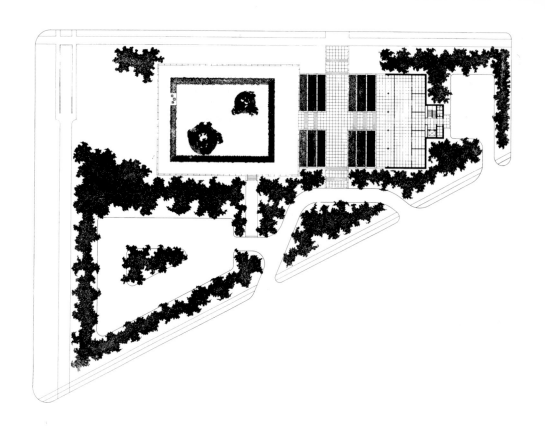

Pavillon am Teich
Philip Johnson
1962
New Canaan, Connecticut

Am Fuß der Anhöhe, auf der das Glashaus steht, sitzt ein offener Pavillon am Rand eines künstlichen Teiches. Der Raumkörper wird von 60 vorgefertigten Stützen aus sandgestrahltem Beton im Achsabstand von ca. 90 cm umschlossen. Die Fassung der Raumkanten durch eine Kolonnade ist ein Experiment in punkto Ausbildung von Eckbereichen – ein Thema, das Johnson an anderen zeitgenössischen Bauten immer wieder beschäftigte. Beim Pavillon am Teich wird die Ecklösung dadurch erzielt, daß die konkave Krümmung der Stützenkanten sich über die Ecke fortsetzt.

Die Gegenüberstellung des im ganzen nur 1,80 m hohen Bauwerks mit einer rund 6 m hohen Wasserfontäne wirkt wie eine Täuschung und verzerrt den Maßstab.

Pavilion at Pond
Philip Johnson
1962
New Canaan, Connecticut

An outdoor pavilion on the edge of a man-made pond is located at the bottom of the hill from the Glass House. It consists of 60 columns of sand blasted pre-cast concrete spaced 3 feet on center. The pavilion's corners are experiments in framing interior and exterior edges with a colonnade – a problem that concerned Johnson in connection with several of his contemporary buildings. The solution here was achieved by continuing the concave curved plane of the column edges as the corner is turned.

The entire building is only 6 feet tall, which combined with the adjacent 20 foot tall fountain spray, creates an illusion and distortion in perceived scale of the building.

Architectural Record, July 1962
«Full Scale False Scale», Show Magazine, June 1963

Grundriß Erdgeschoß
Außenansicht

Ground floor plan
Exterior view

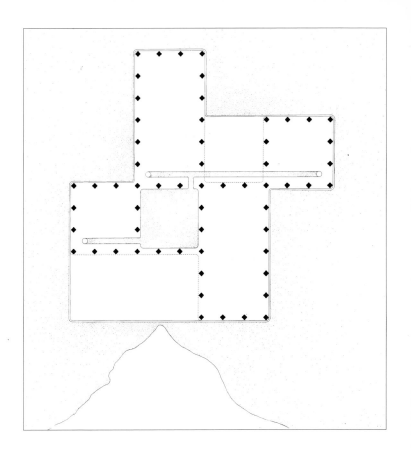

Museum für präkolumbische Kunst in Dumbarton Oaks

Philip Johnson
1963
Washington, D.C.
Statik: Lev Zetlin & Associates
Haustechnik: Jaros, Baum & Bolles
Lichttechnik: Richard Kelly

Der Anbau an das Dumbarton Oaks Museum in Washington, D.C. mit seinen Kuppeldächern entstand einige Jahre vor dem der Bibliothek in Boston, den das Büro Johnson und Burgee entwarf. Die beiden Gebäude sind in Maßstab, Details, Formensprache und Funktion anders geartet, haben aber eine Gemeinsamkeit im Grundriß. Dieser wird in beiden Fällen aus neun, jeweils in Dreierreihen angeordneten Elementen gebildet, die an den Schnittpunkten miteinander verbunden sind. Bei den beiden axialsymmetrischen Bauten liegt der Eingang mittig in einer der vier Außenwände.

Der quadratische Grundmodul der Bibliothek beträgt ca. 18,30 m, die kreisrunden Elemente des Museums haben einen Durchmesser von 7,60 m. Ein Lichthof bildet das Herzstück der Bibliothek, im Museum ist es ein runder, nach oben offener Innenhof.

Die Traufhöhe der Bibliothek nimmt die des Nachbargebäudes von McKim, Mead & White auf; die Kuppeln des Museums orientieren sich an byzantinischer Architektur, insbesondere am schaffensreichen Werk des türkischen Architekten Sinan aus dem 15. Jahrhundert, der durch seine zahlreichen Kuppelbauten bekannt wurde. Johnson sah in Sinans sogenannten «Moscheen mit vielen Räumen» den geeigneten Ausgangspunkt für die Unterbringung einer Kunstsammlung.

Das im Föderalistischen Stil errichtete Herrenhaus von Dumbarton Oaks war in den zwanziger Jahren bereits von McKim, Mead & White restauriert und im gleichen Stil erweitert worden. Die bemerkenswerte Landschaftsarchitektin Beatrix Ferrand gestaltete das 16 Hektar große Areal des Landsitzes – ihrer Arbeit hat Dumbarton Oaks seine besondere Qualität zu verdanken. Im Jahre 1920 wurde das Gut von Robert und Mildred Bliss erworben, einem Ehepaar mit einer Sammlung präkolumbischer und anderer Kunst. Sie bauten den Besitz aus, machten daraus eine Stiftung und übergaben diese der Harvard Universität, in deren Besitz sich Dumbarton Oaks auch heute befindet.

Der Neubau von Johnson sollte sich nach ihrer Auffassung auf unauffällige Weise in die Landschaftsgestaltung von Beatrix Ferrand einpassen. Ihr Gebäude ist daher kurvenförmig und transparent ausgebildet und weist nicht die

Museum for Pre-Columbian Art at Dumbarton Oaks

Philip Johnson
1963
Washington, D.C.
Structural Engineers: Lev Zetlin & Associates
Mechanical Engineers: Jaros, Baum & Bolles
Lighting: Richard Kelly

The domed wing of the Dumbarton Oaks Museum, in Washington, D.C., was designed a couple of years before Johnson and Burgee began work on their addition to the Boston Public Library. Although the two buildings are quite different in scale, function, detail, form and just about everything else, they are similar in one respect: both consist, in plan, of nine elements grouped in a three-by-three pattern, and linked to each other where they touch. And both are symmetrical, with an entrance in the center of one of the four sides.

But the library's units measure about 60 feet square; while the Museum's units are circular, and measure only 25 feet in diameter. And the library is centered on a skylit atrium that is square like the other units, and 60 feet tall; while the Museum has a circular, central court that is open to the sky.

While the library's roof line was determined in profile by McKim, Mead & White's roof next door, the domes that form the Museum's roof recall the forms of Byzantine architecture – specifically, the work of the prolific 15th century Turkish architect Sinan, who is best known for his multi-domed structures. When asked to design a Museum for a collection of art, Johnson thought that Sinan's so-called «multi-unit mosques» were an appropriate point of departure.

The existing building at Dumbarton Oaks is an extension of a Federalist mansion that was reconstructed and expanded by the firm of McKim, Mead & White in the 1920s, and in much the same style. The planning and planting of the 16-acre estate was done by the remarkable landscape gardener Beatrix Ferrand – and her work has given Dumbarton Oaks its special qualities. The estate was acquired in 1920 by Robert and Mildred Bliss, the collectors of pre-Columbian and other art, developed and endowed by them, and donated to Harvard University which still owns and operates Dumbarton Oaks.

When Johnson was asked to design the new pavilion on this beautiful estate, they felt that the new building should be almost invisible – engulfed in the landscaping designed by Beatrix Ferrand. So they created something that is in no way hard-edged (as a neo-Federalist building might be), but curvilinear and transparent. When you

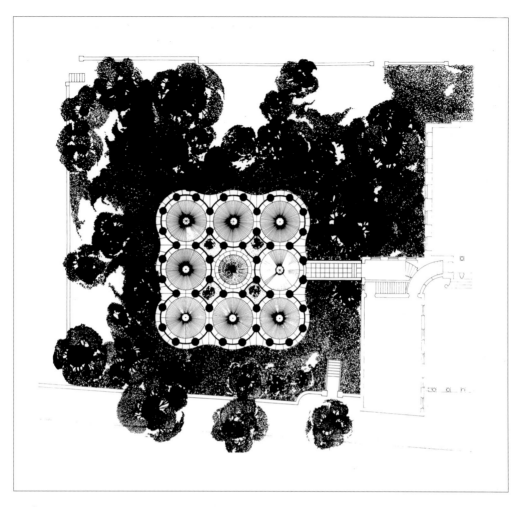

Lageplan, 1:500

Site plan, 1:500

klaren Kanten des neoföderalistischen Stils auf. Im Inneren des Gebäudes scheinen die gebogenen Wand- und Glasflächen nahtlos in der umgebenden Landschaft aufzugehen. «Der Ausblick soll wie eine Täuschung wirken, wie eine Art Rundum-Panorama, das einem den Eindruck von Unendlichkeit vermittelt», merkte Johnson dazu an. Ausblick wird nicht nur durch die Dachkuppeln aus Plastik gewährt, sondern auch durch die raumhohen gebogenen Glasscheiben, die zwischen Rundstützen mit einem Durchmesser von ca. 90 cm sitzen. Die Stützen-

are inside this little Museum, the curved wall and glass surfaces tend to merge with the surrounding landscape. «The views are meant to be illusive, like a cyclorama that represents infinity», Johnson has said. The views are not merely through the curved plastic domes, but also through the curved floor-to-ceiling sheets of glass separated by cylindrical columns, 3 feet in diameter. The columns are sheathed in honed Agatan buff veined marble quarried in Illinois. The effect is one of «organic» images rather than linear, geometric forms and reflections –

verkleidung besteht aus geschliffenem und poliertem Agata-Adermarmor aus einem Steinbruch in Illinois. Die Gesamtwirkung ist eher «organischer» denn linear-geometrischer Natur – das Gebäude scheint förmlich in Beatrix Ferrands Landschaft zu verschwinden.

Astor Moore entwarf die Schaukästen aus transparentem Kunstharz, in denen die präkolumbischen Werke in den acht Galerieräumen ausgestellt sind (der neunte Rundraum in der Mitte beherbergt einen kleinen Garten mit Wasserbecken und Fontäne). Die Architekten sollten das erdenklich beste Gebäude für die Bauherrschaft errichten, aufs Geld kam es nicht an. Es blieb daher nicht bei den marmorverkleideten Stützen – der Boden ist aus Teakholz, und jede Gebäudekante, jeder Wand- und Deckendurchbruch erhielt eine Einfassung aus Bronze. Der pavillonartige Bau wirkt trotz der luxuriösen Details und Oberflächenbehandlung bewundernswert zurückhaltend. Er kann es an Eleganz und Stil durchaus mit den Ausstellungsstücken aufnehmen.

Kann man ihn als einen Bau der Moderne bezeichnen? Selbstverständlich – auch wenn er die Moscheen Sinans zitiert. Das Bauwerk weist einen Grad an Präzision und Offenheit auf, der zu Sinans Zeiten nicht möglich gewesen wäre. Ebenso modern ist das Konzept des fließenden Übergangs von Bauwerk und Landschaft, das sich vor Mies schon in Karl Friedrich Schinkels Werk aus dem frühen 19. Jahrhundert findet. Johnson wiederum lehnt sich, wie schon sein Lehrer Mies van der Rohe vor ihm, immer wieder an Schinkel an – vor allem beim Haus Boissonnas aus dem Jahre 1956 und beim Haus David Lloyd Kreeger sechs Jahre später. Das letztere – übrigens nicht weit von Dumbarton Oaks entfernt – hat mittlerweile auch als Museum Verwendung gefunden. Die Verwandtschaft mit Schinkels Werk läßt sich in Dumbarton Oaks nicht leugnen, auch wenn es von der Geometrie her nicht viel mit Schloß Glienicke gemein hat.

Andrea O. Dean schrieb angesichts der Fertigstellung der kleinteiligen Erweiterung mit den Kuppeldächern in der Zeitschrift des American Institute of Architects: «Der winzige Anbau an die Villa im neo-georgianischen Stil ist in jeder Beziehung klassischer Natur – vom klaren Grundriß und der symmetrischen Anlage über die Wiederholung in der Form bis zur Sorgfalt in den Details. Dies kommt der derzeitigen Vorliebe für das kunstvolle Detail und den Einsatz wertvoller Materialien entgegen und stellt, vor allem mit dem byzantinisch geprägten Grundriß, historische Bezüge her.» Das hat zwar alles seine Richtigkeit, Johnson selbst besteht dennoch darauf, daß der Pavillon in Dumbarton Oaks «sehr stark von Wrights konzentrischen Hausentwürfen beeinflußt» war. Ein durchaus interessanter, wenn auch nicht ganz überzeugender Gedanke.

a structure that seems to dissolve into Beatrix Ferrand's landscape.

In the eight galleries (the central circle is a small garden, with a pool and a fountain) works of pre-Columbian are displayed in cases designed by Astor Moore, and made of lucite. Because the clients wanted the very best structure that the architects could design, there was no pinching of pennies. In addition to the marble-clad columns, there are teak floors and bronze moldings to define the edges of the structure and the various openings in the walls and ceilings. But despite the luxury of the details and the finishes, the little pavilion is beautifully restrained. It easily matches the exhibits in elegance and style.

Is it a modern building? Of course – despite its debt to Sinan's Mosques. It is a structure of a precision and a degree of openness and transparency that could not have been achieved in Sinan's day. But it is a modern building in other ways as well: the extension of a structural frame into the landscape comes as much from the early 19th century work of Karl Friedrich Schinkel as it does from any other antecedent; and like Johnson's teacher, Mies van der Rohe, Johnson pursued Schinkel's ideas in many of his buildings – in particular in the Boissonnas House of 1956, and in 1962 David Lloyd Kreeger House (not far from Dumbarton Oaks) that has become a little museum in recent years also. Although the geometry of the Dumbarton Oaks pavilion is hardly that of Schinkel's structures at Schloss Glienicke, there is an unmistakable kinship.

When the little domed wing at Dumbarton Oaks was completed, Andrea O. Dean wrote in the Journal of the American Institute of Architects that this «tiny addition to a neo-Georgian mansion ... is classical in its clarity of plan, its symmetry, repetition of forms and carefully worked out proportions; it appeals to the current predilection for masterful detailing and use of rich materials, and it alludes to history, especially in its Byzantine plan.» All that is true. But Johnson believes that the Dumbarton Oaks pavilion was «very much influenced by Wright's circular houses.» Very interesting, but not entirely convincing.

Architectural Forum, March 1964
Robin Boyd, «The Puzzle of Architecture»,
AIA Journal, May 1980

Außenansicht
Innenansicht

Exterior view
Interior view

Sheldon Memorial Kunstgalerie

Philip Johnson
1961–1963
Lincoln, Nebraska
Assoziierte Architekten: Hazen and Robinson
Statik: Lev Zetlin & Associates
Haustechnik: Jaros, Baum & Bolles

Das Museum besteht aus einem geschlossenen recht-eckigen Kubus. Eine Reihe von Pilastern, deren Säulen-schaft sich nach oben und unten ausweitet, sorgt für die rhythmische Unterteilung der mit Travertin verkleideten Außenwände. Das Bauwerk ruht auf einem Säulenunter-bau, der über das Pilasterrelief hinausragt. Die monu-mental angelegte, ca. 9,10 m hohe Große Halle, die eine Kassettendecke als oberen Raumabschluß aufweist, be-stimmt das Gebäudeinnere. Die Treppenanlage, die ins Obergeschoß führt, erinnert an Schinkels Altes Museum in Berlin. Die Galerieräume selbst befinden sich zu beiden Seiten der Großen Halle.

Sheldon Memorial Art Gallery

Philip Johnson
1961–63
Lincoln, Nebraska
Associate Architects: Hazen and Robinson
Structural Engineers: Lev Zetlin & Associates
Mechanical Engineers: Jaros, Baum & Bolles

The exterior of this museum is a compact rectangular prism, its travertine walls modulated by pilasters with re-versed entasis. The building rests on a stylobate that pro-jects at the pilasters. The interior has a monumental 30-foot high Great Hall, with a coffered ceiling and stairs somewhat reminiscent of Schinkel's Altes Museum in Berlin leading to the second floor. The galleries are in rooms on both sides of the Great Hall.

Building Construction, November 1964
Architectural Record, August 1963

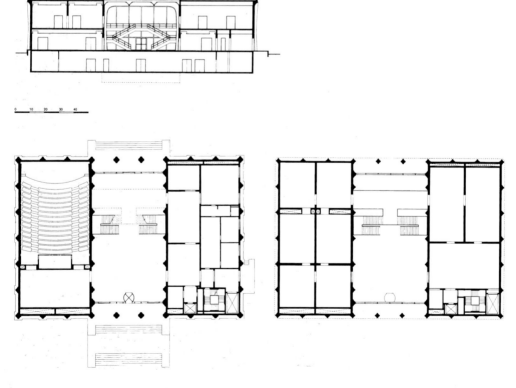

Schnitt, 1:750
Grundriß Erdgeschoß, 1:750
Grundriß Obergeschoß, 1:750
Außenansicht
Innenansicht der Großen Halle

Building section, 1:750
Ground floor plan, 1:750
Upper floor plan, 1:750
Exterior view
Great Hall interior

Haus Boissonnas II

Philip Johnson
1964
Cap Bénat, Frankreich
Statik: Lev Zetlin & Associates

Das Sommerhaus in Südfrankreich liegt auf einem Hügel mit Blick aufs Meer. Mit seinen fünf Pavillons und drei Zwischenhöfen gleicht es einer kleinteiligen «Dorfanlage».
Das Bedürfnis nach Zurückgezogenheit in einer Familie, die drei Generationen und ihre jeweiligen Gäste umfaßt, machte eine Trennung der Schlafräume erforderlich. Nach Nordwesten hin wird das Grundstück in weiten Bereichen durch Mauern vor dem Mistral geschützt.
Drei Pavillons, die Wohn-, Eß- und Schlafbereich beherbergen, sind um einen überdeckten Zwischenhof angeordnet und bilden das Herzstück der Anlage. Vier pyramidenförmig zulaufende Stützen tragen die geschwungene Hofüberdachung aus Beton und bilden einen Raum im Freien, dessen vierte «Begrenzung» der dramatische Blick aufs Meer darstellt.

Boissonnas House II

Philip Johnson
1964
Cap Bénat, France
Structural Engineer: Lev Zetlin & Associates

This summer home on a hilltop on the Mediterranean coast in the south of France, is broken into a small «village» of five pavilions and three outdoor courtyards.
The requirements of three generations of the family with their own guests dictated separation of bedroom spaces for privacy and maintenance. Blocking the force of the seasonal northwest winds (the «Mistral») required the extensive walls enclosing that side of the site.
At its core are three pavilions: living, dining and bedroom surround the covered court. The court has a «wavy» concrete roof structure braced by four pyramidal columns creating an outdoor room: the fourth «wall» has a dramatic view of the sea.

Interiors, December 1965
Architectural Record, June 1967
House and Garden, August 1967

Grundriß Erdgeschoß, 1:500
Schlafpavillons und Hofüberdachung
Blick in den Zwischenhof mit Wohnpavillon

Ground floor plan, 1:500
Bedroom pavilions and concrete roof
Central covered court with living room

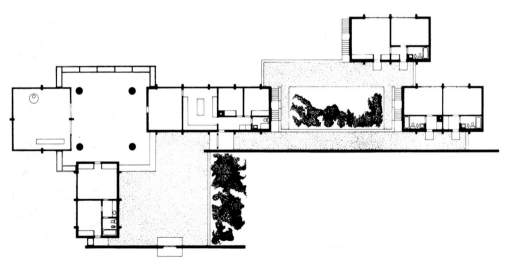

Museum of Modern Art Ostflügel

Philip Johnson
1964
New York, New York
Statik: Severud-Elstad-Krueger
Haustechnik: Jaros, Baum & Bolles

Dieser Anbau an das Gebäude des Museum of Modern Art von Goodwin & Stone von 1939 sollte zusätzlichen Platz für Ausstellungen und Büros bieten. In ähnlicher Weise wie schon Johnsons Erweiterung aus dem Jahre 1950 bestimmt eine in Stahl gefaßte Glasfassade den Bau. Die gleichen Materialien kommen zum Einsatz, allerdings weichen die Stahldetails hier vom Mies'schen Vorbild ab. Statt vorgefertigter Stahlverbindungen werden an den Rahmenecken gebogene Sonderelemente verwendet. Im Dachgeschoß springt die Fassade im Angleich an den Laubengang des Originalbaus um ca. 90 cm zurück. Auf diesem Geschoß entwarf Johnson den «Founders' Room» für die Honoratioren des Museums. Dessen Decke besteht aus neun Kuppelgewölben aus Gips in einem Stahlprofilraster mit eingebauter Beleuchtung.

Museum of Modern Art East Wing

Philip Johnson
1964
New York, New York
Structural Engineer: Severud-Elstad-Krueger
Mechanical Engineer: Jaros, Baum & Bolles

This annex to the original 1939 MoMA building by Goodwin & Stone was to provide additional space for exhibitions and offices. It bears certain resemblances to Johnson's annex of 1950, which also had a glass curtain wall. The same materials are here used again; however, in this addition the detailing of the steel is non-Miesian, and instead of using a vocabulary of stock steel elements, Johnson employed curved connections at the corners of the frames. The entire curtain wall is recessed at the top floor three feet to match the terrace on the original building. On the top floor Johnson designed a «Founders' Room» with nine vaulted plaster domes framed in a steel grid with integral lighting.

Progressive Architecture, July 1964
Progressive Architecture, December 1967
«New York 1960», R. Stern, T. Mellins, D. Fishman, 1995

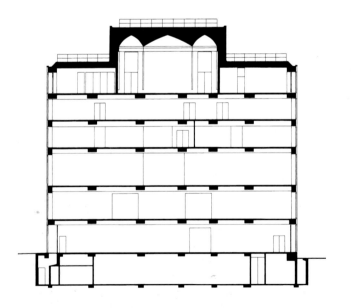

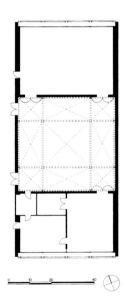

Schnitt, 1:500
Grundriß Dachgeschoß mit «Founder's Room», 1:500
Fassadenschnitt mit Stahlprofil, 1:20
Außenansicht
«Founders' Room»

Building section, 1:500
Top floor plan with Founders' Room, 1:500
Detail axonometric of facade with steel mullion, 1:20
Exterior view
Interior view Founders' Room

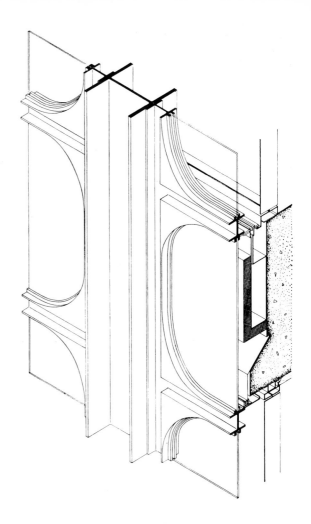

New York State Theater am Lincoln Center

Philip Johnson
1964
New York, New York
Partner: Richard Foster
Statik: Severud-Perrone-Fisher-Strum-
Conlin-Bandel
Haustechnik: Syska & Hennessy
Akustik: Vilhelm Jordan
Lichttechnik: Richard Kelly

Das New York State Theater ist Teil des Lincoln Center in Manhattan. Die auf den Vorplatz ausgerichtete Hauptfassade besteht aus einem Portikus, über dessen gesamte Länge ein Balkon läuft. Die räumliche Abfolge vom Eingang bis in den Theaterraum hinein ist sorgfältig orchestriert, vom niedrig gehaltenen Eingangsfoyer über die symmetrische Treppenanlage zu den Wandelgalerien der einzelnen Stockwerke.

Während der Ausarbeitung schlug Philip Johnson den anderen am Lincoln Center beteiligten Architekten vor, man könne doch die Einzelbauten durch einen umlaufenden Säulengang miteinander verbinden – zum einen, um die Fußgängererschließung zwischen den Gebäuden zu erleichtern, zum anderen, um dem Gesamtwerk architektonisch ein einheitliches Bild zu verleihen. Damit stieß er auf Widerstand, die anderen Architekten zogen es vor, ihre Fassaden gebäudespezifisch zu entwerfen, das Erscheinungsbild eines einheitlich gestalteten Arkadengangs, ähnlich der Place Vendôme und Place des Vosges in Paris, wurde abgelehnt. Eine städtebauliche Chance sondergleichen war somit vertan.

New York State Theater at Lincoln Center

Philip Johnson
1964
New York, New York
Partner: Richard Foster
Structural Engineer: Severud-Perrone-
Fisher-Strum-Conlin-Bandel
Mechanical Engineer: Syska & Hennessy
Acoustical Engineer: Vilhelm Jordan
Lighting: Richard Kelly

The New York State Theater is a component of the Lincoln Center complex in Manhattan, and its main facade fronts on its central plaza. The building's front is porticoed with a balcony extending across the entire facade. The procession from the entrance to the theater inside is carefully controlled, with a low entry foyer leading to two monumental staircases which, in turn, lead to a galleried promenade.

When Philip Johnson worked on this project, he suggested to the other architects designing various buildings for Lincoln Center that it might be a good idea to connect all the Center's buildings with a continuous arcade to facilitate pedestrian circulation and to unify the Center architecturally. The other architects objected, suggesting that each would prefer to design his own facade, rather than subordinate that of his specific building to a uniform arcaded elevation in the manner of the Place Vendôme or the Place des Vosges in Paris. And so a major urban design opportunity was missed.

Award: AIA Honor Award, 1964

Architectural Record, May 1964

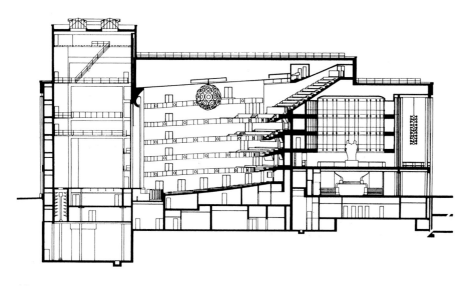

Schnitt, 1:750
Entwurf für einen umlaufenden Arkadengang
(nicht realisiert)
Grundriß Theaterraum
Deckenuntersicht im Theaterraum
Nächste Seite: Außenansicht mit
Vorplatz und Springbrunnen
Foyer

Section, 1:750
Perspective of proposed arcade
Theater floor plan
Auditorium ceiling
Following page: Exterior view with
plaza and fountain
Lobby

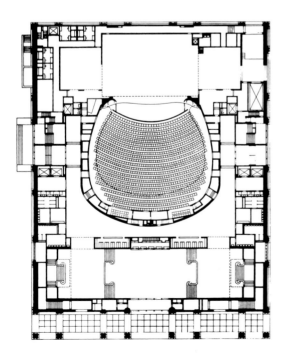

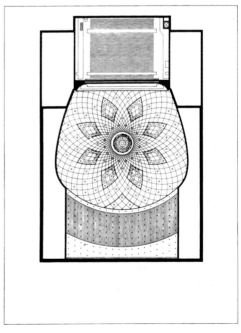

New York State Pavillon
Philip Johnson
1964
New York, New York
Partner: Richard Foster
Statik: Lev Zetlin & Associates
Haustechnik: Syska & Hennessy
Landschaftsplanung: Zion & Breen Associates

Der Bundesstaat New York war 1964 mit diesem Pavillon auf der Weltausstellung vertreten. Der Pavillon ist in drei Abschnitte gegliedert – den mittig angeordneten Hauptraum in Form einer Ellipse, der von einer kabelverspannten Dachtragstruktur in den Abmessungen von 107 m x 76 m überdeckt wird; den drei im Grundriß konzentrischen Aussichtstürmen mit einer Höhe von jeweils ca. 27 m, 56 m und 76 m, die von einer außenliegenden verglasten Aufzugsanlage erschlossen werden; sowie einem konzentrisch angelegten Theater («Circarama») von 30,50 m Durchmesser mit einer 360-Grad-Leinwand zur Filmprojektion.
Der Fußboden des platzartigen Hauptraums zeigt eine vollständige Straßenkarte des Bundesstaates New York. Die Außenwände wurden von New Yorker Popart-Künstlern gestaltet.

New York State Pavilion
Philip Johnson
1964
New York, New York
Partner: Richard Foster
Structural Engineer: Lev Zetlin & Associates
Mechanical Engineer: Syska & Hennessy
Landscape Architect: Zion & Breen Associates

As the pavilion for the State of New York at the 1964 World's Fair, this building consists of three sections: A central elliptical room (and support space) covered by a cable-hung roof structure 350 feet by 250 feet in dimension. Secondly, a set of three circular observation towers 90, 185 and 250 feet tall respectively, and accessed by glass-enclosed exterior elevators; and lastly, a 100 feet diameter circular theater (a «circarama») for the projection of a 360 degree film.
The central plaza-like space had a complete highway map of the State of New York as its paving pattern and the exterior of the pavilion was embellished with murals of various New York «pop» artists.

Architectural Record, July 1964
Architectural & Engineering News, April 1964

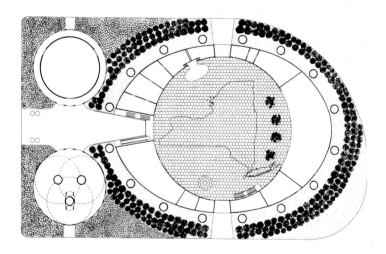

Lageplan, 1:1500

Site plan, 1:1500

Blick in den platzartigen Hauptraum
Außenansicht

Interior view of plaza
Exterior view

Haus Beck
Philip Johnson
1964
Dallas, Texas
Statik: Mullen & Powell Engineers
Haustechnik: Herman Blum Engineer

Im Haus Beck setzt Johnson erneut ein System aus vorgefertigten Betonstützen und -pfeilern ein, das er bereits im Pavillon am Teich auf seinem eigenen Landsitz verwandt hatte. Hinter die Stützen zurückgesetzte, raumhohe Glasscheiben und grau verputzte Betonsteinwände dienen als Raumabschluß. Die im Rhythmus durchlaufenden Stützen und Bogen umschließen den zweigeschossigen Bau, binden ihn in Form eines offenen Arkadengangs an außenliegende Versorgungsbauten an und grenzen die begrünten Terrassen von der freien Landschaft ab.

Beck House
Philip Johnson
1964
Dallas, Texas
Structural Engineer: Mullen & Powell Engineers
Mechanial Engineer: Herman Blum Engineer

The house uses a system of columns and pilasters first developed in the pavilion at the pond of the Johnson estate. Like the pavilion, the columns are of pre-cast concrete; and, when enclosing a room, they are filled in with recessed, full height glass panels or an opaque wall of grey stucco over concrete block. The continuous pattern of columns and arches is used to enclose the two-story house, and extends out in open colonnades to service buildings, and defines the edges of landscaped terraces.

Vogue, May 1964

Lageplan

Site plan

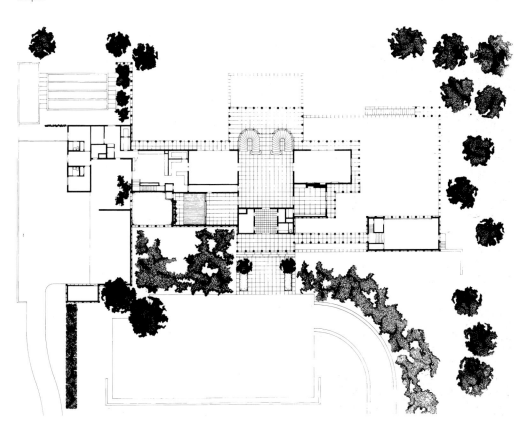

Haus Geier

Philip Johnson und John Burgee
1965
Indian Hills, Cincinnati, Ohio
Assoziierte Architekten: Baxter, Hodell,
Donnelly & Preston, Inc.
Statik: Severud-Elstad-Krueger
Haustechnik: James Greenwood

Das Haus Geier wurde am Abhang eines kleinen Hügels platziert. Sein Hauptmerkmal sind die Zylinder aus «Cor-Ten»-Stahl, die über die Ebene des Daches hinausragen und ihre eigene, abstrakte Dachlandschaft bilden (und unter anderem als Lüftungsschächte, Oberlichter und Kamine Verwendung finden). Das umgebende Erdreich ist angeböscht, wodurch das Gebäude wie eingegraben erscheint – in der Wirkung der Gemäldegalerie auf Johnsons eigenem Grundstück ähnlich, die um die gleiche Zeit entstand. Vor der dem Tal zugewandten, fast vollständig verglasten Seite liegt, lediglich ca. 15 cm unterhalb der Wohnebene, ein künstlicher See.

Geier House

Philip Johnson and John Burgee
1965
Indian Hills, Cincinnati, Ohio
Associate Architects: Baxter, Hodell,
Donnelly & Preston, Inc.
Structural Engineer: Severud-Elstad-Krueger
Mechanical Engineer: James Greenwood

The Geier House is set into a small hill, with «Cor-Ten» steel cylinders (containing functional elements such as vents, skylights, and chimneys) projecting above the roof to form an abstract landscape. The earth around the house is bermed to give the impression that the building is buried – much in the same way as Johnson's own Painting Gallery of the same year. A man-made lake, only 6 inches below the level of the main floor, fronts the expansive glass walls of the down-hill side.

AIA Journal, November 1973

Außenansicht des Eingangs

Exterior view at entry

Gemäldegalerie

Philip Johnson
1965
New Canaan, Connecticut
Statik: Lev Zetlin Associates
Haustechnik: Jaros, Baum & Bolles

1965 errichtete Johnson in der Nähe des Glashauses eine Galerie für seine Gemäldesammlung, deren Eingangssituation dem Grabmal des Atreus in Mykene entlehnt sein soll. Der Hauptteil des Gebäudes besteht aus einer niedrig gehaltenen Eingangszone und einem größeren Raum, in dem sich drei halbkreisförmige, unterschiedlich große Ausbuchtungen mit schwenkbaren Paneelen befinden. Ähnlich wie bei der Sammlung des englischen Baumeisters Sir John Soane können so die Gemälde im Turnus gezeigt werden. Die Wandnischen werden von den ausgeschwenkten Paneelen verdeckt, wodurch der Raum rechtwinklig wirkt. Das Gebäude ist fast völlig von einer Erdböschung umgeben und scheint daher unterirdisch zu liegen. Der Eingang liegt im rechten Winkel zu einer bestehenden Allee.

Painting Gallery

Philip Johnson
1965
New Canaan, Connecticut
Structural Engineer: Lev Zetlin Associates
Mechanical Engineer: Jaros, Baum & Bolles

The entrance to this gallery recalls the Tomb of Atreus in Mycenae, according to Johnson, who built this structure in 1965 next to his Glass House. The principal space of the building is a low entrance and then a larger room containing three bays of rotating screens to hold the paintings, similar to the organization of the painting gallery at the home of Sir John Soane. The circular bays each differ in size, and can effectively transform the plan into a rectilinear space. The building appears to be underground, for it is surrounded by earth berms that bury it into the landscape. The siting is perpendicular to an existing allee of trees, and the gallery is entered from this allee.

Art in America, July 1968
Architectural Record, June 1967

Grundriß Erdgeschoß

Ground floor plan

106

Außenansicht
Innenansicht

Exterior view
Interior view

Henry Moses Forschungsinstitut des Montefiore Krankenhauses

Philip Johnson
1965
Bronx, New York
Statik: Lev Zetlin & Associates
Haustechnik: Caretsky & Associates

Das Kline Wissenschaftszentrum der Yale Universität und das Henry Moses-Institut in der New Yorker Bronx entstanden Mitte der sechziger Jahre. Beide Bauten verdanken dem Richards-Forschungslabor der medizinischen Fakultät, von Louis Kahn etwa sechs Jahre früher für die Universität von Pennsylvania erbaut, entscheidende Entwurfsmerkmale. Bei beiden Bauten handelt es sich um Hochhäuser mit kreuzförmigem Grundriß, deren Erscheinungsbild von Vertikalschächten geprägt wird, die die Laboratorien mit Zu- und Abluft versorgen und gleichzeitig als tragende Elemente dienen.

Kahns Laborgebäude muten wie mittelalterliche Turmbauten an – das Erscheinungsbild ist im Vergleich zum Moses-Institut ausgeprägter, aber die Versorgungs- und Tragsysteme funktionieren weitaus schlechter. Beim Moses-Institut steht die Anordnung dieser Elemente im direkten Zusammenhang mit den Anforderungen der Laboratorien. Die Nutzung der Laborräume bleibt flexibel, da die Zu- und Abluftschächte gleichmäßig um das Gebäude verteilt und von überall her gut zugänglich sind – im Gegensatz zu Kahns konzentrierter Anordnung.

Johnson setzt funktionale Entwurfsbelange gerne herab, er behauptet immer, daß sie ihn nicht besonders interessieren. Beim Moses-Institut handelt es sich jedoch um ein gut organisiertes Forschungsgebäude: Labors, Versorgungstechnik und Tragwerksraster sind im Grundriß in Einklang gebracht. Es ist ein elegantes Stück «Machine Art» mit seiner Verkleidung aus dreifach verstärktem, in den Ecken auf Gehrung geschnittenem Glas, den Vertikalschächten, die mit flachen, römischen Ziegeln in hellbrauner Färbung – Johnsons bevorzugter Sorte – und schmalen Mörtelfugen verkleidet sind. Die Fassade der zurückgesetzten Erdgeschoßzone besteht aus schwarzem Granit und Glas und fällt bei weitem nicht so ins Auge wie die Laborgeschosse mit ihren senkrecht aufstrebenden Schacht- und Fensterelementen. Im Unterschied zum Kline-Hochhaus in Yale, bei dem die vertikalen Ziegelschächte von horizontalen Sandsteinfeldern unterbrochen werden, zeigt das Moses-Hochhaus deutlich eine durchgängige Vertikalität.

Henry Moses Research Institute at Montefiore Hospital

Philip Johnson
1965
Bronx, New York
Structural Engineer: Lev Zetlin & Associates
Mechanical Engineer: Caretsky & Associates

Both the Kline Science Center at Yale University and the Henry Moses Institute in the Bronx, New York, were designed in the mid 1960's, and both owe something to Louis Kahn's Richards Medical Research Building at the University of Pennsylvania, designed half a dozen years earlier. Both are high-rise buildings, both are cruciform in plan, and both are dominated by vertical shafts that form the supporting structure, and also contain vertical supply or exhaust ducts to service the laboratories.

While Kahn's Richards Building at Penn is more medievally towering than the Moses Hospital, its structural and service systems actually do not work nearly as well as those at the Moses Hospital. In the latter, the locations of structure and service shafts are more relationally determined by the actual requirements of the laboratories, and make for a more flexible use of the lab spaces because the supply and exhaust ducts are located all around the perimeter of the building (rather than clustered together), and thus become much more accessible to critical areas of the laboratories within.

Johnson often likes to play down the functional aspects of his buildings, claiming that they don't especially concern him. But the Moses Hospital is , in fact, a remarkably well-organized research tower, with the layout of laboratories perfectly integrated with the service systems and the structural grid. It is a very elegant piece of Machine Art, clad in triple-thickness sheets of glass (with mitered corners) and vertical shafts clad in buff-colored brick of Johnson's favorite, iron-spot variety, in elongated Roman courses, with narrow mortar joints. The recessed ground floor of the tower is clad in black granite and glass; but it is the articulation of the laboratory floors, with their vertical thrust of windows and ducts that makes the little tower so impressive. Unlike the Kline Tower at Yale, in which the vertical brick shafts are interrupted by horizontal bands of sandstone, the Moses Tower has a consistent verticality that reads extremely well.

Award: City Club of New York Honor Award, 1966

Architectural Forum, October 1966
«Philip Johnson Architecture 1949–1965»,
Henry-Russell Hitchcock, 1965

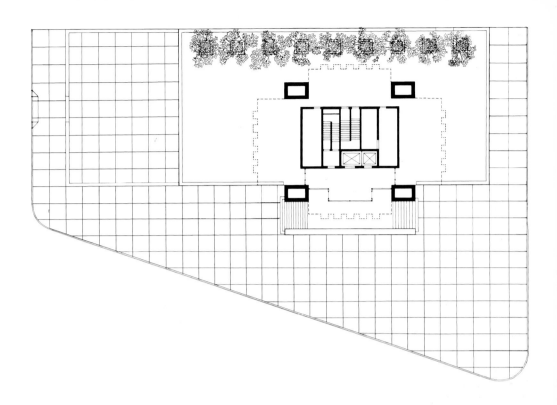

Grundriß Eingangsebene mit Vorplatz, 1:5000
Außenansicht von der Straßenseite

Plaza level plan, 1:500
Exterior view from street

Kline Biologiegebäude der Yale Universität

Philip Johnson und Richard Foster Architects
1966
New Haven, Connecticut
Statik: Lev Zetlin & Associates
Haustechnik: Meyer, Strong & Jones
Landschaftsplanung: Zion & Breen Associates

Als die Yale Universität Johnson mit dem Entwurf eines siebzehngeschossigen Hochhauses als Teil des Naturwissenschaftlichen Zentrums beauftragte, wollte sie nicht nur ein Biologieseminar- und Laborgebäude, sondern auch ein sichtbares Zeichen für die naturwissenschaftliche Fakultät im Stadtbild New Havens – ähnlich den neogotischen Türmen aus früheren Jahren. Johnsons kühner Turm aus violett-roten Ziegeln, Sandstein und Glas wird dieser Aufgabe mehr als gerecht.

Der Turm hat einen kreuzförmigen und gut nutzbaren Grundriß. Der Unterschied zu anderen kompakten Bauten dieser Art liegt im Detail, vor allem in der Detaillierung der Außenwände.

Am auffälligsten ist die Kolonnade aus ziegelverkleideten Stützen, die das gesamte Gebäude in voller Höhe umfaßt. Die Stützen sind Rohre aus Asbestzement mit einem Durchmesser von ca. 50 cm, die mit Beton ummantelt und im Achsabstand von 3,35 m angeordnet wurden. Abluft aus den Laboratorien wird über diese Rohre in einen horizontal verlaufenden Kanal im 13. Obergeschoß geleitet und dort durch einen Schornstein ausgeblasen.

Johnson verkleidete die Hohlstützen mit dem von ihm bevorzugten gebrannten Ziegel, der in einer Farbpalette von weiß über dunkelrot bis schwarz erhältlich ist. Das Material altert hervorragend. Er hat es bei zahlreichen Gebäuden mit ausgezeichneten Ergebnissen eingesetzt. Die Rundstützen mögen in Peter Behrens' Berliner AEG – Kleinmotorenfabrik aus dem Jahre 1910 ihren Ursprung haben. Die Brüstungspaneele aus Sandstein scheinen zwischen den Stützen zu schweben und unterstreichen deren dreidimensionales Erscheinungsbild. Sie beschatten zudem die von der Stützenebene zurückgesetzten Fenster. Das einprägsame Spiel von Licht und Schatten auf den zurückliegenden Flächen verleiht der Außenwand eine plastische Qualität, die das Gebäude wohltuend von einigen der banalen, unartikulierten Vorhangfassaden der Umgebung abhebt.

Johnson säumte ein paar Gärten in der näheren Umgebung des Turms ebenfalls mit Kolonnaden aus Ziegel, um das Gebäude besser in die Gesamtanlage des Wissenschaftszentrums einzubinden. Ebenso kam das Motiv an Nachbargebäuden, die der Erweiterung bedurften, zum

Kline Biology Tower at Yale University

Philip Johnson and Richard Foster Architects
1966
New Haven, Connecticut
Structural Engineer: Lev Zetlin & Associates
Mechanical Engineer: Meyer, Strong & Jones
Landscape Architect: Zion & Breen Associates

When Johnson designed this 17-story tall tower for Yale's Science Center, the University needed not only a building to house its biology classes and laboratories, but one that would identify the Science Center on the New Haven skyline – as clearly as some of the other disciplines had been identified by various Collegiate Gothic towers in earlier years. The bold tower, clad in purplish-red ironspot brick, sandstone, and glass, does that job exceedingly well.

The plan of the tower is cruciform and efficient. What makes the building very different from other compact structures of this sort is its detailing, especially the detailing of the exterior walls.

The most visible detail, of course, is the massive, brick-finished colonnade that surrounds the tower, and reaches from the ground all the way up to the roofline. These columns are hollow, 20 inch diameter cement-asbestos pipes encased in concrete, and placed about 11 feet on centers. The pipes exhaust air from the laboratories and feed it into a horizontal duct at the 13th floor. From there it is exhausted through a roof stack.

The hollow concrete columns are finished with Johnson's favorite hard-fired brick that comes in colors ranging from near white to deep red and black. It ages extremely well, and Johnson has used it in many of his buildings, to excellent effect. The rounded brick columns were probably inspired by the columns used by Peter Behrens in the AEG «Kleinmotorenfabrik» in Berlin, done around 1910. Johnson has given the columns an added three-dimensionality by the connecting slabs of sandstone that act as «floating» spandrels, and also serve to shade the windows recessed between the columns. The result is a wall of great plasticity, with light and shadow reflecting surfaces within the recessed areas making for a memorable facade – very different, needless to say, from the bland, flat curtain walls on some of the neighboring new buildings.

To make the tower more than an isolated incident in the Science Center, Johnson has extended his brick colonnades around some of the gardens surrounding the tower, and used the motif in a few of the nearby buildings that required additions to their facilities. Perhaps the University will, some day, return to this elegant brick and stone motif in giving the entire Science Center an even

Lageplan, 1:4000
Grundriß Normalgeschoß, 1:500

Site plan, 1:4000
Typical floor plan, 1:500

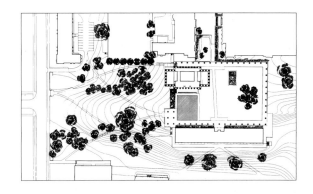

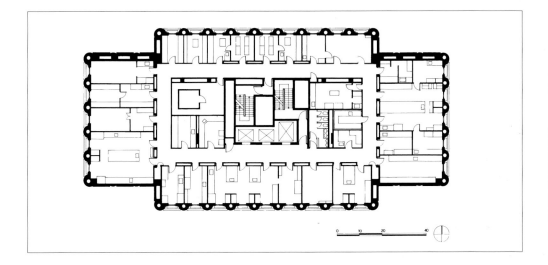

Einsatz. Vielleicht entschließt sich die Universität eines Tages dazu, das elegante Stein- und Ziegelmotiv wieder aufzugreifen, um dem Wissenschaftszentrum als Gesamtkomplex eine einprägsamere Identität zu verleihen. Der Anfang ist mit Johnsons Hochhaus gemacht.

Der Einsatz tragender Stützen, die zugleich als Versorgungsschächte dienen, erinnert an Louis Kahns Bauten für die Universität von Pennsylvania aus derselben Zeit. In funktionaler Hinsicht überzeugt das Kline-Hochhaus jedoch wesentlich mehr als die Richards-Forschungslabors von Kahn. Er trennte die Versorgungselemente vom Tragwerk, während die Funktionen bei Johnson in einem Element zusammengefaßt werden. Puristen kritisierten die Vermischung der Funktionen, vielleicht zu Recht. Die Effizienz der Kombination von Tragwerk und Belüftung in einer einzigen hohlen Säule läßt sich jedoch nicht von der Hand weisen.

more memorable identity. Johnson's tower is a fine start in that direction.

The vertical service shafts (doubling as structural columns) are, of course, reminiscent also of Louis Kahn's buildings of that same period on the campus of the University of Pennsylvania; but the detailing of the Kline Tower seems a good deal more convincing, as a functioning entity, than the design of the Richards Research Labs built by Kahn during those same years. Still, Kahn separated the structural elements from his service towers, while Johnson combined the two functions in a single shaft. To some purists, this seemed like a confusion of functions, which may be true. But, as a matter of fact, Johnson's combination of structure and ventilation in a single hollow column happens to work most efficiently.

Award: AIA Honor Award, 1965

Progressive Architecture, February 1967
Architectural Record, June 1967
«Modern Architecture», Manfredo Tafuri, 1970

Außenansicht

Exterior view

Haus Kreeger

Philip Johnson and Richard Foster Architects
1968
Washington, DC
Assoziierte Architekten: Milton Fisher Associates
Statik: Lev Zetlin & Associates
Haustechnik: Jaros, Baum & Bolles

Johnson entwarf dieses Haus für den Versicherungsmag-
naten David Lloyd Kreeger als Wohnhaus und Ausstel-
lungsgalerie für dessen Sammlung moderner Gemälde
und Skulpturen.
Tageslichtplanung, Haustechnik und der modulare Grundriß sind ganz durch die besonderen Erfordernisse der ausgestellten Kunst bestimmt. Demzufolge ist es mehr als
eine glückliche Fügung, daß das Bauwerk 1994 von den
Kreegers zu einem der Öffentlichkeit zugänglichen Museum erklärt wurde. Dem Grundriß liegt ein Stützenraster
von ca. 6,70 m zugrunde. Glas- und Travertinpaneele sind
zwischen die Stützen eingefügt. Flach gewölbte Kup-
peldächer, die jeweils an den Ecken auf den Stützen auf-
liegen, überdecken die Rasterfelder und geben Oberlicht-
bänder über den massiven Wänden frei.

Kreeger House

Philip Johnson and Richard Foster Architects
1968
Washington, DC
Associate Architect: Milton Fischer Associates
Structural Engineer: Lev Zetlin & Associates
Mechanical Engineer: Jaros, Baum & Bolles

Johnson designed this home for the insurance magnate
Mr. David Lloyd Kreeger as both a residence and a gallery
for his collection of modern painting and sculpture.
Having been designed with concern for the display of art
in its daylighting, mechanical controls, and modular planning, it is appropriate as well as fortunate that the house
was turned into a public museum by the Kreegers in
1994. The house plan is based on piers set on a 22 foot
module, with infill of travertine stone panels and glass.
These bays are topped by shallow domed roofs resting on
corner piers, and these domes arc above the wall to become a series of clerestory windows.

Time, September 13, 1968
House Beautiful, February 1969
Interior Design, June 1995

Grundriß Erdgeschoß
Grundriß Obergeschoß

Ground floor plan
First floor plan

Ansicht von der Gartenseite

Exterior view from garden

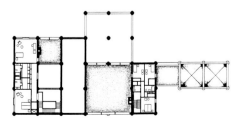

Kunsthalle Bielefeld

Philip Johnson
1968
Bielefeld
Assoziierter Architekt: C. Pinnau
Statik: Severud-Elstad-Krueger
Haustechnik: Jaros, Baum & Bolles

Diese kleine Kunsthalle in Bielefeld ist eines von Johnsons etwa einem Dutzend Kunstmuseen und in vielfacher Hinsicht interessant. Ihre Einteilung eignet sich für ein Museum dieser Art besonders gut – die Ausstellungsflächen sind im Erdgeschoß und zwei Obergeschossen; der Vortragssaal, die Bibliothek und andere Nutzbereiche im Untergeschoß. Tageslicht und Kunstlicht stehen in einem ausgewogenen Verhältnis. Das Gebäude, ein freistehender Pavillon, thront auf einem zurückspringenden Sockel inmitten einer der schönsten Parkanlagen der Stadt.

Es ist eines der wenigen Bauwerke Johnsons, die Le Corbusiers Einfluß erkennen lassen: ein klarer Kubus auf – so etwas ähnlichem wie – Pilotis vom Boden abgehoben und oben zum Himmel hin geöffnet. Der Grundriß ist quadratisch und mißt ca. 24,40 m x 24,40 m.

Johnson sähe das Bauwerk gerne etwas vorteilhafter proportioniert – das oberste Geschoß höher und die beiden darunterliegenden Geschosse niedriger. Oder umgekehrt. Das mag sein; dennoch funktionieren die Proportionen, wenn auch nicht perfekt. Die glatten Wände des Obergeschosses schließen es von der Außenwelt ab, und Tageslicht dringt nur durch Oberlichter ein, die die gesamte Dachfläche einnehmen. Die beiden darunterliegenden Geschosse können ebenfalls nach außen abgeschlossen werden, wobei die Exponate dann mit Kunstlicht ausgeleuchtet werden. Johnson, der davon wahrscheinlich mehr versteht als viele seiner Zeitgenossen, zieht für Ausstellungsräume Kunstlicht vor – weil es sich gezielter als Tageslicht einsetzen läßt.

Die Kunsthalle in Bielefeld bietet beides, und das scheint eine gute Kompromißlösung, eingedenk der Tatsache, daß sich Museumsdirektoren – die ihre Posten ähnlich häufig wie bei der «Reise nach Jerusalem» tauschen – nie einig sind, wie Kunstwerke am besten auszuleuchten seien. In diesem Museum gibt es deshalb vielerlei Möglichkeiten zur Präsentation der Gemälde und Skulpturen.

Das Tragwerk verdient besonderes Augenmerk. Die massiven Betonwände sind windmühlenartig angeordnet, im Innen- und Außenbereich mit südafrikanischem Granit verkleidet und stehen im Wechsel mit Wänden aus Glas. Terrassen säumen den Pavillon und erweitern die Galerieräume nach außen. Auf allen vier Gebäudeseiten finden sich Wasserbecken und Skulpturengärten.

Bielefeld Art Gallery

Philip Johnson
1968
Bielefeld, Germany
Associate Architect: C. Pinnau
Structural Engineer: Severud-Elstad-Krueger
Mechanical Engineer: Jaros, Baum & Bolles

This small museum in Bielefeld, in northwest Germany, is one of about a dozen art galleries designed by Johnson over the years, and it is interesting in a number of ways: to start with, it is an almost perfect diagram for such a museum – galleries on three floors, with an auditorium, library, and other facilities underground; and both natural and artificial lighting available in more or less equal amounts. Moreover, the building is a free-standing pavilion, gracefully perched on a recessed base, and located in one of the city's nicest public parks.

Finally, it is one of the very few buildings done by Johnson over the years that clearly owes something to the work of Le Corbusier: it is a «pure prism» raised off the ground on «pilotis» (more or less), and open to the sky (also more or less) on its top floor. The building is square in plan, and its footprint measures 80 by 80 feet.

Johnson feels that the building should have been somewhat differently proportioned – either taller in its top floor and shorter in the two lower floors, or the other way around. Perhaps so. But its proportionate division, while not perfect, seems to function extremely well: the top floor has blank walls facing the outer world (and is naturally lit through skylights that make up the entire roof); while the two lower floors can be closed off from the outside world, and the works of art can be artificially lit. Johnson prefers artificially lit galleries, because you can adjust artificial light to the art more easily.

Because of its configuration, the Bielefeld Art Gallery offers both artificial and natural lighting, which seems like a reasonable compromise since Museum Directors, who tend to change jobs as if they were hopping around on musical chairs, can never agree on the best way to light works of art.

One of the most intriguing aspects of this building is its structure – an arrangement of massive concrete walls in a loose pinwheel pattern, with glass walls alternating with solid panels finished with South African granite, inside and out.

Terraces on different levels surround the little pavilion, with reflecting pools and sculpture gardens on all sides.

Progressive Architecture, May 1965
Architectural Record, December 1969

Grundriß 1. Obergeschoß,
1:750, Grundriß 2.
Obergeschoß, 1:750
Innenansicht des Foyers
Außenansicht

First floor plan, 1:750,
Second floor plan, 1:750
Interior view of lobby
Exterior view

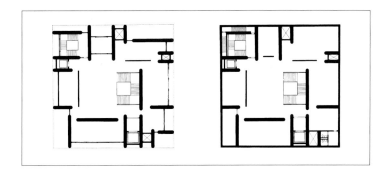

John F. Kennedy Gedenkstätte
Philip Johnson
1970
Dallas, Texas
Statik: George Emerson

Der Kenotaph zum Gedenken an Präsident Kennedy steht drei Straßenblöcke vom Ort des Attentats entfernt. Der 1965 begonnene Entwurf besteht aus einer einfachen, 9,10 m hohen Mauer, die die 15,20 m x 15,20 m große, nach oben offene Gedenkstätte umschließt. Die Mauer ist aus senkrecht angeordneten Betonschwellen mit einem Querschnitt von je 76 cm, die auf horizontal verlaufenden, an den Ecken sichtbaren Stahlankern aufgefädelt sind. Längere, von den Ecken aus eingerückte Betonelemente heben den Rahmen um 76 cm von der Erde ab. In der Mitte des Raumes befindet sich ein 1,20 m x 1,20 m großer, schwarzer Granitblock mit eingravierter Widmung. Das Projekt klingt an den Entwurf an, den Mies van der Rohe im Jahre 1930 für den Innenraum von Schinkels Neuer Wache in Berlin vorschlug.

John F. Kennedy Memorial
Philip Johnson
1970
Dallas, Texas
Structural Engineer: George Emerson

This cenotaph to honor President Kennedy was built three blocks from the site of his assassination. The design, started in 1965, is a simple enclosure defining an outdoor room 50 feet by 50 feet with 30 foot high walls. The memorial walls are pre-cast concrete slabs 2 1/2 feet square in section, connected by horizontal steel tie rods expressed at the corners. The entire assembly is raised 2 1/2 feet above the ground by off-corner columns.
A black granite slab, 4 feet square, is placed at the center with a carved dedication. The project derived inspiration from Mies van der Rohe's proposed 1930 World War I memorial inside Schinkel's Neue Wache in Berlin.

Design Magazine, March 1966
New York Times, June 25, 1970

Blick von oben auf die Gedenkstätte

Exterior view from above

Skulpturengalerie

Philip Johnson
1970
New Canaan, Connecticut
Statik: Severud Associates
Haustechnik: Cosentini Associates

Die Skulpturengalerie, die Johnson für seinen Landsitz in New Canaan entwarf, wurde 1970 errichtet und ist, neben dem Glashaus und dem Gästehaus, einer von sieben skulpturalen Bauten dort und, in mancher Hinsicht, der gelungenste.

Das Bauwerk wäre in jeder Hinsicht gelungen, wäre es von außen nicht so merkwürdig unscheinbar. Das Besondere daran wird erst innen augenscheinlich.

Johnson spricht vom Innenraum gerne als einer Treppenanlage oder einer Abfolge von Stufen zwischen fünf verschieden hohen Podesten, die sich um einen abgesenkten Zentralraum entwickeln. Die zugrundegelegte Geometrie ist, laut Johnson, teils Quadrat, teils Fünfeck, wobei Wände und Stufen der jeweils am besten geeigneten Richtung folgen. Johnson hatte sich schon lange mit dem Problem einer Skulpturengalerie beschäftigt, in der mehrere Exponate vor- und hintereinander zu sehen wären. Um der visuellen Überlagerung zu begegnen und die einzelnen Werke zur Geltung zu bringen, schien ihm die Ausbildung von Nischen und Ecken für seine Skulpturen von entscheidender Bedeutung.

Die zwölfseitige Skulpturengalerie wird fast vollständig über ein schräg verlaufendes Oberlicht ausgeleuchtet, das sich über den gesamten Raum erstreckt und dessen Schattenwurf schwarze Furchen auf den weißgetünchten Wänden zieht. Das Schattenbild wirkt wie ein Teil der Sammlung und gehört in gewisser Weise zu den besten Beispielen abstrakter Kunst in der Galerie – dem Lichteinfall von Sonne, Mond und Sternen unterworfen und nachts hervorgehoben durch künstliche Lichtstrahlen, die vom Stahlrahmen des Glasdaches herabfallen. In der Photographie scheint es, als ob die Schattenfurchen die Skulpturen visuell zerteilen oder zumindest von ihnen ablenken. Das ist aber nicht der Fall.

Der vorrangige Grund für die Errichtung des Bauwerks war Platzmangel. Johnson konnte seine Skulpturen in der bestehenden Gemäldegalerie mit ihrem drehbaren, einem Postkartenständer nicht unähnlichen Ausstellungssystem nicht unterbringen. «Ich habe mit dem Entwurf dieser schwenkbaren Wände in der Gemäldegalerie einen schrecklichen Fehler gemacht», gestand er vor kurzem. «Man kann doch nicht jedesmal die Skulpturen beiseite schieben, wenn sich das riesige Postkartenkarussell zu drehen beginnt.» Die Skulpturensammlung brauchte of-

Sculpture Gallery

Philip Johnson
1970
New Canaan, Connecticut
Structural Engineer: Severud Associates
Mechanical Engineer: Cosentini Associates

The Sculpture Gallery Johnson built on his New Canaan estate was constructed in 1970. It is one of seven sculptural works that Johnson constructed for himself in addition to the Glass House and Guest House complex; and it is, in some respects, the most successful.

In some respects, but not all: oddly enough, it is a rather indifferent building when seen from the outside. It becomes something truly extraordinary once you get into it. Johnson likes to describe the interior as a stair – or a series of steps that connect five different landings. The stairs wind around a sunken space in the center, and the geometry of this layout, according to Johnson, is part square and part pentagon, with walls and stairs following whatever direction seemed to work best. He had long worried about sculpture galleries in which several pieces would be viewed overlapping each other, front and back, in incompatible ways; and so he was determined to give his gallery a series of niches and corners that would form separate settings for separate works.

The twelve-sided sculpture gallery is lit, almost entirely, from above, through a slanting skylight that covers the entire space and projects its striated shadows over the whitewashed interior walls. In a way, these striated patterns are the most impressive abstractions in the gallery's collection – changing with the light of the sun and the moon and the stars, and reinforced at night by artificial lights mounted on the steel frame of the glass roof. In photographs, these striations seem as if they might distract from, or dissect, the forms of sculpture displayed on the different levels. In reality, they don't.

The principal reason Johnson designed and built this gallery is that his painting gallery, with its rotating «postcard rack»-like walls, simply could not accommodate sculpture as well. «I'd made a perfectly horrifying mistake in designing those rotating walls in the painting gallery», he said recently. «How can you move the sculpture each time the great postcard rack starts turning?» Obviously, he needed a very different and very special place to house his sculpture collection, and so «I had to build another building.» The real reason, he admits, was that he had always wanted to build another building, anyway.

Another reason, without questions, was that he had always wanted to build a building that would explore certain ideas that had always fascinated him: the very nature

fensichtlich eine andere, geeignetere Behausung, also «...mußte ich noch ein Gebäude errichten.» Der Wunsch, wieder etwas Neues zu bauen, war, wie er zugibt, jedoch der eigentliche Vater des Gedankens.

Zudem wollte er einige Ideen weiter erkunden, die ihn schon lange beschäftigten: das Wesen von Treppen und Podesten mit dem dazugehörigen Thema der Abfolge und der Fortbewegung, das Wesen von Licht und Raum und deren Zusammenspiel sowie die Möglichkeit der Flucht vor der Natur.

Letzteres ist ein erneutes Beispiel für das Vergnügen, mit dem Johnson die Konventionen und anerkannten Regeln der Moderne in Frage stellt. Warum soll Symmetrie Sünde sein? Warum ist Klassizismus unmodern? Warum hat die Funktion artikuliert zu werden – und warum folgt ihr die Form? Warum sollen Gebäude «ehrlich» sein? Und schließlich – welchen Vorteil hat es überhaupt, den Außenraum in den Innenraum einzubeziehen?

Die Errichtung eines Gebäudes, in dem der Außenraum außen und der Innenraum innen bleibt, kann Johnson eingedenk der Tatsache verziehen werden, daß er die meiste Zeit in einem Glashaus lebt, in dem der Außenraum stets Innenraum ist – und oftmals umgekehrt. Nach Fertigstellung der Skulpturengalerie war er mit dem Ergebnis so zufrieden, daß er sich überlegte, dort einzuziehen und die Skulpturensammlung im Glashaus auszustellen. Das Glashaus schien als Galerie für Skulpturen ungeeignet – ebenso wie so manche Galerie im MoMA –, also ließ er die Idee fallen. Und vielleicht läßt die Skulpturengalerie durch ihr Glasdach doch schon zuviel Außen nach Innen.

Natürlich ist die Galerie nicht nur Innenraum. Wenn man sich auf den Stufen von einem Podest zum anderen bewegt, fühlt man sich an die schönen, weißgetünchten Dörfer am Mittelmeer erinnert, wie man sie auf den griechischen Inseln und an der italienischen oder spanischen Küste findet. Die Galerie gleicht in der räumlichen Abfolge einer Mittelmeersiedlung auf einer steilen Klippe, jedes Podest eine Piazza oder ein Haus, die Treppe ein Weg, der den Hügel erklimmt. Wer Gelegenheit hatte, dies vor Ort zu erleben, der weiß, warum es auf Johnson einen so unauslöschlichen Eindruck hinterließ.

of stairs and landings, and the kind of progression or procession that only stairs can generate; the nature of light and space, and their interaction; and the possibility of escape from nature.

This latter notion is one more example of Johnson's delight in questioning all of the conventional, accepted rules of the modern movement. Why would symmetry be a sin? Why is classicism anti-modern? Why does function have to be expressed – and why should form follow it? Why do buildings have to be «honest»? And, finally, what's so good about bringing the outdoors inside?

Living, as he does much of the time, in a glass house in which the outdoors is always inside (and the inside is often outdoors), he could be forgiven for doing a building that would keep the outdoors out, and the indoors in. When he had built the sculpture gallery he found the result so successful that he briefly thought of moving into it, and putting his sculpture collection into the Glass House. But the Glass House as a sculpture gallery seemed all wrong – very much like MoMA's galleries in fact – and so he shelved the idea. And perhaps the sculpture gallery, with its glassy roof, let in too much of the outdoors after all.

The sculpture gallery isn't all indoors, of course. A walk up and down those steps, from one landing to the next, reminds you of nothing so much as the experience of walking through those beautiful white walled Mediterranean villages, on Greek islands or on the coasts of Italy and Spain. The gallery is really a procession through one of those cliff-hanging Mediterranean settlements, with each landing being another piazza or another house, and with the stairway a street winding up and down the hillside. It is an experience that anyone familiar with that part of the world will never forget; Johnson certainly never did.

Award: Bricklayers, Masons and Plasterers 1975
Louis Sullivan Award

Architectural Forum, December 1972
Architectural Forum, January 1973

Grundriß Erdgeschoß, 1:250
Innenansicht

Ground floor plan, 1:250
Interior view

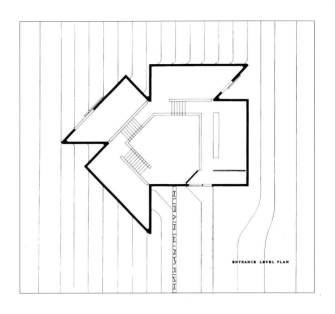

ENTRANCE LEVEL PLAN

Außenansicht

Exterior view

Albert und Vera List Kunstinstitut der Brown Universität

Philip Johnson Architect
1971
Providence, Rhode Island
Assoziierte Architekten: Samuel Glaser & Partner
Statik: Albert Goldberg & Associates
Haustechnik: Thompson Engineering

Die Arbeiten an diesem Gebäude, das für die Kunstfakultät der Brown Universität entworfen wurde, begannen 1963. Es besteht aus fünf Büro- und Ateliergeschossen auf einem langgestreckten, schmalen Grundstück. Man betritt es durch eine überdachte Kolonnade auf der Schmalseite, die von Pilotis aus Beton gebildet wird, ähnlich Le Corbusiers berühmten Bauten. Wie bei diesen besteht auch hier die Fassade aus Ortbeton und weist die für Sichtbeton charakteristischen Abdrücke der Holzschalung auf.

Albert and Vera List Art Building at Brown University

Philip Johnson
1971
Providence, Rhode Island
Associate Architects: Samuel Glaser & Partner
Structural Engineer: Albert Goldberg & Associates
Mechanical Engineer: Thompson Engineering

This building was designed for the Art Department of Brown University, and work on it began in 1963. It consists of five stories of offices and studios on a long narrow site, and is entered by a colonnade at the short side. This colonnade makes a covered entryway of concrete pilotis quite similar to some of Le Corbusier's most famous structures. Like those buildings, it has a facade of poured-in-place concrete with an articulated grid of the formwork pattern.

Architectural Forum, January 1973
Brown Daily Herald, July 1973

Grundriß Erdgeschoß mit Auditorium und Ausstellungssaal

Ground floor with auditorium and exhibition space

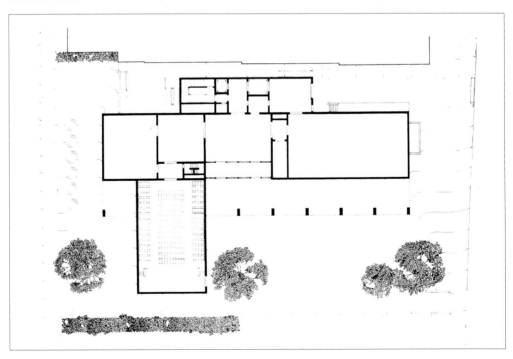

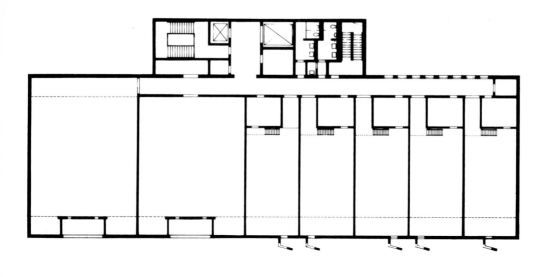

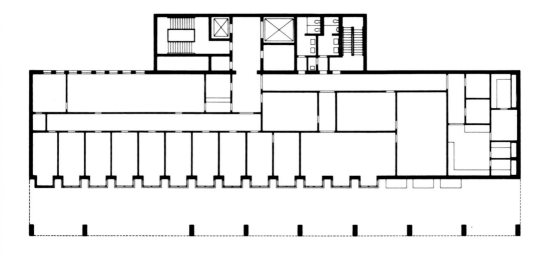

Grundriß 4. Obergeschoß mit Ateliers,
Belichtung durch Oberlichter
Grundriß Normalgeschoß mit Büro- und
Unterrichtsräumen
Außenansicht von der Straßenseite

Fourth floor with skylit studios
Typical floor plan, offices and classrooms
Exterior view from street

Kunstmuseum für das südliche Texas

Johnson/Burgee Architects
1969–1972
Corpus Christi, Texas
Assoziierte Architekten: Barnstone & Aubry
Statik: Cunningham & Lemus Inc.
Haustechnik: Thomas John & Associates

Das Kunstmuseum für das südliche Texas wurde 1972 fertiggestellt und gleicht keinem der bis dahin von Philip Johnson entworfenen Gebäude. Es verdankt sein äußeres Erscheinungsbild der Kapelle in Ronchamp, die Le Corbusier Anfang der fünfziger Jahre entworfen hatte und die mit ihren skulptural geschwungenen, weiß verputzten Außenwänden all jene schockierte, die Le Corbusiers Werk mit scharfkantigen, kubistischen Formen gleichsetzten. Die skulpturalen Elemente, die Le Corbusier in Ronchamp und seinen eindrucksvollen Bauten in Indien verwendete, verblüfften seine Anhänger weltweit und Johnson sicherlich auch. Mehr noch: sie faszinierten ihn. Es dauerte nicht lange, und er begann mit Strukturen und Fensterrastern zu experimentieren, die eindeutig dem Spätwerk Le Corbusiers entlehnt waren.

Die Faszination verflog zwar rasch, beeinflußte jedoch die Entstehung einiger interessanter Bauten. 1971 wurde das Albert und Vera List Kunstinstitut an der Brown Universität fertiggestellt, das von Le Corbusiers Klosteranlage in La Tourette inspiriert war. Auch das Kunstmuseum für das südliche Texas sowie verschiedene kleinere Bauten der darauffolgenden Jahre künden gleichermaßen von Le Corbusiers Formensprache wie von Johnsons anderen Interessen.

Der Grund, warum das Museum in Corpus Christi zu den besten in dieser Reihe zählt, ist einfach. Es steht an einem eindrucksvollen Ort am Golf von Mexico, gesegnet mit mediterranen Lichtverhältnissen, die ein so blendend weißes Bauwerk erst richtig zur Geltung bringen. Im trüben Norden der USA, wo die meisten Bauten Johnsons sind, würde es an den meisten Tagen einen eher düsteren Eindruck machen.

Das Museum sticht aus Johnsons Werk nicht allein ob des Sonnenscheins und der schönen Lage hervor, auch seine skulpturale Qualität ist besonders bemerkenswert, ähnlich Le Corbusiers kubistischem Appartement für Charles Beisteguy aus dem Jahre 1930. Die Innenräume des Museums sind jedoch viel lebhafter gestaltet als viele Bauten Le Corbusiers, die einem verhältnismäßig knappen Budget unterworfen waren. Die räumlich durch eine Verbindungsbrücke unterteilte und durch Oberlichter ausgeleuchtete Hauptausstellungshalle ist ein besonderer Ort. Das zentral gelegene, öffentlich zugängliche Atrium wirkt

Art Museum of South Texas

Johnson/Burgee Architects
1969–1972
Corpus Christi, Texas
Associate Architects: Barnstone & Aubry
Structural Engineer: Cunningham & Lemus Inc.
Mechanical Engineer: Thomas John & Associates

The Art Museum of South Texas was completed in 1972, and it seems about as different from most buildings designed by Philip Johnson as it could possibly be. The Museum's exterior clearly owes a good deal to Le Corbusier's Ronchamp chapel of the early 1950s, a building whose white, curvilinear, sculptured stucco walls shocked all those who had long associated Le Corbusier's work with hard-edged cubist forms. Ronchamp, and several of the sculptural elements in Le Corbusier's impressive buildings going up in India, stunned the architect's admirers everywhere. They probably stunned Johnson as well, but they also fascinated him. And before long he began to experiment with forms and textures and window patterns clearly taken from Le Corbusier's latest work.

His fascination was relatively short-lived, but it did produce some intriguing buildings. In 1971 he completed the Albert and Vera List Art Building for Brown University, which was clearly influenced by Le Corbusier's monastery of La Tourette. The Art Museum of South Texas shown here was completed in the year after that; and several years later there were various smaller structures that were clearly shaped as much by Le Corbusier's examples as they were by Johnson's other concerns.

The Corpus Christi Museum is probably the best of these, and for a simple reason: the building has a spectacular site on the Gulf of Mexico and the light is distinctly Mediterranean. An all-white stucco building needs that kind of sunlight to dazzle properly; and it would look dreary, much of the time, if constructed in the much gloomier northern climes of the U.S. where most of Johnson's buildings have gone up.

Yet the beautiful site and the dazzling sunlight are not the only aspects that make this museum something very special in Johnson's work. It is, above all, a very interesting piece of sculpture, much in the manner of Le Corbusier's cubist penthouse for Charles Beistegui in 1930; but the interiors of the museum are much livelier, spatially, than most of Le Corbusier's rather tightly budgeted spaces. The main exhibition hall, bisected by a «catwalk» and skylit here and there, is a very special place – a central public atrium that forms a kind of indoor piazza and provides access to other elements of the building – an auditorium, smaller galleries, and curatorial offices. In fact, the interior

Außenansicht
Innenansicht

Exterior view
Interior view

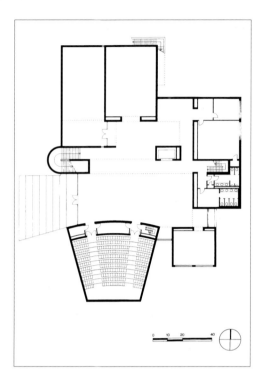

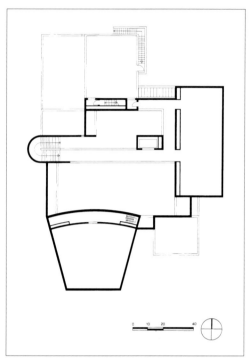

Grundriß Erdgeschoß, 1:750

Ground floor plan, 1:750

Grundriß Obergeschoß, 1:750

First floor plan, 1:750

wie eine überdachte Piazza, von der aus andere Gebäu-
debereiche wie der Vortragssaal, die kleineren Galerieräume und die Büros der Kuratoren zugänglich sind.
Innen ist das Museum in Texas der Nationalgalerie, die
I.M. Pei Jahre später in Washington entwarf, nicht unähn-
lich, ist jedoch erheblich kleiner.

Die meisten Bauten Johnsons aus dieser Zeit waren eher
symmetrisch und formal, mit einem leicht verständlichen
Grundriß. Das Museum weicht von diesem Schema auf
bemerkenswerte Weise ab. Mit seinen Aus- und Durch-
blicken, den verschiedenen Lichtverhältnissen, Fußboden-
höhen und Raumkonfigurationen steckt es so voller Über-
raschungen, daß man sich ein weiteres Ausreizen dieser
Formensprache wünscht. Und in der Tat hat er niemals
aufgehört, damit zu experimentieren.

Zum Zeitpunkt dieser Zeilen beschäftigt er sich mit dem
erstmals 1957 in Angriff genommenen Entwurf einer Kapelle für die St. Thomas-Universität in Houston, Texas, die
vielleicht einmal – wie Ronchamp – zu den wichtigen Kir-
chenbauten des 20. Jahrhunderts zählen wird. 1980 errichtete Johnson eine Studierklause auf seinem Landsitz
in New Canaan, die ebenfalls Le Corbusiers Einfluß erkennen läßt und beweist, daß auch ihm es leicht fällt, sich
in dieser Formenwelt zu bewegen.

is not unlike the East Building of Washington's National
Gallery, designed several years later by I.M. Pei, and considerably larger in size than Johnson's little Art Museum
of South Texas.

Since most of Johnson's buildings of that period tended
to be symmetrical, formal, and admirably «obvious» in
plan, this building is a remarkable departure. It is so full
of little surprises, views, vistas, lights and unexpected
changes in level and spatial configuration that one wishes
Johnson would pursue these directions farther. As a matter of fact, he already has and probably will continue to
explore them farther in the years to come.

As this is written, he is working on a chapel for the campus of St. Thomas University in Houston, begun in 1957,
that may well compete with Ronchamp for a prominent
place in 20th century ecclesiastic architecture. And in
1980, he constructed a tiny study retreat for himself on
his New Canaan estate, which clearly owes a great deal
to Le Corbusier, and shows that Johnson is able to handle that idiom with as much facility as anyone.

Architectural Forum, January 1973

Elmer Holmes Bobst-Bibliothek der New York Universität

Philip Johnson and Richard Foster Architects
1967–1973
New York, New York
Statik: Severud-Perrone-
Strum-Bandel Associates
Haustechnik: Jaros, Baum & Bolles

Die Bobst Bibliothek der New York Universität am Washington Square in Manhattan ist ein umstrittenes Bauwerk, dessen Fertigstellung zehn Jahre in Anspruch nahm.

Mit einer Traufhöhe von ca. 46 m paßt es sich zwar den im Osten gelegenen Bauten der Jahrhundertwende an – die Bewohner von Greenwich Village, darunter die bekannte Kritikerin Jane Jacobs, protestierten dennoch gegen einen Neubau dieser Größe.

Die Bibliothek, die dem Universitätsgelände ein Zentrum verleiht, entwickelt sich um ein mittig gelegenes Atrium von 30,50 m im Quadrat und ca. 46 m in der Höhe. Dieses nimmt die Erschließung auf und bildet einen räumlichen Bezug für die elf Geschosse, auf denen verschiedene Funktionen untergebracht sind.

Das Gebäude ist mit unregelmäßig gestocktem, rotem Sandstein verkleidet. Pilasterartig ausgestanzte Reliefbänder sorgen im Wechsel mit massiven oder verglasten Fassadenfeldern für die rhythmische Artikulation in der Vertikalen. Das horizontale Fensterband der Verwaltungsbüros läßt das 11. Obergeschoß visuell zum «Gesims» des Gebäudes werden.

Johnson regte an, die älteren Nachbarbauten mit der gleichen Sandsteinfassade zu versehen und den Straßenzug im Osten mit einem Glasdach zu überdecken. Damit sollten die Gebäude ein einheitliches Erscheinungsbild erhalten, das der Universität als Kennzeichen dienen sowie dem verstreut liegenden Campus ein Zentrum verschaffen könnte. Dem Vorschlag fehlte jedoch die nötige finanzielle Unterstützung.

Elmer Holmes Bobst Library at New York University

Philip Johnson and Richard Foster Architects
1967–1973
New York, New York
Structural Engineer: Severud-Perrone-
Strum-Bandel Associates
Mechanical Engineer: Jaros, Baum & Bolles

The Bobst library was a controversial building on Washington Square in Manhattan, for New York University that required ten years to complete.

Although the building with its 150 foot cornice height matches the turn of the century buildings to the east, the Greenwich Village community (including Jane Jacobs) protested new construction of that size on this site.

This central library acts as a center to the campus, it is organized around a central atrium space with dimensions of 100 feet square and 150 feet tall. This open volume acts as a reference point and circulation for 11 floors of different functions that open onto it.

The exterior of the building is longmeadow red sandstone with a random chisel pattern finish. The rhythmic vertical articulation is a series of recessed «negative pilasters» and either solid or glass infill panels. The assembly is completed at the top by contrasting horizontal fenestration having the 12th floor Administration Offices act as a «cornice.»

Johnson proposed to extend the same stone facade pattern over the older adjacent buildings and include a glass roofed street to the east. The objective was to establish a uniform image to all buildings, a clear identity for the school and a center to the scattered urban campus. This proposal, however, did not get the necessary funding.

Progressive Architecture, June 1966
New York Times, November 7, 1973
«New York 1960», R. Stern, T. Mellins, D. Fishman, 1995

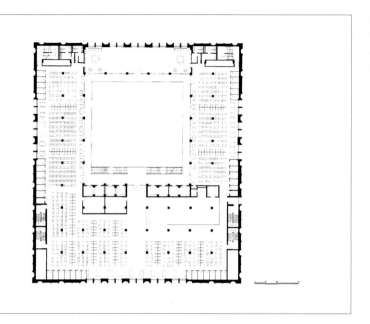

Grundriß Normalgeschoß, 1:1000
Außenansicht

Typical floor plan, 1:1000
Exterior view

Kevorkian-Studienzentrum für den Nahen Osten

Philip Johnson und Richard Foster Architects
1970–1973
New York, New York
Statik: Zoldos-Mahony-Salerno
Haustechnik: Robert K. Bedell

Das Studienzentrum gehört zur Fakultät für Kunst und Wissenschaften an der New York Universität. Der viergeschossige Bau liegt auf einem kleinen Eckgrundstück und beherbergt Büroräume in den beiden obersten Geschossen, eine Bibliothek im ersten Obergeschoß sowie Unterrichtsräume und die Eingangshalle im Erdgeschoß. Durch seine skulptural behandelte Fassade, die von tief eingeschnittenen Fenstern geprägt wird, nimmt sich der Bau am Washington Square im Maßstab zurück und schafft einen Übergang zu den größeren Nachbargebäuden.

Kevorkian Center for Near Eastern Studies

Philip Johnson and Richard Foster Architects
1970–1973
New York, New York
Structural Engineer: Zoldos-Mahony-Salerno
Mechanical Engineer: Robert K. Bedell

The Center is an academic entity within the Faculty of Arts and Science at New York University. In a small corner lot, the four-story building contains offices on the top two floors, a library on the second, and a lobby and classrooms on the ground. Because of its location on Washington Square and its larger neighbors, the building hides its true scale by its sculptural organization of deep cut-out bands that contain the windows and entrance.

Architectural Design, August-September 1979

Grundriß Normalgeschoß, 1:250
Außenansicht

Typical floor plan, 1:250
Exterior view

IDS Center

Johnson/Burgee Architects
1973
Minneapolis, Minnesota
Assoziierter Architekt: Edward F. Baker Associate, Inc.
Statik: Severud-Perrone-Sturn-Conlin-Bandel
Haustechnik: Cosentini Associates
Innenarchitektur Hotel: Johnson/Burgee

Das IDS Center in Minneapolis besteht aus mehreren Teilen – dem Bürohochhaus mit 51 Geschossen, einem achtgeschossigen Trakt mit Büromietflächen für erhöhten Raumbedarf, dem Hotel mit 19 Geschossen und 285 Zimmern, sowie einem zweigeschossigen Gewerbebau mit Läden, einer Bank und zusätzlichen Mietbereichen.

Die vier Gebäude nehmen einen ca. 114 m x 114 m großen Block im Stadtkern ein und umschließen eine ansprechende kleine innenliegende Piazza mit einer Fläche von etwa 1800 m². Ein pyramidenartiges Gebilde aus stahlgerahmten Glas- und Plastikelementen überdeckt diesen öffentlichen Raum bis in eine Höhe von ca. 37 m. Der Innenhof, als «Crystal Court» bekannt, gibt der Gesamtanlage ihre städtische Qualität.

Der Stadtkern von Minneapolis erfreut sich seit geraumer Zeit einer findigen Art der Erschließung: Kurz nach dem Zweiten Weltkrieg wurde damit begonnen, die Blöcke im ersten Obergeschoß durch geschlossene Fußgängerbrücken miteinander zu verbinden, da die Witterungsverhältnisse während der Wintermonate die Bürgersteige so gut wie unpassierbar machen. Inzwischen gibt es 30 bis 40 dieser zumeist verglasten Fußstege. Darüber hinaus sind alle Gebäude mit mehrgeschossigen, unterirdischen Parkhäusern verbunden, wodurch die Gewerbezonen in der Stadtmitte leichter erreichbar sind. Es lag also nahe, das IDS durch die in der Stadt üblichen Fußgängerbrücken allseitig an die Bauten der Umgebung anzubinden.

Der auf zwei Ebenen aus allen Himmelsrichtungen zugängliche Crystal Court ist der gelungenste Teilbereich des IDS. Normalerweise und bei günstigem Wetter nutzen die Fußgänger den Haupteingang im Erdgeschoß, direkt vom Bürgersteig aus. Zusätzlich ist er vom ersten Obergeschoß über ein Zwischengeschoß mit umlaufender Galerie erreichbar, die mit den Fußgängerbrücken außerhalb des Gebäudes verbunden ist. Von dort aus führen effektvoll plazierte Rolltreppen nach unten, auf denen der Fußgängerbetrieb gleichsam inszeniert wird. (Johnson stellt sich den Raum und seine Menschen als eine Art Laienbühne vor, wobei die Rollen von Schauspielern und Publikum beständig wechseln. Allerdings, meint er, bringen die Zuschauer im Erdgeschoß wohl die meiste Zeit damit zu, den Publikumsverkehr auf der Rolltreppe zu beobachten.

IDS Center

Johnson/Burgee Architects
1973
Minneapolis, Minnesota
Associate Architect: Edward F. Baker Associate, Inc.
Structural Engineer: Severud-Perrone-Sturn-Conlin-Bandel
Mechanical Engineer: Cosentini Associates
Hotel Interior Designer: Johnson/Burgee

The IDS Center, in Minneapolis, consists of several buildings: a 51-story high office tower; an 8-story office building annex that provides extra size floors for rental purposes; a 19-story hotel with 285 rooms; and a 2-story commercial structure for shops, a bank, and other rental spaces.

These four buildings are grouped on a downtown city block measuring 375 feet by 375 feet; and they form a wonderful little piazza between them – a public space that measures about 20,000 square feet in size, and is covered by a pyramidal structure of glass and plastic (framed in steel), and rising to a high point of 121 feet above the main floor of the piazza. The piazza is known as the Crystal Court; and it is that space – the Crystal Court – that makes this complex such a splendid place for this city.

Downtown Minneapolis has long been blessed with an innovative pedestrian system: because the weather, in the winter months, makes it virtually impossible for pedestrians to circulate on open sidewalks, Downtown Minneapolis, shortly after World War II, began to link its city blocks with enclosed walkways at second floor level that would connect all the major blocks to each other and to downtown, multi-level parking garages that made it easier for people to reach the commercial facilities in the center of town. There are now some 30 or 40 such pedestrian bridges (usually glass-enclosed), and the block on which IDS was constructed could be and was connected to all four neighboring city blocks by the kind of elevated walkways that the people of the city have come to depend upon.

The Crystal Court thus made accessible to pedestrians from all directions is the most successful aspect of the IDS block. In addition to its main floor at sidewalk level – and this is, of course, used much of the year by pedestrians when the weather is tolerable – there is a second floor, mezzanine level with a perimeter gallery that overlooks the Crystal Court. That level is linked to the elevated walkways outside, and to the Court itself by way of a dramatically exposed escalator where, in a sense, all the action is. (Johnson thinks of the space and the people moving through it as a public theater, with actors and audience

Grundriß Erdgeschoß, 1:2000
Grundriß 1. Obergeschoß mit Fußgängerbrücken, 1:2000

Ground floor plan, 1:2000
First floor plan with skybridges, 1:2000

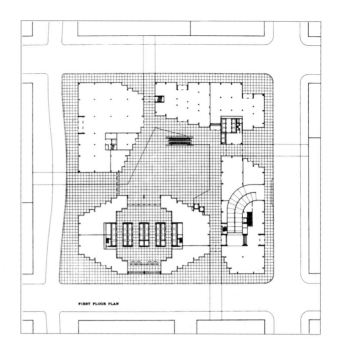

FIRST FLOOR PLAN

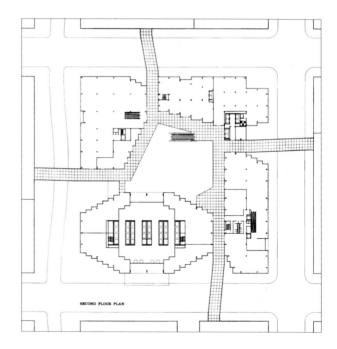

SECOND FLOOR PLAN

Außenansicht
Innenansicht

Exterior view
Interior view

Vom Crystal Court aus besteht ebenerdig und im Zwischengeschoß Zugang zu Restaurants, Ladengeschäften sowie den Aufzügen. Die Gebäude, die den Hof umgeben, werden in dem rund um die Uhr anhaltenden Getümmel gern übersehen. Dabei sind sie alles andere als nebensächlich. In der Abwicklung ist jeder der vier Bauten mit mehrfach abgewinkelten Glasfassaden versehen, wodurch die meisten Büros und Hotelzimmer Eckfenster erhalten – eine ansprechende Besonderheit des Entwurfs, zumal IDS bis heute das höchste Bauwerk der Stadt ist und somit nach allen Seiten einen ungestörten Blick bietet. Im obersten Geschoß des Bürohochhauses befinden sich ein weiteres Restaurant und eine Aussichtsplattform – für den Fall, daß einem der Blick auf die Stadt bis dahin entgangen sein sollte.

Johnson behauptet gern, daß städtebauliche Belange der herkömmlichen Art in seinem Werk keine Rolle spielten und man Architektur nur in freistehenden Bauten betreiben kann – wenigstens behauptet er das. Allerdings ist ihm hier womöglich der beste öffentliche Stadtraum seiner Laufbahn gelungen, und die Qualität der ihn bildenden Bauten mag deshalb sogar von geringerer Bedeutung sein.

almost interchangeable – although he feels that most people on the main floor level spend their time watching those riding up and down the escalators!)

The Crystal Court contains sidewalk and mezzanine restaurants as well as stores and access to the various elevator lobbies. The buildings that form the Court are easily overlooked in all this around-the-clock activity. Yet they are by no means secondary. All of them have multi-faceted glass facades that give most offices and hotel rooms corner windows – a very attractive feature, especially since IDS, as of this writing, is still the tallest tower in town, with views in all directions. On the top floor of the office tower there is another restaurant and an observation deck, just in case you missed the view from the lower elevations.

One of the amusing aspects of this complex is the fact that Johnson tends to play down urban design issues of a conventional sort in his work – he thinks that architecture can be made only in free-standing buildings, or so he sometimes says. At IDS, he has produced perhaps the most successful public space of his career; and the quality of the individual buildings that form it may be of secondary importance.

Awards: AIA Honor Award 1975

AIA Journal, August 1978
Forum, November 1973

Stadtbibliothek Boston

Philip Johnson
1964–1973
Boston, Massachusetts
Assoziierte Architekten: The Architects Design Group, Inc.
Statik: LeMessurier Associates, Inc.
Haustechnik: Francis Associates

Ende der sechziger Jahre wurde Johnson mit einem großen Anbau an die Stadtbibliothek in Boston von McKim, Mead und White betraut. Zu dem Zeitpunkt schlugen sich die meisten amerikanischen Architekten mit Themen wie Kontextualismus, Postmoderne und Denkmalpflege herum, zumeist im Zusammenhang mit einem Entwurf neben einem unter Denkmalschutz stehenden Bauwerk.

Drei verschiedene Lösungsansätze schienen möglich: erstens, den Anbau im Stil dem Originalgebäude anzupassen, zweitens, sich völlig über das historische Vorbild hinwegzusetzen und ihm ein zeitgenössisches Erscheinungsbild, das der Qualität des Originals standhalten kann, zu verleihen, oder drittens, einen laienhaften Anbau hinzustellen, der aussieht, als ob er von der Müllabfuhr abgesetzt wurde. Die meisten Anbauten aus dieser Zeit gehören zur letzteren Sorte.

Johnson war zunächst versucht, McKims Originalfassaden zu kopieren, allerdings erwies sich diese Art der Granitverkleidung, Fenstergestaltung und Detailausbildung als entschieden zu teuer. Etwas besseres als eine Fälschung bar jeden Einfühlungsvermögens würde ihm allemal einfallen, befand Johnson und sollte damit Recht behalten.

Sein Anbau an das prächtige, zwischen 1888 und 1895 im Stil der Neo-Renaissance errichtete Bauwerk am Copley Square zählt vielleicht zu den sensibelsten amerikanischen Beiträgen zum Thema Einfügung in den historischen Kontext.

Der Anbau umfaßt ca. 16.000 m² und ist damit beinahe doppelt so groß wie der Originalbau. Die Brüstungs- und Dachhöhen sind peinlich genau auf die des Nachbarbauwerks abgestimmt, ebenso die Oberflächenbehandlung der Fassaden — sogar soweit, daß man den Steinbruch, aus dem die ursprünglich verwendeten Steine stammten, wieder öffnen ließ. Die Profilierung des Anbaus zitiert die Vor- und Rücksprünge der Originalfassade.

Dennoch ist der Anbau ein gänzlich modernes Bauwerk. Die Abmessung der Stützenfelder, die von graziös wirkenden Bogen in Beton überspannt werden, beträgt jeweils 18,30 m, eine Spannweite, die zu McKims Zeiten nicht realisierbar gewesen wäre. Die Fassaden sind klar und glatt, bar jeglicher Renaissance-Details. Der Grundriß, be-

Boston Public Library

Philip Johnson
1964–1973
Boston, Massachusetts
Associate Architects: The Architects Design Group, Inc.
Structural Engineer: LeMessurier Associates, Inc.
Mechanical Engineer: Francis Associates

When Philip Johnson was asked, in the late 1960s, to design a major addition to McKim, Mead & White's great 1895 Boston Public Library, architects in the United States and elsewhere were struggling with issues like contextualism, postmodernism, and historic preservation – most of them having to do with the questions of how to design a new building next to a bona fide historic landmark.

There seemed to be only three possible ways of approaching a problem of that sort: you could either build an extension in the same style as that employed by the architects of the original landmark; or you could ignore the historic precedent and design and build something that was entirely of our time, and make that addition as good a job as the architects of the original landmark had made theirs; or you could simply do a workmanlike addition that would look as if the addition had been put up by the local Department of Sanitation. Most of the additions constructed in those years fell into the latter category.

Johnson was tempted, briefly, to duplicate and extend the original McKim facades; but using the same granite finishes and the same fenestration (and details of that sort) would have been unacceptably expensive to duplicate. Johnson felt that he could probably do better without fakery or insensitivity. And he was right.

His addition to the splendid, Renaissance revival building, constructed on Copley Square in 1888–1895, may be one of the most sensitive efforts at historic accommodation undertaken in the United States.

The addition – a building of 170,000 square feet, almost twice the size of the original – is meticulously aligned in its parapet and roof lines with its neoclassical neighbor; its exterior granite finishes match those of the original library – in fact, the quarry of the original stone was reopened to supply an exact match. And various projections and recesses in the facades of the original are faithfully recalled in the profiles of the addition.

Still, the addition is an entirely modern building. Its bays are more than 60 feet wide and topped by graceful concrete arches that would have been almost impossible to span in McKim's day. The facades are neat and smooth, uninterrupted by Renaissance detail. And the plan – nine squares, roughly 60 feet by 60 feet in size – is reminiscent of the way Louis Kahn organized his buildings, around a

Grundriß Erdgeschoß, 1:1000
Grundriß 1. Obergeschoß, 1:1000
Schnitt, 1:1000

Ground floor plan, 1:1000
First floor plan, 1:1000
Building section, 1:1000

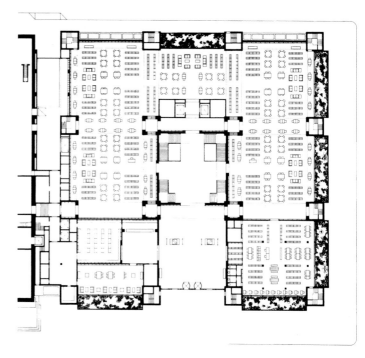

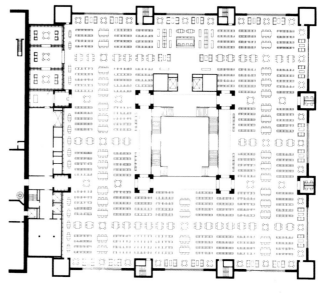

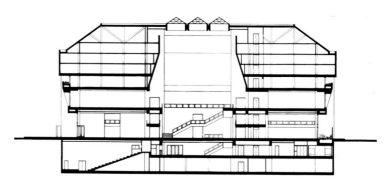

stehend aus neun 18,30 m x 18,30 m großen Quadraten, erinnert an Louis Kahns Bauten mit ihren dreidimensionalen Rastern aus Vertikalelementen, in denen Feuertreppen, Kanäle und andere Versorgungseinrichtungen untergebracht sind.

Wie viele Bauten Johnsons ist auch dieser Anbau symmetrisch angelegt. Der klar definierte, achsmittige Eingang und der 18,30 m hohe Lichthof in der Gebäudemitte erlauben dem Besucher eine schnelle Orientierung, trotz der Größe des Gebäudes.

Ein herkömmlicher zeitgenössischer Entwurf im Stil der Moderne hätte wahrscheinlich einen Verbindungsbau mit Eingang und Foyer zwischen der alten Bibliothek und dem neuen Anbau vorgesehen. Auf dem Papier wirkt dies sehr einleuchtend, wesentlich einleuchtender als in Wirklichkeit – solch ein «moderner» Regelgrundriß hätte das Zurechtfinden erschwert, und die Verbindung zwischen Alt und Neu hätte wahrscheinlich Maßstabs- und Detailprobleme ergeben. Der Architekturhistoriker Henry-Russell Hitchcock kritisierte Johnson gegenüber einen Maßstabssprung zwischen dem Anbau mit seinen weit gespannten Bogen und dem Originalbauwerk. Das stimmt, war aber sicherlich beabsichtigt. Der Anbau gehört einer anderen Generation an, ist kühner, vielleicht großzügiger und jedenfalls unverwechselbar modern.

Ebenso eindeutig ist er mit McKims Bauwerk verwandt, so wie dieses mit dem Palazzo Rucellai in Florenz – und dennoch nicht identisch. Hätten sich die Architekten der alten Bibliothek dazu entschlossen, die Fassaden ihres Bauwerks der auf der anderen Seite des Copley Square gelegenen Trinity Church von Richardson anzupassen, die zwölf Jahre früher entstanden war, wäre Johnson womöglich versucht gewesen, desgleichen zu tun.

Aber genau wie McKim sich im Maßstab, im Detail und im Baustil nicht an Richardson Kirche als Vorlage hielt, so geht Johnson in vieler Hinsicht über die ursprüngliche Stadtbibliothek von Boston hinaus. Auf diese Weise gelang ihm eine hervorragende Erweiterung, die gleichzeitig den Originalbau noch besser zur Geltung bringt.

three-dimensional grid of vertical shafts that would contain fire stairs, ducts and other services.

Like so many of Johnson's buildings, the addition is a symmetrical structure with a clearly defined central entrance. This works extremely well, since the size of the addition makes it important to permit visitors to orient themselves without trouble – and a central entrance leading into a central 60 foot high atrium space makes the orientation quite easy.

In a more conventional modern scheme of that time, the entrance would probably have been placed in some sort of «link» between the original library and the new addition – a perfectly workable arrangement, with the entrance lobby in the link between the old and the new wings.

A workable arrangement on paper, but much less so in fact: such a typical «modern» plan would have made it much more difficult for visitors to orient themselves, and it probably would have created problems of scale and of detail in the connecting element between old and new. The architectural historian Henry-Russell Hitchcock, told Johnson that he thought the addition, with its great arches, was out of scale with the original. Quite right, but that was surely the idea. The addition is of a different generation, bolder, more generous perhaps, and unmistakably modern.

But it is just as unmistakably a close relative of McKim's building, just as the latter is a close relative of the Palazzo Rucellai in Florence but hardly its twin. If the architects of the original library had decided, in the 1880s to make the facades of their building echo those of Richardson's Trinity Church, built opposite the library on Copley Square about a dozen years earlier, then Johnson might have been tempted to make his addition closer in scale and detail to its neighbor.

But just as McKim made his building different in style, in detail, and in scale from Richardson's church, so Johnson went beyond the original Boston Public Library in most respects. And, in doing so, he constructed not only a splendid addition, but enhanced the original work by McKim, Mead & White as well.

Progressive Architecture, February 1973
New York Times, September 24, 1973
Architecture and Forum, February 1973

Außenansicht
Innenansicht des zentralen Lichthofs
mit Zwischengeschoß

Exterior view
Interior view of central atrium with
mezzanine floor

Messezentrum Niagara Falls

Johnson/Burgee Architects
1974
Niagara Falls, New York
Statik: Zelin, Desimone, Chaplin & Associates
Haustechnik: Syska & Hennessy, Inc.
Akustik: Ranger Farrell & Associates

Das Messezentrum ist ein entscheidender Teil des umfangreichen städtischen Erneuerungsprojekts, mit dem Ende der sechziger Jahre dem Verfall der Innenstadt begegnet werden sollte.

Das Gebäude besteht aus einer gekrümmten, von Stahlfachwerkträgern gehaltenen Dachfläche, die einen stützenfreien Hauptraum von 97,50 m Länge überspannt. Die ca. 7.700 m² große Fläche wird für Ausstellungen genutzt und kann in ein Sportstadion mit 10.000 Sitzplätzen umgewandelt werden.

Die Träger sind auf beiden Seiten in große Widerlager eingespannt, die mit Kalksandstein verkleidet wurden und die Krümmung der Träger zum Boden hin optisch fortsetzen. In diesen seitlichen Bereichen liegen Restaurants, kleine Konferenzräume, Ballsäle, Versorgungseinrichtungen sowie Technikräume.

Der Bau liegt am Ende einer bestehenden Straße und begrenzt dadurch die Achse einer neuen Fußgängerzone, an deren Ende ein Park mit Aussicht über die Niagarafälle liegt.

Niagara Falls Convention Center

Johnson/Burgee Architects
1974
Niagara Falls, New York
Structural Engineer: Zelin, Desimone, Chaplin & Associates
Mechanical Engineer: Syska & Hennessy, Inc.
Acoustical: Ranger Farrell & Associates

This convention center was a key element of a major urban renewal project in the late 1960s to revitalize a decaying downtown.

The building is a simple steel trussed arch that spans 320 feet over the main area. This area of 83,500 square feet is used for convention displays; it can be transformed to a 10,000 seat sports auditorium.

The trusses structurally and visually end at limestone clad piers at either end that continue the curve of the truss to the ground. Inside these volumes are support facilities, restaurants, small meeting rooms, ballrooms, and mechanical services.

The Center is sited so as to close off an existing street and thereby end the axis of a new pedestrian mall that leads to a park overlooking the Niagara Falls.

«Johnson/Burgee Architecture», N. Miller, 1979

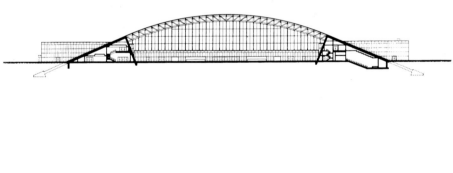

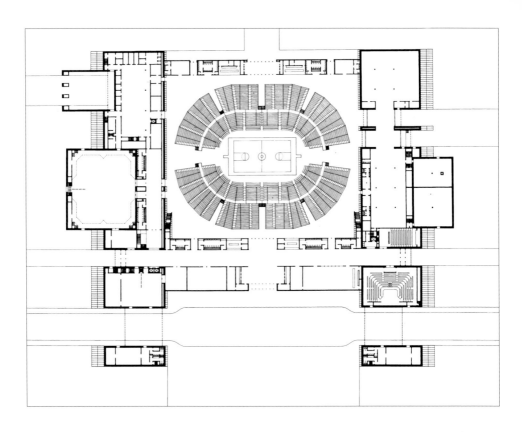

Längs- und Querschnitt, 1:2000
Grundriß Erdgeschoß, 1:2000
Außenansicht

Longitudinal and transverse section, 1:2000
Ground floor plan, 1:2000
Exterior view

Wassergarten in Fort Worth

Johnson/Burgee Architects
1970–1974
Fort Worth, Texas
Statik: Desimone & Chaplin
Haustechnik: J.S. Hammel Engineering Inc.

Amon G. Carter war einer der legendären Millionäre, die Texas zu dem gemacht haben, was es heute ist – ein Ort wie kein zweiter in ganz Amerika. Die Stadt Fort Worth war gleichsam seine Erfindung, an der nach seinem Tod 1955 seine Nachfahren beständig weitergearbeitet haben.

Die Amon G. Carter-Stiftung beschloß 1975, der Stadt einen Garten in der Größe von Texas zu schenken – in Tat und Wahrheit nahm er später nur etwa 1,7 Hektar in der Nähe des Stadtzentrums ein. Nach der Eröffnung schrieb Paul Goldberger, der Architekturkritiker der New York Times, daß hier ein «herrlich nutzloser Ort» entstanden sei.

Dem war und ist noch immer so. Zahllose Wasserfälle, die über rosafarbene Betonterrassen in eine Art Krater hinunterrauschen, prägen das Bild des Wassergartens in Fort Worth. Es gibt drei oder vier solcher Krater, und jeder dieser abgesenkten Räume hat seinen eigenen, vom Wasser geprägten Charakter. Der Kraterrand ist jeweils von Bäumen – Eichen, Birnbäumen und Zypressen – und Blumen gesäumt und der Kratergrund wird von einmal hohen, dann wieder niedrigen Fontänen zum Leben erweckt.

Abgetreppte Pfade führen die Besucher an den Wasserfällen vorbei und durch sie hindurch, in die Krater hinunter, wo ein grandioser Ausblick über die glitzernden Betonstufen auf sie wartet. Das dreidimensionale Gebilde erinnert an Gemälde des frühen Expressionismus aus der Zeit nach dem Ersten Weltkrieg, die Johnson seit langem bewunderte.

Der Wassergarten hat nicht nur einen bemerkenswerten Grundriß. Auf beeindruckende Weise wird eine Abfolge von Blickbeziehungen und Räumen geschaffen, eine unantastbare Welt des Scheins. Das Geräusch des Wassers,

Fort Worth Water Garden

Johnson/Burgee Architects
1970–1974
Fort Worth, Texas
Structural Engineer: Desimone & Chaplin
Mechanical Engineer: J.S. Hammel Engineering Inc.

Amon G. Carter was one of those legendary millionaires who really invented Texas, and made that state different from every other place in North America. As a matter of fact, Amon Carter practically invented the city of Fort Worth, and his descendants have been reinventing it ever since he died in 1955.

In 1975, the Amon G. Carter foundation decided to give their City a huge Texas-sized garden (actually, it was only 4.3 acres in area), located near the center of town. When that garden was opened to the public, Paul Goldberger, the architecture critic of the New York Times, said that the place was «at once useless, and absolutely splendid.»

And so it was and is. Most of the Fort Worth Water Garden is a series of cascading water falls that spill over pinkish concrete steps and descend into some sort of crater. There are three or four such craters or sunken «rooms,» each with its own special character generated by the sound of its own water falls, by the edge of trees (live oaks, bradford pears and bald cypress) that frame each of the «rooms», by the flowers in surrounding flower beds, and by the varying sprays of fountains that animate the pools at the bottom of each «room.»

There are walkways down into those craters – steps that take visitors past and through the water falls, to extraordinary views up and down and across the glistening concrete terraces. It is a three-dimensional composition in the manner of the early Abstract Expressionist painters of the years after World War I, whose work Johnson had long admired.

But the Water Garden is remarkable not only because of the intriguing formation of its plan; it is extraordinary in the way it uses intangible effects and images to create a succession of wonderful vistas and spaces.

Lageplan
Blick in eines der Wasserbecken

Site plan
View of fountain

140

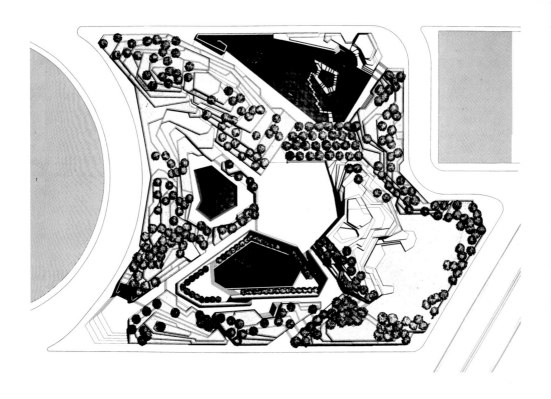

die tosenden Wasserfälle und plätschernden Brunnen, bringen dort einen unvergleichlichen Ort in der brutal anmutenden Stadtlandschaft hervor. Am Ende ihres Abstiegs haben die Besucher den Blick auf die Stadt hinter sich gelassen und sehen sich von nichts als Wasser und Bäumen umgeben. Man glaubt sich eher in einem Märchenland aus Schluchten und reißenden Strömen, denn in einer prosaischen amerikanischen Stadtlandschaft – ein Geschenk an die Bewohner von Fort Worth.

In Johnsons Vorstellung sind Architektur und Landschaft eins, die graue Wirklichkeit aus Stein und Beton ist um keinen Deut handhabbarer als Geräuschkulissen oder Licht- und Schattenspiele. Der Wassergarten ist eine Welt des Scheins und des ewigen Wandels. (Nachts leuchten 24 m hohe Lichtmasten und bodennahe Lampen den Garten aus.) Die rauschenden Wasserfälle und die stillen Wasserbecken schlagen einen geradeso in ihren Bann wie manches herkömmliche Gebilde aus Ziegel und Stein.

Die Krater des Wassergartens gleichen Amphitheatern. Hans Scharouns Berliner Philharmonie könnte Pate gestanden haben bei den terrassenartig abgestuften Auditorien, von denen jedes sein Publikum und seine Schauspieler anzieht. Diese sind selbstredend die Besucher, die sich hier eingefunden haben, um die Stufen entweder selbst zu erklimmen oder um andere bei dem waghalsigen Manöver zu beobachten. Wie die meisten Theater wandelt sich der Wassergarten mit jedem neuen Schauspiel und mit ihm die Beleuchtung, die Geräuschkulisse und die Bewegungen. Philip Johnson, als Schauspieler selbst nicht unbegabt, ist sich der Scheinwelt wohl bewußt, die seinen Bauwerken und Gärten Leben einhaucht und setzt sie gekonnt in Szene. Beim Wassergarten in Fort Worth übernahm er die Rollen des Bühnenbildners sowie des Produzenten, und das Ergebnis kann sich mehr als sehen lassen.

The sound of water – both the sound of roaring water falls, and the sound of delicate fountains – creates an ambiance in the midst of a rather brutal cityscape that cannot be duplicated by any other means. And the angled views out of the craters blot cut the unimpressive skylines of surrounding city blocks – so that visitors climbing down the terraces and past the fountains and water falls completely lose sight of the urban skyline and find themselves surrounded by a silhouette of trees and bushes and flowers. It is a magic landscape of canyons and torrential streams, quite unexpected in a prosaic American cityscape, and a beautiful gift to the citizens of Fort Worth.

To Johnson, architecture and landscape are quite inseparable; and the realities of stone and concrete are no more tangible than the effects of sound and movement and light and shade. The Water Garden is made up of such intangibles, and they are all subject to constant change. (At night, the Water Garden is dramatically lit from lights mounted on 80-foot tall poles, as well as from below.) And the sounds made by the water falls, and the stillness of pools in some of the craters, are as compelling as any conventional composition in brick or stone.

The four or five «rooms» or craters that make up the Water Garden are really more like theaters-in-the-round than anything else. Each seems like a terraced auditorium, in the manner of Hans Scharoun's Berlin Philharmonic Hall; and each has its own performance, and its own performers. The actors, needless to say, are locals who have come to visit and to climb up and down; and audience are other locals, watching the performers go through their perilous motions. And like most theaters, the Water Gardens change with each performance – the light changes, the movement changes, even the sound changes. Philip Johnson, who is not a bad performer himself, is very much aware of all those intangibles that animate his buildings and his gardens, and he is capable of orchestrating them all. Here, in the Forth Worth Water Garden, he performed both as a stage designer and as a theatrical producer, and the results are quite spectacular.

Progressive Architecture, January 1975
Architectural Record, November 1978
«Water and Architecture», Charles Moore, 1994

Post Oak Central

Johnson/Burgee Architects
1973–1975 – Haus 1
1977–1979 – Haus 2
1980–1982 – Haus 3
Houston, Texas
Assoziierte Architekten:
Wilson, Morris, Crain & Anderson (Haus 1);
Richard Fitzgerald & Partners (Haus 2 und 3)
Statik: Colaco Engineers, Inc.
Haustechnik: I.A. Naman & Associates, Inc.

Post Oak Central ist eine Gebäudegruppe, die aus drei Bürohäusern an einer der meistbefahrenen Autobahnen Houstons besteht. Das Erscheinungsbild wird von den horizontal gestreiften Vorhangfassaden bestimmt. Ein dreigeschossiges Parkhaus nimmt drei Seiten der 68.800 m² großen Gesamtanlage ein, in deren Zentrum die drei unterschiedlich genutzten Bürohäuser mit jeweils 20 Geschossen angeordnet sind.
Die abgerundeten Gebäudeecken und horizontalen Fensterbänder erinnern an das im Art Deco Stil gehaltene Starret Lehigh Lagerhaus in Manhattan von 1931 sowie an die Wohnhausprojekte der Gebrüder Bowman im Stil der Moderne, die in der MoMA-Ausstellung «International Style» gezeigt wurden.

Post Oak Central

Johnson/Burgee Architects
1973–1975 – Building 1
1977–1979 – Building 2
1980–1982 – Building 3
Houston, Texas
Associate Architects:
Wilson, Morris, Crain & Anderson (Building 1);
Richard Fitzgerald & Partners (Building 2 & 3)
Structural Engineer: Colaco Engineers, Inc.
Mechanical Engineer: I.A. Naman & Associates, Inc.

Post Oak Central is a group of 3 horizontally banded curtain wall office buildings next to a major highway in Houston. The entire complex occupies 17 acres with a three story parking garage around three sides of the site. In the center of the complex are the three 20-story office towers which are of the same height but differ in their use. The buildings themselves, with their rounded curves and ribbon windows recall the art deco Starrett Lehigh warehouse (1931) in Manhattan and the modern apartment projects of the Bowman Brothers displayed in MoMA's «International Style» exhibition.

«Johnson/Burgee Architecture», N. Miller, 1979
«The Skyscraper», Paul Goldberger, 1981

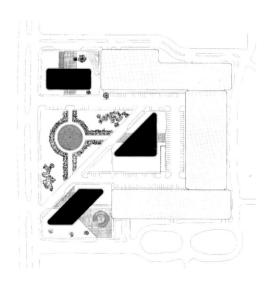

Lageplan, 1:5000

Site plan, 1:5000

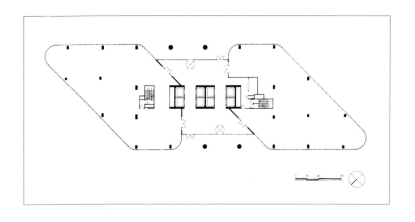

Grundriß Erdgeschoß,
Post Oak Central 2, 1:1000
Außenansicht Post Oak Central 2

Ground floor plan,
Post Oak Central 2, 1:1000
Exterior view of Post Oak Central 2

Innenausbau Avery Fisher Hall
Johnson/Burgee Architects
1976
New York, New York
Statik: Amman & Whitney
Haustechnik: Syska & Hennessy
Akustik: Dr. Cyril M. Harris
Lichttechnik: Claude R. Engle

1976 kam der Auftrag für einen komplett neuen Innenausbau der New Yorker Philharmonie am Lincoln Center,
ursprünglich von Harrison und Abramovitz errichtet. Die
Anzahl der Sitzplätze wurde auf 2.742 erhöht und die
Bühnenfläche auf 216 m² vergrößert. Die Akustik des
Bühnenraums sollte verbessert und die Technik hinter der
Bühne erweitert werden.
Im Zuge der Renovierung wurde der ursprünglich fla-
schenförmig angelegte Grundriß in ein rechteckiges Volumen umgewandelt. Die Anzahl der Balkonränge wurde
auf drei erhöht, die alle mit konvex gekrümmten Elementen zur Streuung des Schalls versehen sind. Die Wand-
und Deckenflächen, die in schmale, im stumpfen Winkel
zueinander angeordnete Streifen vielfach aufgebrochen
sind, wurden auf möglichst geringe Schalldurchlässigkeit
hin angelegt.

Avery Fisher Hall Interior
Johnson/Burgee Architects
1976
New York, New York
Structural Engineer: Amman & Whitney
Mechanical Engineer: Syska & Hennessy
Acoustical Engineer: Dr. Cyril M. Harris
Lighting: Claude R. Engle

A totally new interior built for the New York Philharmonic
at Lincoln Center, originally designed by Harrison and
Abramovitz. Seating capacity is now 2,742 with a stage
area of 2,321 square feet. The design was developed to
improve acoustics and larger backstage support facilities
were developed.
In the reconstruction, the room became a conventional
rectangular box instead of its previous bottle configuration. It now has three levels of balconies faced with con-
vex curves to scatter sound. Wall and ceiling planes are
broken into strips of thin chevrons and constructed to be
as impervious to sound transmission as possible.

Interiors, February 1977
Progressive Architecture, March 1977

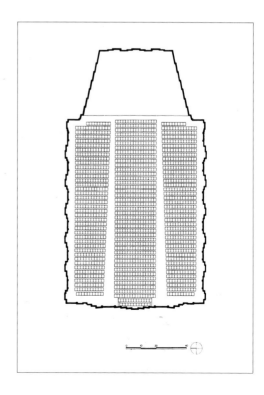

Grundriß Hauptebene, 1:750

Main floor plan, 1:750

Blick auf die Bühne

View toward stage

Pennzoil Place
Johnson/Burgee Architects
1976
Houston, Texas
Assoziierte Architekten: Wilson, Morris, Crain & Anderson
Statik: Ellisor Engineers, Inc.
Haustechnik: I.A. Naman & Associates
Lichttechnik: Claude R. Engle

Das AT&T-Gebäude in New York und der Transco Tower in Houston sind mit Sicherheit Philip Johnsons bekannteste Hochhäuser, aber im Laufe der Jahre gesellten sich noch etliche hinzu, die durchaus von Belang sind.

Pennzoil Place – ebenfalls in Houston – ist mit Abstand der beste. Die Anlage besteht aus zwei verglasten Bürotürmen, die lediglich durch einen ca. 3 m breiten und 152 m hohen Einschnitt voneinander getrennt sind. Von Osten und Westen sticht das Gebäude wie ein Schlaglicht aus der Stadtsilhouette Houstons heraus. Unter Johnsons bisherigen Hochhausentwürfen mag der 1976 fertiggestellte Doppelwolkenkratzer der einzige sein, der es an Qualität mit Mies van der Rohes Hochhäusern – zumindest den zu seinen Lebzeiten gebauten – aufnehmen kann und sie vielleicht gar übertrifft.

Pennzoil Place erhebt sich über einem quadratischen Baublock mit 76 m Seitenlänge im Herzen der Stadt. Die komplexe Gebäudegeometrie entwickelt sich aus dem Quadrat – die Außenhaut folgt den durch die Straßen gebildeten rechten Winkeln, im Innenbereich entstehen zwei dreieckige Eingangsbereiche durch die Überlagerung zweier, zur Achsmitte parallel verlaufender Begrenzungslinien mit der Diagonalen. Im 28. von insgesamt 36 Stockwerken sind die vierseitigen Türme im 45° Winkel abgeschrägt, die verglaste Schrägfassade wird von weiß lackierten Stahlträgern gehalten.

Die dreieckigen Bereiche im Erdgeschoß, die passagenartig miteinander verbunden sind, werden ebenfalls durch verglaste Schrägfassaden überdeckt. Auch wenn sich die Gebäudegeometrie – wie man sieht – nur schwer beschreiben läßt, ist es leicht, sich im Gebäudeinneren zurechtzufinden.

Die diagonal durch den Baublock verlaufende «Galleria», die den Grundriß bestimmt, ist kein beliebig eingesetzter Kunstgriff. Sie wurde ganz bewußt entwickelt, um das benachbarte Geschäftszentrum mit seinen konventionellen Bürohochhäusern an ein Kulturzentrum anzubinden, das zu der Zeit im Entstehen war. Die Gebäudeform, die sich aufgrund dieser Überlegungen allmählich herausschälte, verlangte nach etwas wie einem Wahrzeichen. So entstand der Schlitz, der die trapezförmigen Türme schlaglichtartig trennt und im Herzen Houstons zu einer unver-

Pennzoil Place
Johnson/Burgee Architects
1976
Houston, Texas
Associate Architects: Wilson, Morris, Crain & Anderson
Structural Engineer: Ellisor Engineers, Inc.
Mechanical Engineer: I.A. Naman & Associates
Lighting: Claude R. Engle

Although Philip Johnson's best known skyscrapers, undoubtedly, are the AT&T Building in New York and the Transco Tower in Houston, there are several other highrise buildings that he completed over the years that seem at least as interesting.

The best of these, surely, is the twin-tower Pennzoil Place (also in Houston) – an extraordinary complex of two, glass-enclosed office shafts separated by a slot of air 10 feet wide and 500 feet tall, that stands like a sliver of light on the Houston skyline when seen from the East and West. The twin-tower complex was completed in 1976, and it may be the one high-rise designed by Johnson, so far, that is equal to the best that Mies van der Rohe was able to build in his lifetime – equal to, or better than.

Pennzoil Place stands on a square downtown city block that measures about 250 by 250 feet in plan. The twin towers are formed by that square, with two opposite sides of glass aligned with the edges of two parallel streets; on the third side, the glass walls follow a diagonal in outline; and on the fourth side the towers are squared off again and run parallel to the two perimeter streets referred to earlier. At the 29th floor level (there are 36 stories in all) this geometry gets even more complicated – for here the towers are sliced off with 45-degree slopes of glass, supported on white-painted steel trusses inside.

At the street level, the two towers are linked by a spectacular, glass-roofed «galleria» that bisects the block diagonally. Although the geometry of the Pennzoil Place complex is impossible to put into words (see above), it is not in the least bit confusing if you are anywhere inside the building.

The diagonal «galleria» that bisects the city block and helps shape the plan of Pennzoil Place is no arbitrary device: it was designed to link a developing cultural district in downtown Houston to a nearby business center consisting of several conventional office skyscrapers. But as the geometry began to take shape from these considerations, it became clear that a slot or sliver of light between the two trapezoidal towers would create an unmistakable «landmark» in downtown Houston – visible, if only for a few seconds, from a perimeter beltway that circles downtown, then disappearing in a flash, then reappearing in

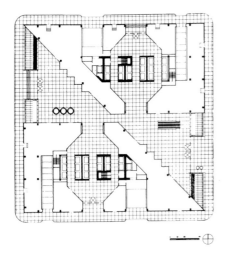
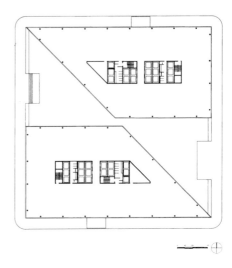

Grundriß Erdgeschoß, 1:1500
Grundriß Normalgeschoß,
1:1500
Innenansicht des Atriums mit
Blick auf den Eingang
Außenansicht

Ground floor plan, 1:1500
Typical floor plan, 1:1500
Interior view of atrium
with entry
Exterior view

wechselbaren Erscheinung wurde. Von der Ringautobahn wird er in immer neuer Form sichtbar, taucht sekundenschnell auf, um gleich darauf wieder zu verschwinden. Dieser Einschnitt ist ein Geniestreich aus Luft – der Architektur zur Kunst erhebt.

Wie die meisten Architekten läuft Johnson zu voller Form auf, wenn er es mit einem erstklassigen Bauherren – beispielsweise sich selbst – zu tun hat. Im Falle von Pennzoil Place handelte es sich um einen Investor mit ausgeprägtem Vorstellungsvermögen namens Gerald D. Hines, sowie den Vorsitzenden des Aufsichtsrates von Pennzoil, J. Hugh Liedtke, der ersterem in nichts nachstand und ausgezeichnete Entwurfsvorschläge zum Doppelhochhaus parat hatte.

Johnson selbst gab bei der Projektpräsentation vor Pennzoil und anderen Interessenten sein Bestes. Er erklärte das Projekt anhand eines maßstabsgetreuen Modells von Pennzoil Place: «Es ist nicht das von jedem Standort aus verschieden anmutende Erscheinungsbild des Gebäudes allein. Es ist das Erlebnis, das der Eintritt in diese Lichterwelt birgt, ein Funkeln, das wie Sternschnuppen durch das Glas herab zu fallen scheint...» Er wirkte sehr überzeugend, genauso wie die auf 15 Bildschirmen flimmernde Multi-Media-Schau, die seine Vorstellung untermalte. Am meisten überzeugte das Doppelhochhaus selbst – ein Anblick, den man in dieser Art noch nicht gesehen hatte und so schnell nicht wieder vergaß. Obwohl in Houston zwischenzeitlich höhere Bauten entstanden sind, die es, je nach Blickwinkel, klein erscheinen lassen, bleibt Pennzoil Place so eindrucksvoll präsent wie am Tag seiner Eröffnung.

another configuration. That slot, that sliver of air, is a work of pure genius – the kind of intangible that turns architecture into art.

Like most architects, Johnson is at his best when he has a first-rate client, and that includes himself. In the case of Pennzoil Place, Johnson dealt with an enormously imaginative developer whom he knew well, Gerald D. Hines and with an equally imaginative Chairman of Pennzoil's Board of Directors, J. Hugh Liedtke, who contributed some of the most interesting suggestions to the design of the twin towers.

Johnson himself participated most effectively in the presentation of the project to Pennzoil and to other potential tenants. «It's not just the look of the building as you approach it from different angles,» he said, pointing at a scale model of Pennzoil Place. «It's the feeling you experience when you are about to enter this world of light, twinkling down through the glass from above...» He was very convincing, as was the 15-screen, multi-media show that accompanied his words.

But the most convincing argument was the twin-tower building itself. It was a sight that one had never quite seen before, and that one was unlikely to forget. Although taller buildings in downtown Houston now sometimes dwarf Pennzoil Place from certain angles, the presence of the twin towers is just as powerful as it was on the day the ribbon was cut.

Awards: R.S. Reynolds Memorial Award 1978

Progressive Architecture, August 1977

Platzgestaltung Thanksgiving Square

Johnson/Burgee Architects
1976 (Ergänzung 1996 durch Philip Johnson Architects)
Dallas, Texas
Statik: Datum Structures Engineering, Inc.
Haustechnik: Herman Blum
Buntglas: Gabrielle Loire
Lichttechnik: Claude R. Engle

Der Thanksgiving Square nimmt ein ca. 1,2 ha großes, dreieckiges Grundstück im Stadtzentrum von Dallas ein. Er ist als friedliche Oase gedacht, ein Platz der Rast in einer angeböschten Grünanlage, in deren Herz eine ca. 27 m hohe, spiralförmige Kapelle steht, die von den Minaretten der Moschee von Samara inspiriert ist. Im Inneren findet sich ein einziger Raum, in den das Licht von oben durch ein fortlaufendes spiralförmiges Band aus farbigem Glas fällt. Der Entwurf für eine Kapelle im Glockenturm der Kristallkathedrale in Garden Grove, Kalifornien, nimmt das Motiv Jahre später wieder auf. Landschaftsgestalterisch wurden die verschiedensten Gewächse verwendet, unter anderem Grindelias, Myrten, Ulmen und Eichen. Wasser kommt als Element in Form von zwei Brunnen am westlichen Eingang und als zwei spiegelnde Wasserbecken neben der ökumenischen «Danksagungskapelle» vor.

Thanksgiving Square

Johnson/Burgee Architects
1976 (1996 additions by Philip Johnson Architects)
Dallas, Texas
Structural Engineer: Datum Structures Engineering, Inc.
Mechanical Engineer: Herman Blum
Stained Glass Artist: Gabrielle Loire
Lighting: Claude R. Engle

Thanksgiving Square occupies a three-acre triangular site in downtown Dallas. It is conceived as a peaceful node, offering a resting place with sloping greenery. At its center is a 90 foot tall chapel in the form of a spiral inspired by the minarets of the Mosque of Samara; it is a single room sky lit by a continuous stained glass spiral strip. This room is recalled in the later design for the small chapel at the Crystal Cathedral Bell Tower, in Garden Grove, California. The landscaping consists of live oaks, sweet gums, a large cedar elm and crepe myrtle trees. The water effects are a pair of fountains at the west entry, with two reflecting pools at the small non-denominational «Chapel of Thanksgiving».

«Johnson/Burgee Architecture», N. Miller, 1979
«Philip Johnson – The Architect in His Own Words», Hilary Lewis, John O'Connor, 1994

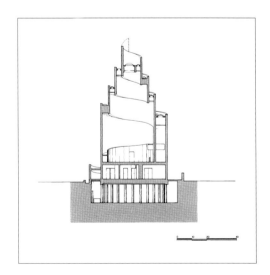

Schnitt durch Kapelle, 1:750

Section at chapel, 1:750

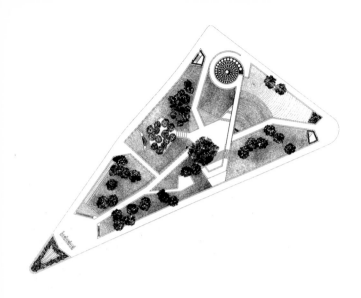

Lageplan, 1:2000
Außenansicht der Kapelle
Deckenuntersicht mit farbigem Glasband

Site plan, 1:2000
View of chapel
View of chapel ceiling with stained glass

Zentrum der Schönen Künste am Muhlenberg College

Johnson/Burgee Architects
1977
Allentown, Pennsylvania
Assoziierte Architekten:
Coston-Wallace & Watson Associates
Statik: Coston-Wallace & Watson Associates
Haustechnik: T.A. Coughlin & Coston

Das Gebäude beherbergt Unterrichts-, Galerie- und Theaterräume, die an einer 61 m langen, mit Glas überdachten «Straße» liegen. Die innenliegende Straße folgt dem Grundstücksgefälle als sanft ansteigende Rampe, wobei ihre Raumhöhe von ca. 9,10 m auf ca. 15,85 m zunimmt. Johnson setzte die rückgratähnliche Grundrißanordnung bereits bei früheren Entwürfen für andere Auftraggeber ein – so zum Beispiel im Century Center in South Bend, Indiana und dem Bürgerhaus in Peoria, Illinois.

Fine Arts Center at Muhlenberg College

Johnson/Burgee Architects
1977
Allentown, Pennsylvania
Associate Architects:
Coston-Wallace & Watson Associates
Structural Engineer: Coston-Wallace & Watson Associates
Mechanical Engineer: T.A. Coughlin & Coston

An «interior street» skylit and 200 ft long is the organizational spine for this collection of classrooms, gallery spaces and theaters. The street adjusts to the slope of the site by being a gentle ramp that gives the space a height that varies from 30 to 52 feet.
The organizing principle of this building was used by Johnson to solve problems in other sites and for other clients, such as the Century Center in South Bend, Indiana and the Peoria Civic Center, in Illinois.

Architectural Record, November 1977
«Johnson/Burgee Architecture», N. Miller, 1979

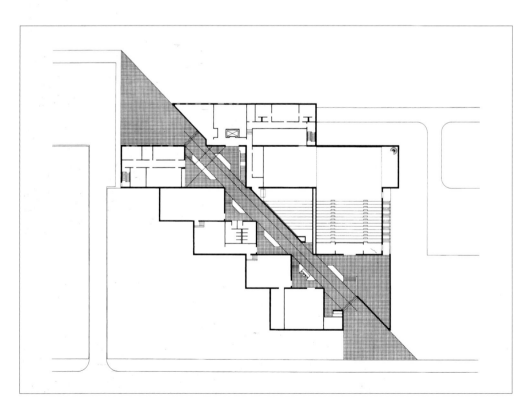

Grundriß Erdgeschoß, 1:1000
Ansicht Eingangsbereich
Innenansicht der «Straße»

Ground floor plan, 1:1000
Exterior entry
Interior «Street»

Fassade 1001 Fifth Avenue

Johnson/Burgee Architects
1977–1978
New York, New York
Architekt des Gebäudes: Philip Birnbaum
Statik: Robert Rosenwasser
Haustechnik: I.M. Robbins

Gegenüber dem Metropolitan Museum an der Fifth Avenue wurde ein Appartementhaus geplant. Aufgrund von Bürgerprotesten gegen die vorgesehene «moderne» Fassade wandte man sich an Johnsons Büro mit der Bitte, dem Gebäude mittels einer anderen Fassade einen angemesseneren Ausdruck zu verleihen.

Das Wechselspiel in der Vertikalen zwischen den ausgebuchteten, dunkel verglasten Fensterbändern und den flachen Kalksandsteinpilastern bestimmt das Fassadenbild ebenso wie die horizontal verlaufenden Steingesimse. Die Gesimse sind auf die glatte Fassadenfläche aufgesetzt, um die Steinversätze und Gesimsbänder der beiden neoklassizistischen Nachbarbauten aufzunehmen und in der Flucht weiterzuführen.

Der obere Abschluß des Gebäudes ist beidseitig leicht abgeschrägt und erzeugt in der Ansicht den Eindruck eines traditionellen Mansardendachs.

1001 Fifth Avenue Facade

Johnson/Burgee Architects
1977–1978
New York, New York
Building Architect: Philip Birnbaum
Structural Engineer: Robert Rosenwasser
Mechanical Engineer: I.M. Robbins

A new apartment building was designed for Fifth Avenue across from the Metropolitan Museum, and Johnson's office was asked, to «upgrade» its facade in response to the request of various community groups and individuals who protested against the previous «modern» design.

The facade consists of contrasting vertical dark glass bay windows and a series of horizontal stone moldings. The limestone facade acts as a thin flat surface to which moldings are applied, their location determined by alignment with various courses and cornices of the two adjacent neo-classic structures.

The top of the structure is cut away at a shallow angle creating a frontal illusion of a traditional mansard roof.

«Johnson/Burgee Architecture», N. Miller, 1979

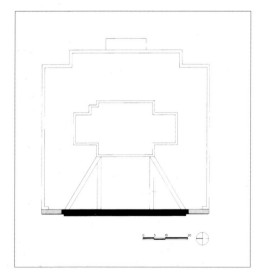

Dachaufsicht, 1:500, mit Fassadenstützkonstruktion
Außenansicht

Roof plan showing facade construction
Exterior view

Fassade Marshall Field & Co.

Johnson/Burgee Architects
1978–1979
Houston, Texas
Assoziierte Architekten: S.I. Morris Associates
Statik: COLACO Engineers, Inc.
Bildhauerischer Entwurf: Claes Oldenburg

Die fünfgeschossige Eingangsfassade für das Kaufhaus Marshall Field & Co. wurde mit texanischem Muschelkalk verkleidet, der Sockel besteht aus Granit. Die ellipsenförmig gekrümmte Scheibe wirkt wie eine Willkommensgeste über den endlosen Parkplatz hinweg. Der eigentliche Eingang, ein achsmittig angeordneter, giebelförmiger Einschnitt, wurde mit goldfarbenen Mosaikfliesen aus Glas versehen. Der – vom Bauherrn abgelehnte – Entwurf von Claes Oldenburg sah die Anbringung von «Farbklecksen» aus gestrichenen Aluminium-Gußteilen auf der Fassade vor.

Marshall Field & Co. Facade

Johnson/Burgee Architects
1978–1979
Houston, Texas
Associate Architect: S.I. Morris Associates
Structural Engineer: COLACO Engineers, Inc.
Sculpture Proposal: Claes Oldenburg

This structure is a five story facade of Texas shellstone on a base of granite. The elliptical curve gestures as an entrance across the vast scale of the parking lot and an entrance angular arched opening is covered in gold-colored glass mosaic tile. The proposal by Claes Oldenburg for cast aluminum painted «paint drops» was not accepted by the client.

Progressive Architecture, August 1979
Claes Oldenburg, Large Scale Projects 1977–1980, R.H. Fuchs, 1980
Philip Johnson/John Burgee Architecture 1979–1985, Carleton Knight, 1985

Fassadenskulptur von Claes Oldenburg
Ausgeführte Fassade

Proposed Sculpture by Claes Oldenburg
Final Exterior View

Kristallkathedrale
(Garden Grove Gemeindekirche)

Johnson/Burgee Architects
1980
Garden Grove, Kalifornien
Statik: Severud-Perrone-Strum-Bandel
Haustechnik: Cosentini Associates
Akustik: Kleppe Marshall King Associates
Lichttechnik: Claude R. Engle

Auf die Frage hin, welches halbe Dutzend Gebäude aus der zweiten Hälfte unseres Jahrhunderts als wahrhaft modern zu bezeichnen wäre, würden sich in den meisten Antworten das Glashaus in New Canaan (1949), das AT&T-Gebäude in Manhattan (1979) und die Kristallkathedrale, die Kirche für die Gemeinde Garden Grove (1977) wiederfinden. Sie gehören zwar nicht zu den radikal modernen Bauten, aber zu den bekanntesten.

Es ist schon bemerkenswert genug, daß alle drei von Philip Johnson stammen, und der Umstand, daß man sich kaum unterschiedlichere Bauten vorstellen könnte, unterstreicht das noch. Das Glashaus aus den Nachkriegsjahren war als Wohnhaus der Avantgarde seiner Zeit tatsächlich voraus. Die Kristallkathedrale ist wahrscheinlich außer Cape Kennedy der Ort mit dem theatralischsten High-Tech-Firlefanz und vermutlich ebenso bekannt, da der Sonntagsgottesdienst von dort aus in 177 Städten im Fernsehen zu sehen ist. Das AT&T-Gebäude ist wahrscheinlich der erste postmoderne Wolkenkratzer, der seit Cass Gilberts Hochhaus für Woolworth (1913) die Amerikaner an eine Vergangenheit erinnert, die sie nie hatten. Die Kristallkathedrale, die die ursprüngliche Kirche von Richard Neutra (1962) ablöste, sollte eine Art «Zelt» für einen der charismatischsten Prediger Amerikas werden. Einst verkündete er seine frohe Botschaft einigen wenigen von irgendeinem Kioskdach aus, nun erreicht er mittels Radio und Fernsehen Millionen ergebener Anhänger. Seine Sendung, bekannt als die «Hour of Power», wird regelmäßig jeden Sonntag ausgestrahlt. Reverend Dr. Robert H. Schuller wußte genau was er wollte, als er sich, wahrscheinlich auf göttliche Eingebung hin, an Philip Johnson wandte. Ihm schwebte ein Kirche von fantastischen Ausmaßen vor, groß genug, um 3000 Gläubige aufzunehmen und eindrucksvoll genug, um Millionen von Fernsehzuschauern in ihren Bann zu schlagen. Dazu fehlte nur noch ein Architekt. Da weder Joseph Paxton (der Erbauer des ersten Kristallpalastes von 1851) noch Alexander Graham Bell (der sich 1906 mit dem Raumtragwerk einen Namen gemacht hatte) noch direkt ansprechbar waren, sollte es zumindest jemand sein, der über Paxton und Bell – und vor allem über Charisma – genauestens

Crystal Cathedral
(Garden Grove Community Church)

Johnson/Burgee Architects
1980
Garden Grove, California
Structural Engineer: Severud-Perrone-Strum-Bandel
Mechanical Engineer: Cosentini Associates
Acoustical Engineer: Kleppe Marshall King Associates
Lighting: Claude R. Engle

If one were to identify half a dozen American buildings of the second half of this century that the general public would surely recognize as being «radically modern,» they would have to include the Glass House in New Canaan (1949), the AT&T Building in Manhattan (1979), and the Crystal Cathedral in Garden Grove, California (1977). They are not necessarily among the very best «radically modern» structures of their time; but they are surely among the very best known.

The fact that all three were designed by Philip Johnson is in itself remarkable; and the fact that no three buildings of any period could be much more different makes all this even more so. The Glass House is probably the most avantgarde residence of the postwar years; the Crystal Cathedral may be the most dramatic high tech extravaganza outside Cape Kennedy, and at least as well known to those who watch the 177 TV programs broadcast from the Cathedral every Sunday; and the AT&T Building is probably the first post modern skyscraper since Cass Gilbert's Woolworth Tower (1913) reminded Americans of a past that never was.

The Crystal Cathedral, which supplanted the previous 1962 church by Richard Neutra, was designed to serve as a «tent» for one of the most charismatic preachers in the U.S. – an evangelist who graduated from preaching on the roof of a snack bar to addressing millions of devoted followers via radio and TV, through a regular Sunday program known everywhere as the «Hour of Power.» The preacher, the Reverend Dr. Robert H. Schuller, seemed to know exactly what he wanted when he approached Philip Johnson, probably at the Almighty's suggestion: he wanted a fantastic church, big enough to hold 3,000 worshippers, and memorable enough to attract millions more via the tube – and he was looking for an architect capable of doing exactly that, and more. Since neither Joseph Paxton (of the original Crystal Palace in 1851) nor Alexander Graham Bell (of Space-Frame fame in 1906) were available, Schuller looked for someone who would know all about Paxton, Bell and, especially about charisma, and decided that Johnson was the one. He was quite right.

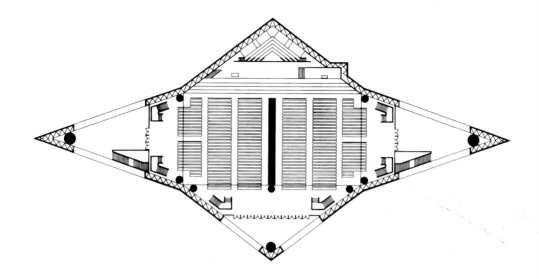

Grundriß Erdgeschoß, 1:1000

Ground floor plan, 1:1000

Bescheid wußte. Er entschied sich für Johnson. Zu Recht. Die Kristallkathedrale ist mehr als nur eine verblüffend gute Nachbildung von Vorläufern aus früheren Zeiten. Sie ist ein raffiniertes und einfallsreiches Gebäude, größer und wesentlich ausgefeilter als bekanntere zeitgenössische Raumfachwerk-High-Tech-Gebilde. Der zeltdachartige Umriß über dem rautenförmigen Grundriß hat eine silberbeschichtete Spiegelverglasung, die nur 8 Prozent Sonneneinstrahlung durchläßt und bündig mit den Aluminiumprofilen sitzt, die wiederum von Raumfachwerkträgern in Form eines Tetraeders aus Rundstahl gehalten werden. Alles wunderbar auf engstem Raum untergebracht.

Balkone mit ansteigenden Sitzreihen kragen in drei der vier Raumecken aus, im vierten Raumwinkel ist eine Bühne angeordnet, auf der der Chor und die Kanzel stehen und von der aus Dr. Schuller seine Vorstellung gibt. Auf der einen Seite der Bühne verspringt die Glasfassade und bildet zwei 27,40 m hohe Pendeltüren, die von der

The Crystal Cathedral, however, is not merely a dazzling reconstruction of an earlier precedent; it is an extremely sophisticated and innovative building, larger and considerably more polished than most of the better known High-Tech, space-frame structures designed and built by some of the famous High-Tech, space-frame innovators of our time. Its configuration is rather surprising: it is diamond shaped in plan and tent shaped in silhouette; it is sheathed in silver-coated, reflective glass that screens out all but 8 percent of sunlight; and the glass is framed flush in an aluminum grid attached to a tubular steel, tetrahedral space frame. It is a beautifully tight fit.

Three of the four triangular ends of the diamond-shaped plan contain balconies with stepped-up seating; the fourth contains a platform for the choir and the pulpit, where Dr. Schuller performs. At one end of this platform, the glass wall juts out and forms two 90 feet tall pivoting doors that can be controlled from the pulpit and made to swing open to direct the service to a 300-car parking lot

Kanzel aus gesteuert werden können und sich auf den für 300 Autos ausgelegten Parkplatz hin öffnen, der dann in den Gottesdienst mit einbezogen wird – Autoinsassen können den Ton zum Bild auf ihrem Radio empfangen. Mit seinen ferngesteuerten Türen, den diversen audio-visuellen Hilfsmitteln und den ferngesteuerten Fontänen, die auf Kommando himmelwärts spritzen, wird die Kristallkathedrale zu einem riesigen High-Tech-Theater, das sich zur umgebenden Landschaft und zum Himmel fast vollständig öffnet. Wenn sich die Riesentore auftun, erwartet man, daß eine Saturnrakete auf ihrer Abschußrampe ausgefahren wird, um dem Allmächtigen alsbald näher zu kommen.

Seit Fertigstellung der Kristallkathedrale 1980 haben Johnson und Dr. Schuller ein weiteres Gebilde direkt daneben gesetzt – einen 87 m hohen Campanile aus hochglanzpoliertem Edelstahl, gekrönt mit Stahlprismen, einem Glockenspiel aus 52 Bronzeglocken und einem

just beyond the doors. (Those inside the parked cars can listen to the service on their radios.) These remotely-controlled doors, in addition to various audio-visual devices and remotely-controlled fountains that jet skyward on demand, make the Crystal Cathedral a vast, high-tech theater virtually open to the surrounding landscape and to the heavens. When the huge doors swing open, you fully expect a Saturn V to come rolling out on its launching pad, and to take off in the general direction of the Almighty. Since the great Crystal Cathedral was completed in 1980, Johnson and Dr. Schuller have erected another structure next to it – a 286 foot tall, polished stainless steel campanile, with steel prisms on top and a carillon of 52 bronze bells plus an airplane beacon to finish it all off. This stainless steel tower, with its little domed temple at ground level, may not be quite the bundle of joy that it apparently seems to Johnson and Schuller; it's more like a bundle of giant shish kebab skewers, scaled and styled

Außenansicht mit
Glockenturm im Hintergrund
Innenansicht

Exterior view with bell tower
in background
Interior view

Warnblinklicht für Flugzeuge. Der ebenerdig mit einer kleinen überkuppelten Kapelle versehene Edelstahlturm erinnert allerdings weniger an einen Strahlenkranz, den Johnson und Schuller anscheinend in ihm sehen, als an ein riesiges Bündel Schaschlikspieße, vom Maßstab und Stil her eher für ein Hollywood-Picknick geeignet. Es ist ein Segen, daß man ihn von dem wunderbaren Innenraum der Kirche nicht sehen kann...

Johnson hat immer wieder das Glück gehabt, an einen erstklassigen Bauherrn zu geraten, und Dr. Schuller war da keine Ausnahme. Er paßte ebensogut zu Johnson wie Johnson zu ihm. Schuller wußte, was er wollte, und Johnson wußte, wie er es ihm zu servieren hatte, inklusive Spieße. Mit Auftraggebern wie Dr. Schuller, Gerald Hines, Nelson Rockefeller, Phyllis Lambert (aus dem Seagram Imperium) und, nicht zuletzt, Johnson höchstpersönlich konnte man kaum fehlgehen. Beim Entwurf der Kristallkathedrale ist Johnson eindeutig zu voller Form aufgelaufen.

for a Hollywood picnic. Fortunately, it is not very visible from inside the wonderful Cathedral...

One of Johnson's great fortunes has been the quality of many of his clients, and Dr. Schuller is no exception. He seemed almost ideally suited to Johnson and Johnson to him. Schuller knew exactly what he wanted, and Johnson knew exactly how to give it to him, skewers and all. With clients like Dr. Schuller, and Gerald Hines, Nelson Rockefeller, Phyllis Lambert (of Seagram) and, of course, with Johnson himself, it would have been very difficult to go very far wrong. At the Crystal Cathedral, Johnson was clearly at his best.

Progressive Architecture, December 1980

Glockenturm der Kristallkathedrale

Philip Johnson
1990
Garden Grove, Kalifornien
Assoziierte Architekten: Gin Wong Associates
Statik: Leslie E. Robertson

Zur Abrundung der Originalanlage entstand ein Jahrzehnt nach Fertigstellung der Kristallkathedrale der Glockenturm – der Crean Tower – mit einer Kapelle im Sockel. Er besteht aus hochglanzpolierten Edelstahlprismen, die auf einen 87 m hohen tragenden Stahlrahmen montiert wurden. Die Mary Hood Kapelle wird von einer Kuppel überdeckt, die von 44 Monolithen aus Marmor in allen Arten und Färbungen gehalten wird.

Crystal Cathedral Bell Tower

Philip Johnson
1990
Garden Grove, California
Associate Architect: Gin Wong Associates
Structural Engineer: Leslie E. Robertson

This bell tower (the Crean Tower) and chapel was finished a decade after the completion of Johnson's Crystal Cathedral, and complements his original plan for the Cathedral itself. It is made of polished stainless steel prisms on a structural steel frame which stands 286 feet above the ground. The Mary Hood Chapel is domed and supported by 44 marble monoliths of various types and colors.

Architecture and Urbanism, April 1991

Erdgeschoßgrundriß der Kapelle, 1:200
Horizontalschnitt durch Tragstruktur und Verkleidung, 1:200

Ground floor plan showing chapel, 1:200
Horizontal section showing structure and cladding, 1:200

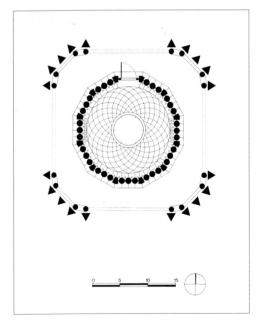

Studierklause und Bibliothek
Philip Johnson
1980
New Canaan, Connecticut
Statik: Robertson, Fowler & Associates
Haustechnik: Stanford Hess
Lichttechnik: Claude R. Engle

In der Nähe seines Glashauses hat Philip Johnson mitten in eine große Wiese dieses kleine verspielte Gebilde gesetzt, das an ein Miniaturgebäude aus einem Landschaftsgarten des 18. Jahrhunderts erinnert. In dem Haus, dessen klare kubistische Formen den Bauten Le Corbusiers aus den zwanziger und dreißiger Jahren ähneln, ist seine Architekturbibliothek untergebracht. Der Außenputz ist weiß gestrichen, wie es in sonnendurchfluteten Mittelmeerländern der Brauch ist. Das einzige Fenster ist auf das nahegelegene Geisterhaus ausgerichtet. Oberlichter gewähren zusätzliches Tageslicht.

Library Study
Philip Johnson
1980
New Canaan, Connecticut
Structural Engineer: Robertson, Fowler & Associates
Mechanical Engineer: Stanford Hess
Lighting: Claude R. Engle

Sited in the center of a large meadow near Philip Johnson's Glass House, this small building is a «garden folly» that houses his architectural library. Its abstract, cubist forms are not unlike those built by Le Corbusier in the 1920 and 1930s. The exterior is white-washed stucco, in the sun-drenched Mediterranean tradition, with a single window pointed at the Ghost House nearby. Several skylights supply additional light.

Architectural Record, July 1983

Grundriß, 1:100

Floor plan, 1:100

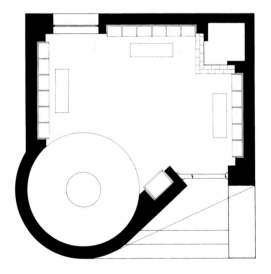

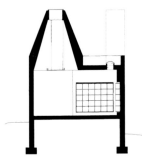

Schnitt durch das konisch zulaufende Oberlicht, 1:250
Außenansicht

Building section at cone skylight, 1:250
Exterior view

101 California Street

Johnson/Burgee Architects
1980–1982
San Francisco, Kalifornien
Assoziierte Architekten: KWA Inc. Architects
Statik: Gillum-Colaco Consulting Structural
Engineers, Inc.
Haustechnik: I.A. Naman & Associates, Inc.
Landschaftsgestaltung: Zion & Breen Associates

Das zylindrische, mit Spiegelglas verkleidete Bürohochhaus zählt 48 Geschosse und übernimmt eine Gelenk-
funktion am Schnittpunkt zweier gegeneinander verdreh-
ter Straßenraster in der Innenstadt San Franciscos. Die
Geschoßfläche des kreisrunden Gebäudes beträgt ca.
2.200 m².
Sieben dreieckige Geschosse bilden den mit Granit verkleideten Sockel. Die Überlagerung der Baukörper wird
durch einen Einschnitt markiert, der die Randstützen des
Hochhauses freigibt. Unter dem vom Boden abgehobenen
Turmbereich liegt das ca. 27 m hohe Eingangsfoyer, durch
eine Schrägverglasung überdeckt. Der verbleibende Grund-
stücksanteil wurde als öffentliche Freifläche gestaltet.
Um die im Bebauungsplan zugelassene Gebäudehöhe
von 183 m ausnutzen zu können, folgt der facettierte Fas-
sadenabschnitt den Vorschriften in der Bauordnung und
weist im oberen Teil des Hochhauses drei Rücksprünge
auf.

101 California Street

Johnson/Burgee Architects
1980–1982
San Francisco, California
Associate Architects: KWA Inc. Architects
Structural Engineer: Gillum-Colaco Consulting Structural
Engineers, Inc.
Mechanical Engineer: I.A. Naman & Associates, Inc.
Landscape Architect: Zion & Breen Associates

This cylindrical mirror glass office tower is 48 stories tall
and positioned as a hinge-like form between two shifting
grids in the street layout of downtown San Francisco. The
circular plan of the tower is 24,000 square feet in area.
The granite clad base is a 7 story triangular building
which at the point of intersection with the tower de-
scribes a cut away form that exposes the perimeter
columns of the tower and develops an angular skylight for
the 88 foot tall lobby space. The remainder of the site is
developed as public plaza.
The top of the tower obeys zoning restrictions to set back
in a sawtooth recess three times reaching the full 600
foot total height allowed.

«Philip Johnson/John Burgee Architecture 1979–1985»,
Carleton Knight, 1985

Lageplan

Site plan

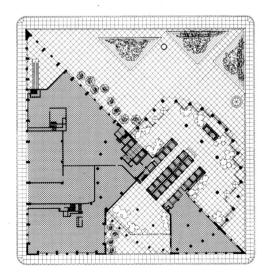

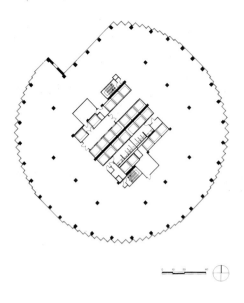

Normalgeschoß Hochhaus, 1:1000
Blick auf den Turm

Typical tower floor plan, 1:1000
View of tower

Platzanlage mit niedrigem Gebäudeteil und Turm
Eingangsfoyer mit niedrigem Gebäudeteil

Exterior view showing tower, plaza and low rise building
Exterior view showing lobby and low rise building

Transco Tower

Johnson/Burgee Architects
1979–1983
Houston, Texas
Assoziierte Architekten: Morris * Aubry Architects
Statik: CBM Engineers, Inc.
Haustechnik: I.A. Naman & Associates, Inc.
Landschaftsplanung: Zion & Breen Associates, Inc.
Assoziierte Architekten Landschaftsplanung:
Richard Fitzgerald and Partners
Lichttechnik: Claude R. Engle

Der ca. 275 m hohe Wolkenkratzer mit 65 Geschossen und einer Bruttogeschoßfläche von ca. 150.000 m² steht am Stadtrand von Houston. Er bricht mit der herkömmlichen Tradition moderner Architektur, der sich Philip Johnsons Zeitgenossen verschrieben haben: der Transco Tower ist alles andere als «Internationaler Stil» im Sinne eines Mies van der Rohe oder Le Corbusier. Er entspricht im Ausdruck eher Bertram Goodhues modernistischem State Capitol in Nebraska aus dem Jahr 1916, ein eklektisches Spätwerk in Beaux-Arts-Manier, das auch über die Grenzen Nebraskas hinaus bewundert wurde. Entgegen der Standardausstattung im Internationalen Stil hat der Transco Tower weder ein zurückgesetztes Sockelgeschoß noch Pilotis noch beides in Kombination. Stattdessen ruht er auf einem fünfgeschossigen, neoklassizistischen Sockel, der wesentlich ausladender als der vertikale Schaft ist.

Der Bau ist auch kein Mies'scher Prototyp eines Hochhauses aus Stahl und Glas – obwohl er durchgängig verglast ist, entspricht seine Ausbildung in Maßstab und Färbung der eines steinernen Bauwerks. Mit Sicherheit stellt er keine primäre Form in der Definiton Le Corbusiers dar und hat nichts mit dessen Konzept einer vertikalen Stadt zu tun. Transcos Umriß hat Vor- und Rücksprünge wie ein neogotischer Turm. Den oberen Abschluß der zinnenartigen Abtreppung bildet nicht etwa ein Flachdach, sondern eine abgeflachte Pyramide.

Der Turm steht am einen Ende eines 110 m langen, abgesenkten Grünbereichs, das andere Ende wird von einer 18,30 m hohen, halbkreisförmigen Wandscheibe gebildet, über die ein Wasserfall rauscht. Das Wasser sammelt sich in einem Becken, das durch eine Art Vorbühne aus Ziegel und Kalksandstein in klassischer Manier abgeschirmt wird. Der imposante Brunnen wurde zu einem bevorzugten Schauplatz für Hochzeiten in Houston, wobei die mittig angeordnete, kreisrunde Plattform als Bühne fungiert.

Ein bißchen viel Aufwand für einen Erdgasvertrieb und eine Immobilienfirma? Das mag schon sein, aber mit einem eindrucksvollen Ergebnis: die abgestufte Glasfas-

Transco Tower

Johnson/Burgee Architects
1979–1983
Houston, Texas
Associate Architects: Morris * Aubry Architects
Structural Engineer: CBM Engineers, Inc.
Mechanical Engineer: I.A. Naman & Associates, Inc.
Landscape Architect: Zion & Breen Associates, Inc.
Associate Architects for the Park:
Richard Fitzgerald and Partners
Lighting: Claude R. Engle

This 900-foot tall, 65 story, 1.6 million square foot tower just outside Houston, Texas, violates almost every conventional maxim of modern architecture as subscribed to by Philip Johnson's contemporaries: the Transco Tower, as it is known, is hardly an «International Style» building à la Mies van der Rohe or Le Corbusier – instead, it is a building in the manner of Bertram Goodhue's 1916 «modernistic» Nebraska State Capitol, a piece of late Beaux Arts eclecticism greatly admired by some both outside and inside Nebraska. Unlike a typical «international style» tower, Transco is not supported on pilotis or a recessed base (or both) – instead, it sits on a neoclassical pedestal considerably broader than its vertical shaft, and five stories high.

Nor is it a glass-and-steel building in the manner of Mies van der Rohe's prototypes, but a building that is scaled and tinted to look like a stone tower (although it is, in fact, clad in glass.) And it is certainly not a vertical «pure prism» in the manner of Le Corbusier's drawings for a vertical city, but a shaft with a serrated silhouette, in the manner of a «Gothic Revival» tower. Its top is not flat, but stepped and almost crenellated, and capped with a flattened-out pyramid.

And it is placed to overlook a 360-foot long sunken lawn that is terminated in a 60 foot tall, semi-circular screen wall transformed into a waterfall. The pool into which all that water falls is further screened by a classically detailed, brick and limestone proscenium; and this stately fountain has become a place where Houstonians now like to have their weddings, and the circular platform at the center of the composition acts as a stage for such ceremonies.

If all this seems quite a lot of pomp and circumstance for a building designed to house a company that sells gas, and another company that sells real estate – well, it probably is. But the result is something quite wonderful: the serrated glass curtain wall picks up reflections of sun and sky in constantly changing patterns, some of them dazzling, vertical silver streaks of light, others subtle and subdued.

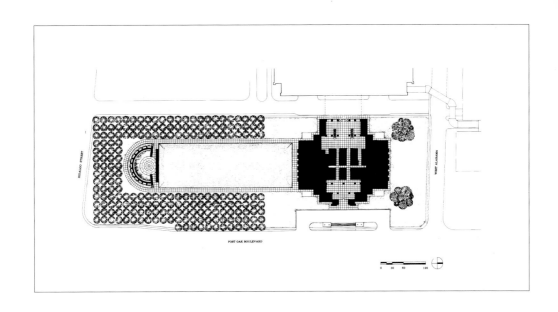

Lageplan, 1:3000
Grundriß der oberen Geschosse, 1:1000
Ansicht mit Turm, Parkhaus, Grünbereich und Brunnen

Site plan, 1:3000
Plan of top floors, 1:1000
View showing tower, parking garage, garden and fountain

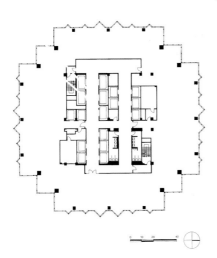

sade reflektiert Sonne und Himmel immer anders – manchmal gleißt das Licht wie Silberstreifen, dann wieder wirkt es unauffällig und gedämpft.

Der Umriß des 275 m hohen Turms ist weithin sichtbar – in keiner anderen amerikanischen Stadt findet sich ein so hohes, freistehendes Gebäude außerhalb des Geschäftsviertels im Stadtkern. Ein Signalfeuer auf der Spitze der Dachpyramide wirft sein Licht 35 Kilometer weit nach allen Richtungen in die Nacht.

Es liegt auf der Hand, daß es Johnson hier, ähnlich wie bei früheren Bauten, um den kleinen Unterschied ging. Den Unterschied zu Mies, zu seinen Harvard-geschulten Studienkollegen, zur gefeierten Formensprache des Internationalen Stils, derer er sich in MoMA-Ausstellungen angenommen hatte, sowie zu den geschäftsmäßigen Bauten im geschäftsbewußten Texas. Beim Transco Tower läßt sich so gut wie nichts mit rein funktionalen Belangen rechtfertigen – schon gar nicht der 18,30 m hohe, formale Eingangsbogen aus Granit, zumal die meisten Besucher das Gebäude über eine verglaste Verbindungsbrücke betreten, nachdem sie ihr Auto im gegenüberliegenden Parkhaus abgestellt haben.

Kurz, der Transco Tower ist seit seiner Eröffnung Tagesgespräch in Houston, und das wird noch geraume Zeit so bleiben. Ihm ist derselbe atemberaubende Effekt eigen, den Johnson und viele andere Chartres zuschreiben – wenn man, von Paris her durch endlose Felder kommend, die beiden Türme der Kathedrale, noch lange vor der Stadt selbst, am Horizont auftauchen sieht. Der Transco Tower ist ebenso weithin sichtbar, bei Tag und bei Nacht.

Ist er des Guten zu viel? Nicht direkt; Johnson dekoriert im Gegensatz zu dem einen oder anderen amerikanischen Architekten der Postmoderne seine Schuppen nicht – und seine Wolkenkratzer genausowenig (mit der berühmten Ausnahme an der Madison Avenue). Dieser klare, geradlinige Wolkenkratzer in Nadelstreifen spricht für sich – und manchmal scheint er gar zu pfeifen.

The silhouette of the 900 foot high shaft is visible from miles away – it is the tallest, free-standing building outside a downtown business center anywhere in the U.S. – and at night there are shafts of light from a beacon on top of the pyramidal roof. This beacon swings around, and pierces 22 miles into the night in all directions.

It is clear that Johnson, in this building and in others, was determined to be different from everyone else – from Mies, from the Harvard-trained architects with whom he went to school, from the International Style vocabulary that he had espoused and celebrated in MoMA exhibitions, and different from the business-oriented buildings of business-oriented Texas. There is almost nothing about the Transco Tower that can be fully justified by purely functional concerns – certainly not the 60 foot high ceremonial granite arch that marks the formal entrance to the Tower, especially since most people arrive by car, and enter the building through a glass-enclosed bridge from a garage on the opposite side of the tower.

The Transco Tower, in short, has been the Talk of Houston from the day its doors opened to the public, and it is likely to be for years to come. It has the dramatic visibility that Johnson and others have noted whenever they approached the town of Chartres from the direction of Paris, driving across the open fields and experiencing the stunning sights of the Cathedral's two towers visible on the horizon, long before there are any other signs of the town. The Transco Tower has that same dramatic visibility, from miles away, and (thanks to its beacon) by night as well as by day.

Is it all a bit much? Not really – unlike some American postmodernists, Johnson has rarely decorated his sheds, or, for that matter, his skyscrapers, except, perhaps, on Madison Avenue, in Manhattan. The Transco Tower's clean, linear forms and shining pin stripes speak for themselves; and sometimes they even seem to whistle.

Progressive Architecture, February 1984
«Philip Johnson/John Burgee Architecture 1979–1985», Carleton Knight, 1985
«Presence, the Transco Tower», Ann Holmes, 1985

Neues Schauspielhaus Cleveland

Johnson/Burgee Architects
1980–1983
Cleveland, Ohio
Assoziierte Architekten: Collins & Rimer
Statik: Robertson, Fowler & Associates
Haustechnik: Cosentini Associates
Akustik: Klepper, Marshall, King Associates
Lichttechnik: Claude R. Engle

Der Anbau an das schöne, kleine Theater von 1927, im romanischen Stil von Charles Rowley und Philip Small entworfen, erwies sich als schwierige Aufgabe. Das Bauprogramm war dreimal so umfangreich wie das des Originalbauwerks und jeder Bereich sollte mit dem großen benachbarten Lager verbunden werden. Die Architekten hielten sich im Maßstab, Stil und Material an das ursprüngliche Theater und lösten das Gesamtvolumen in mehrere Pavillons auf, die in der Größe auf das Original eingingen und an einer Erschließungsachse liegen. Die kleineren Volumina sind den größeren Baukörpern der Theaterräume mit ihren Schnurböden vorgeschaltet.

Man betritt die Gebäudecollage über einen tempelartigen, dramatisch wirkenden Baukörper, der bildhaft Bezug auf Santa Costanza und Berninis Santa Maria dell'Assunzione in Arriccia nimmt. Die Rotunde gewährt Zugang zum alten und neuen Bauteil. Die neuen Theater bestehen aus einem flexiblen Black-Box-Studio und dem «Bolton»-Theater mit 644 Sitzplätzen. Das letztere entspricht einem traditionellen Theaterraum mit Vorbühne und mehreren Rängen aus vorgetäuschten Balkonen, die als Beleuchtungsebenen dienen. Im Ausdruck knüpft es an die Hoftheater vergangener Epochen an.

The New Cleveland Playhouse

Johnson/Burgee Architects
1980–1983
Cleveland, Ohio
Associate Architect: Collins & Rimer
Structural Engineer: Robertson, Fowler & Associates
Mechanical Engineer: Cosentini Associates
Acoustical: Klepper, Marshall, King Associates
Lighting: Claude R. Engle

This structure is an addition to a small 1927 Romanesque theater, designed by Charles Rowley & Philip Small. The addition had a program that was three times the size of the original, and the requirement was to link all elements to a huge adjacent warehouse. Johnson proceeded to use the existing style, materials and scale of the first theater in a series of pavilions, and then lined them up along the circulation spine, as small volumes in front of the larger volumes of the new theaters and their fly lofts.

The entire assembly is entered by a dramatic «temple» inspired by Santa Costanza and Bernini's Santa Maria dell'Assunzione in Ariccia. From this rotunda you enter both new and existing theaters. The new theaters are a black box multi-purpose studio, and the 644 seat «Bolton» theater.

Awards: Cleveland Building Exchange,
Craftsmanship Award 1985

Progressive Architecture, February 1984
«Speaking a New Classicism», Smith College Museum, 1981
«Philip Johnson/John Burgee Architecture 1979–1985», Carleton Knight, 1985

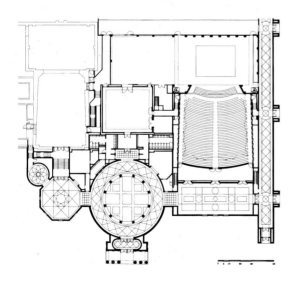

Grundriß Erdgeschoß, 1:1000
Ansicht von Norden
Innenansicht des Theaterraums

Ground floor plan, 1:1000
Exterior north elevation
Interior theater

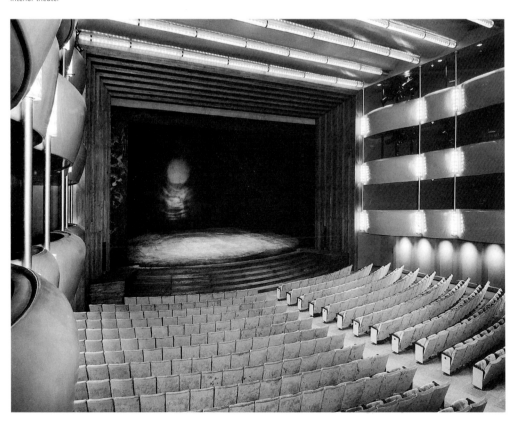

PPG Hauptsitz

Johnson/Burgee Architects
1979–1984
Pittsburgh, Pennsylvania
Statik: Skilling, Helle, Christiansen &
Robertson Inc.
Haustechnik: W.A. Digiacomo Associates
Lichttechnik: Claude R. Engle

Bei dem Entwurf des Hauptsitzes für die Pittsburgh Plate Glass Company (sowie einiger Mieter) lag ein Glasgebäude nahe. Die Frage war vielmehr, welche Art von Glasbau und mit welchem architektonischen Erscheinungsbild?

Ein moderner Architekt mit Philip Johnsons Referenzen hatte wenigstens zwei Möglichkeiten: er könnte sich an Joseph Paxtons Kristallpalast aus dem Jahre 1851 anlehnen oder versuchen, Mies van der Rohes erste Hochhausskizzen umzusetzen.

Johnson tat keines von beidem. Die aus sechs Gebäuden bestehende Gesamtanlage im Zentrum von Pittsburgh ist weder Mies noch Paxton. Im Grundriß erscheint es als Rockefeller Center im Kleinformat, wobei die Ausdrucksmittel weitaus ausgeprägter sind als etwaige Besonderheiten des New Yorker Bauwerks. Davon später mehr.

Die gläserne Gotik ist selbstredend das eindrücklichste und augenscheinlichste Merkmal des PPG Place, gänzlich nicht-modern und gänzlich Johnson. Bei einem wohlhabenden Bauherrn unterliegt er oft der Versuchung, Possen zu reißen. Man fühlt sich dabei an den wunderbaren Film aus den dreißiger Jahren, «The Ghost Goes West», erinnert, in dem eine amerikanische Zillionärsfamilie ein uraltes Schloß in Schottland erwirbt (inklusive Schloßgespenst, gespielt von Robert Donat), es anschließend zerlegt, nach Südflorida verschifft und dort wieder aufbaut, mit ein paar zusätzlichen, pseudo-europäischen Kleinigkeiten – als da wären venezianische Kanäle, Gondeln und Gondoliere in Maharadscha-Klamotten...

Bei flüchtiger Betrachtung wirkt PPG Place wie ein neogotisches Bühnenbild für diesen Film, man wartet auf das Gespenst in Gestalt von Sir Charles Barry, der sich ja mit neogotischen Turmbekrönungen, Glas und vor allem Spiegelglas bestens auskannte. Auf den zweiten Blick wird klar, daß PPG in städtebaulicher Hinsicht ein von Johnson seit Lincoln Center langgehegtes Ideal verfolgt – eine moderne Version Bolognas, eine durch Arkadengänge verknüpfte Stadtanlage.

Johnson regte in seinen Bauten und Projekten wiederholt an, Bauwerke, Straßen und Plätze mit Arkaden zu säumen, um dadurch die fußgängerorientierte Stadt wieder aufleben zu lassen – eine Stadt, in der man ungeachtet der Witterung überallhin trockenen Fußes gelangt, weil

PPG Headquarters

Johnson/Burgee Architects
1979–1984
Pittsburgh, Pennsylvania
Structural Engineer: Skilling, Helle, Christiansen &
Robertson Inc.
Mechanical Engineer: W.A. Digiacomo Associates
Lighting: Claude R. Engle

If you are an architect asked to design a complex that will house the Corporate Headquarters for the Pittsburgh Plate Glass Company (plus other tenants), you will, obviously, design a glass building. The question is – what sort of glass building? And what sort of image will you try to project?

To a modern architect with Philip Johnson's credentials, there might be at least two alternatives: you might try something reminiscent of Joseph Paxton's Crystal Palace of 1851; or you might try to relate to one of Mies van der Rohe's early sketches for skyscrapers in glass.

Johnson did neither. His complex of six buildings in the center of Pittsburgh's Golden Triangle is neither Miesian or Paxtonian; it is, in plan, a very interesting miniature of Rockefeller Center, with a number of features distinctly more advanced than those that make Rockefeller Center so significant. More about that in a moment.

The most memorable and visible aspect of PPG Place, needless to say, is its Glassy Gothic – a distinctly un-modern characteristic that is also distinctly Johnsonian: whenever Johnson does a building for a particular wealthy client, he seems tempted to poke just a little fun, in the manner of that wonderful 1930s movie, The Ghost Goes West, in which a family of American zillionnaires buys an ancient Scottish castle, dismantles it, transports the pieces to Southern Florida, and rebuilds it there with several Euro-chic embellishments, like Venetian canals, gondolas, and black gondoliers dressed roughly like maharajas...

At first sight, PPG Place looks like a neo-Gothic stage set for the movie's sequel (and makes you look for the ghost of Sir Charles Barry). But after the first chuckle or two, PPG becomes a very interesting exercise in urban design, specifically in an aspect of urban design that has interested Johnson ever since he worked on Lincoln Center: the idea of an Arcaded city, a modern version of Bologna. In several of his most successful buildings and projects, Johnson has suggested that arcaded buildings and streets and squares might be an excellent way of recreating a pedestrian city – a city in which people on foot will be protected in all kinds of weather, because all buildings will have recessed ground floors and covered sidewalks. He suggested this for on Lincoln center, where he thought that all separate theaters should be linked by a continu-

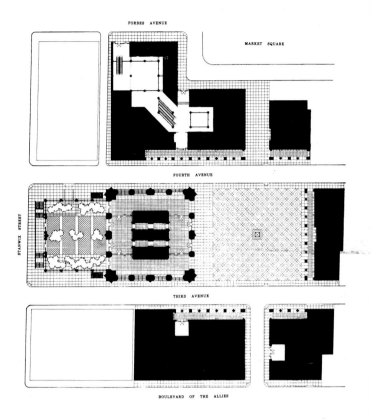

alle Gebäude im Erdgeschoß Rücksprünge und daher überdeckte Bürgersteige haben.

Beim Lincoln Center bestand sein (unwirklichter) Vorschlag in einer vorgesetzten, umlaufenden Fassade, die die Theaterbauten nach dem Vorbild der Rue de Rivoli und der Place des Vosges miteinander verbinden sollte. Beim Universitätsgelände von St. Thomas in Houston konnte er die Idee 1956 in die Wirklichkeit umsetzen, wobei ihm Thomas Jeffersons Arkadengang um den mittig angeordneten Grünbereich der Universität von Virginia als Vorlage diente. Das Konzept fand auch bei einigen Landhäusern Verwendung, wo er einzelne Pavillons durch überdachte Wege verband.

Johnson schöpfte aus der Quelle seines beträchtlichen architekturgeschichtlichen Wissens und verwendete Formen der Vergangenheit in einem zeitgemäßen Gewand. Die gläsernen Turmspitzen, die alle sechs PPG-Bauten krönen, gehören zu den augenfälligsten Beispielen. Ebenso bedeutsam sind die erwähnten hinter Arkaden geführten Wege, die bei allen Bauten die Fußgänger vor Wettereinwirkung schützen. Der förmliche, verglaste Wintergarten nördlich ca. 193 m hohen Turms nimmt Bezug auf die Gartenanlagen Italiens und Frankreichs aus dem

ous facade pattern à la Rue de Rivoli or the Place des Vosges. He built it when he did the St. Thomas campus in Houston in 1956 which was patterned after Jefferson's arcaded central lawn of the University of Virginia; and he pursued the idea even in one or two large villas that consisted of separate pavilions connected by arcaded walkways.

In designing the PPG Complex, Johnson drew upon his considerable knowledge of architectural history, and translated some of the most interesting precedents from the past into entirely modern images. The most obvious, of course, is the spiky glass skin that covers all six of the buildings at PPG Place. Less obvious, but perhaps more important, are the arcaded sidewalks that ring all the buildings. Still another historic reference is the formal, glass-enclosed Winter Garden behind the 635 feet tall tower at the north end of the complex – a Winter Garden patterned after the formal 17th-century gardens found in Italy and France; and there are other references to moments of the past translated into an idiom of the present: many of the 231 «Glassy Gothic» spires in the PPG complex have fluorescent lamps inside them. These lamps add to the shimmer of the reflective glass facades of the

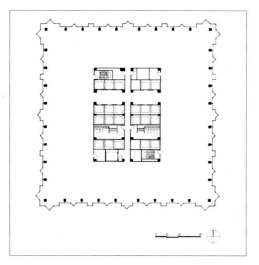
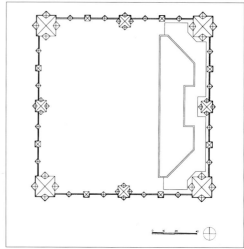

17. Jahrhundert. Ein weitere Anspielung auf traditionelle Formen ist die Neonbeleuchtung in vielen der 231 gläsernen Turmspitzen. Diese leuchtet des Nachts über Pittsburgh und verleiht den Spiegelglasfassaden des Bauwerks zusätzlichen Glanz. Durch ihre Facettierung vermeiden sie die Monotonie der üblichen, allgegenwärtigen Vorhangfassade. Sie spiegeln die Stadt mosaikartig in vielfach gebrochenen Bildern, wie eine avantgardistische Collage.

PPG weist eine Fülle ausgesuchter Details zum Thema Vergangenheit und Gegenwart auf – in der Mitte des Vorplatzes steht ein verkürzter Obelisk (dankenswerterweise keine gläserne Pyramide!), die Lampen in Höhe des ersten Obergeschosses nehmen das Motiv der neogotischen Turmspitzen wieder auf. Ihren eigentlichen dekorativen Schliff erhält die Anlage jedoch vom Spiel von Licht und Schatten auf den abgewinkelten Glasflächen. Die Felder der blaugrauen Spiegelglasfassade wechseln zwischen rechteckigen und dreieckigen Elementen in einem Gitterwerk aus Aluminium, das die Glasscheiben hält. Die Sonne läßt alle 60°-Elemente gleißend aufblitzen während sie die 90°-Elemente ins Dunkel taucht – die Fassaden erscheinen senkrecht gefurcht.

PPG Place gehört vom Ausdruck her Johnsons postmoderner Periode an. Städtebaulich betrachtet ist es ein moderner Entwurf, die verwendeten Materialien sind auf interessante Weise eingesetzt und ausgesprochen modern – allerdings eine Moderne, die aus der Geschichte gelernt hat. Vom Absolventen einer Architekturschule, die ihre Geschichtsbücher der Endlagerung überantwortet hat, hätte man mit Sicherheit kein solches Ergebnis erwartet.

buildings. And those reflective glass facades, being jagged rather than flat, avoid the dead monotony of more conventional glass curtain walls of the sort that afflict most modern cities. They are full of reflections and re-reflections, creating mosaics of urban images, rather than flat duplicates of a boring world. They look like flashing collages of a most avant-gardist sort.

PPG Place is full of nice touches that further enhance its historic references and its contemporary assets: there is a truncated obelisk at the center of its square (no glass pyramid, thank you!); and there are polygonal lanterns at the second floor level, suspended from all the glass facades, that echo the forms of the neo-Gothic spikes up in the sky. But the most lively decorative touches are supplied not by tangible details, but by the constant changes in light and dark, in reflections and refractions on the angled glass. The curtain wall of bluish-gray reflective glass consists of alternating rectangular and triangular bays, and there is an overlay of aluminum tracery that holds the glass in place. The reflections are fascinating: Sixty-degree angles create highlights; ninety-degree angles turn black. And so the facades are vertically striated as you move around, and in response to the sun.

Although PPG Place is probably considered an example of Johnson's postmodernistic phase, it is really an important contribution to modern urban design; an intriguing exercise in the use of some very modern materials; and it is, finally, all of these things not in opposition to the past, but with respect for it.

Progressive Architecture, February 1984
Architecture, December 1989

Grundriß Normalgeschoß des Turms, 1:1000
Dachaufsicht, 1:1000
Blick auf die Gesamtanlage

Typical floor plan tower, 1:1000
Roof plan, 1:1000
Exterior view of complex

Republic Bank Center (Nationsbank Center)

Johnson/Burgee Architects
1981–1984
Houston, Texas
Assoziierte Architekten: Kendall/Heaton Associates, Inc.
Statik: CBM Engineers, Inc.
Haustechnik: I.A. Naman & Associates Inc.

Das Gebäude der Republic Bank in Houstons Stadtmitte, auch Nationsbank Center genannt, steht direkt gegenüber dem Pennzoil Doppelhochhaus. Beide Bauten wurden von Philip Johnson im Abstand von fünf Jahren für den Investor Gerald Hines entworfen, hätten aber kaum unterschiedlicher ausfallen können.

Pennzoil ist ein minimalistisches Werk mit scharfen Aluminium- und Glaskanten, wahrscheinlich die beste und mit Sicherheit die größte moderne Skulptur der Stadt. Die Republic Bank hingegen ist eine Gesamtanlage im neogotischen Stil, die sich an norddeutsche und holländische städtische Gebäude aus dem 15. und 16. Jahrhundert mit steil ansteigenden Treppengiebeln anlehnt.

Als Gerald Hines mit dem Auftrag für die Republic Bank erstmals an Philip Johnson herantrat, schwebte diesem etwas in der minimalistischen Formensprache des Pennzoil Place vor. Hines war davon wenig begeistert. «Der Markt verlangt das Neue und Andersartige», warf er ein. «Das Gebäude muß im Kontrast zu Pennzoil stehen.» Johnson war immer für Stilwechsel zu haben (wenigstens seitdem er sich von Mies losgesagt hat), und so reagierte er mit dem, was er nach wie vor sein «Lieblingsgebäude in Houston» nennt.

Chacun à son goût, könnte man sagen. Das Bauwerk löst eine Reihe komplexer Probleme auf unbestreitbar intelligente Weise. In einer Ecke des Grundstücks, einem quadratischen Stadtblock von 68,50 m Seitenlänge, befand sich bereits ein zweigeschossiges Umspannwerk der Western Union. Es zu versetzen wäre viel zu teuer gewesen, und Johnson beschloß, darum herum zu bauen. Ein mittiges Achskreuz aus mit Oberlichtern versehenen Fußgängerarkaden teilt den Grundriß in vier Quadranten und dient vorrangig der Erschließung. Die Arkaden sind klimatisiert – eine während der drückend heißen Sommermonate in Houston durchaus willkommene Annehmlichkeit. Die Aufteilung in Quadranten erscheint sinnvoll: Zwei Quadranten dienen als Aufzugsfoyer des Bürohochhauses, der dritte wird vom Hauptmieter des Gebäudes als Schalterhalle genutzt, und das Umspannwerk nimmt den vierten ein. Der Raum unmittelbar über dem Umspannwerk dient der Schalterhalle als Zwischengeschoß. Dieser 36,50 m hohe Bereich erinnert an ein gotisches holländisches Rathaus, zumindest von außen.

Republic Bank Center (Nationsbank Center)

Johnson/Burgee Architects
1981–1984
Houston, Texas
Associate Architects: Kendall/Heaton Associates, Inc.
Structural Engineer: CBM Engineers, Inc.
Mechanical Engineer: I.A. Naman & Associates Inc.

The Republic Bank Building in downtown Houston is literally across the street from the Pennzoil Towers. Both are by Philip Johnson; both were built for the developer Gerald Hines; and the two complexes were designed within five years of each other. They could hardly be more different.

The Pennzoil Towers are a hard-edged, minimalist composition of glass and aluminum, probably the best – and certainly the largest – piece of modern abstract sculpture in the city. Whereas the Republic Bank is a neo-Gothic complex reminiscent of the north-German and Dutch Gothic municipal buildings of the 15th and 16th centuries whose serrated, ascending facades were applied to whatever was contained within.

When Gerald Hines first asked Johnson to work on this project, the architect thought that Republic Bank should be a building that would relate to Pennzoil Place – probably a building in the same, minimalist idiom. Hines thought that was a terrible idea. «This has to be sold as a new building, a different building,» Hines said. «It has to contrast with Pennzoil.» Nobody had ever found Johnson reluctant to explore a new direction – at least, not since his Miesian days – and so he designed what he today calls his «favorite building in Houston.»

«Chacun à son goût», as Johnson probably said at some point. The new building is certainly a very intelligent solution to some very complex problems. The site, a downtown city block 225 feet square, already contained a Western Union switching station that was two stories high and occupied a corner quadrant of the site. It would have been too expensive to move the building, and so Johnson decided to build around it: he bisected the site with two skylit pedestrian arcades, and made these the principal access routes to the lobby and to other features on the ground floor. The arcades were air-cooled, an attractive and desirable feature in Houston, especially during the stifling summer months.

The four quadrants created by the arcades made excellent sense in terms of the plan of the complex: two of the quadrants became the ground floor elevator lobby of the office tower; one would be turned into a grand Banking Hall for the building's principal tenant; and the fourth would contain the switching station – with the space

Grundriß Normalgeschoß Turm, 1:1000
Grundriß Erdgeschoß Turm, 1:1000

Typical floor plan tower, 1:1000
Ground floor plan tower, 1:1000

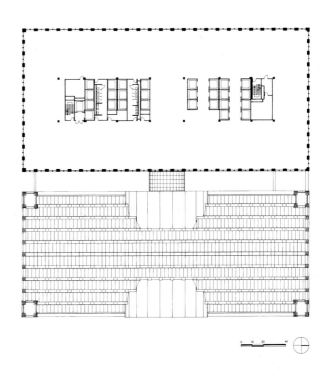

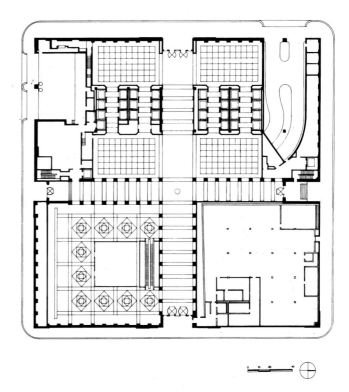

Das Endresultat erweckt den Eindruck zweier verwandter, doch getrennter Bauwerke. Der niedrigere Teil ist eine moderne Fassung eines Ratsgebäudes aus dem 16. Jahrhundert, das dreifach abgestufte Hochhaus von 244 m Höhe wirkt wie dessen großer Bruder.

Sowohl die Außenhaut aus rotem, schwedischem Granit als auch die verbleiten Kupferdächer sind feinsinnig durchdetailliert. Bedauerlicherweise verhinderten Bauvorgaben und -programm die Ausbildung des bei Rathäusern üblichen Bogengangs und beschränkten die Befensterung auf ein Mindestmaß. Die verhältnismäßig kleinen, quadratischen Lochfenster in der massiven, geschlossenen Wandfläche wirken im Vergleich zur historischen Vorlage verunglückt und obendrein unfreundlich. Dazu muß natürlich gesagt werden, daß es in Houston nur wenige Fußgänger auf den Bürgersteigen gibt und schon gar nicht im Sommer, wo sie sich vorzugsweise in klimatisierten unterirdischen Passagen oder klimatisierten Wagen bewegen. Eine 18,30 m hohe, geschlossene Wandfläche ist aber vielleicht doch etwas zu abweisend. Hinzu kommt, daß der Eingangsbogen zur Schalterhalle von 24,30 m Höhe in diesem neogotischen Kontext auch eher befremdlich wirkt. Es gibt hier etliche eigenartige Kehrtwendungen für einen der Geschichte sonst so eng verbundenen Architekten. Trotz der merkwürdigen Verfremdung historischer Elemente bilden die beiden durch 68,50 m lange, überglaste Arkadengänge miteinander verbundene Bauten ein bemerkenswertes Ensemble.

Zum einen erinnern Johnsons Arkadengänge, die er bei mehreren seiner Hochhausbauten einsetzte, an ein Element europäischen Städtebaus, das in den USA kaum zum Einsatz kommt. Zum anderen ist die große Schalterhalle vielleicht einer seiner gelungensten Bezüge auf die Architekturgeschichte, in diesem Fall Otto Wagners Postsparkasse in Wien von 1904. Sollte dies sein Vorbild gewesen sein, ist Johnsons Schalterhalle in Houston eine exzellente Weiterentwicklung. Auch die Rücksprünge des Turms sind besser gelungen als bei den vielen Hochhäusern mit zurückgestaffelten Geschossen, die seit den zwanziger Jahren vom Bebauungsplan hervorgebracht wurden.

Der Pennzoil-Doppelwolkenkratzer und sein Nachbar unterscheiden sich in einem weiteren Punkt. Pennzoil ist unverkennbar aus Glas und Metall, so glatt, geschmeidig und raffiniert, wie man in den siebziger Jahren gern sein wollte. Die Außenhaut der Republic Bank hingegen besteht aus Granit in drei verschiedenen Bearbeitungen; Gebäudesockel, Gebäudeecken und Fensterrahmen sind ebenfalls in Stein detailliert. Die Stufen der Treppengiebel sind allesamt mit bleiverkleideten Kupfer-Fialen versehen, sechs an der Zahl. Man griff hier auf Altbewährtes zurück,

above that turned into a mezzanine extension of the Banking Hall. The Hall itself, and the space above the switching station, became a 120-foot high «Dutch Gothic Town Hall» – at least when viewed from the street.

The result of all this is what looks like two closely related but separate buildings. The 120-foot high structure reads like a modernized, 16th century Town Hall; while the three-stepped, 800-foot high skyscraper next to it looks like its Big Brother.

It is a nicely detailed composition, rendered in red Swedish granite and topped by lead-coated copper roofs. Unfortunately, the requirements of the site and the program robbed the «Town Hall» of the arcades of Gothic arches you would expect to see at sidewalk level, and limited the fenestration to relatively small, square windows set into massively blank walls – a somewhat unhappy departure from the usual Gothic arcades, and a rather unfriendly face to the sidewalk. (Admittedly, few pedestrians in Houston use sidewalks, especially during the summer months; they prefer air-conditioned underground walkways, or air-conditioned limousines; but nearly blank walls some 60 feet high are just a trifle forbidding, nonetheless). Moreover, Johnson's monumental, 80 foot tall archway into the Banking Hall seems rather startling in this neo-Gothic setting – an odd departure for someone as faithful to the past as this architect... Still, despite these curious violations of historic precedents, the two buildings, side by side and joined by 225-foot long, glass-roofed arcades make a very remarkable couple.

For one thing, Johnson's pedestrian arcades in several of his urban, high-rise structures are a very welcome reminder of an urban prototype found in many European cities, but rarely encountered in the United States. For another, the huge skylit Banking Hall may be one of Johnson's most successful historic references, possibly to Otto Wagner's 1904 «Postsparkasse» in Vienna. If that was the point of departure, his Houston Banking Hall is a distinct improvement over the precedent. And, finally, the stepped profile of the office tower is an impressive departure from almost all the stepped high-rise silhouettes on American skylines, and far better than most of those shaped by zoning laws since the 1920s.

There is another difference between the Pennzoil Towers and their new neighbors across the street: Pennzoil is unmistakably glass and metal – smooth, sleek, slick, and as modern as you wanted to be in the 1970s. Whereas the Republic Bank is a tower (and appendage) clad in granite finished in three different ways, with stone details at its corners, at its base, and round its windows. The serrated roofline is further punctuated with 76 lead-coated copper obelisks or finials. The building represents a return

Außenansicht der Gesamtanlage

Exterior view of complex

nachdem sich in den siebziger Jahren mit neu entwickelten Beschichtungsmaterialien allerhand Probleme ergeben hatten. Unter den amerikanischen Architekten war Johnson führend in der Rückkehr zu traditionellen Baustoffen, vor allem bei diesem Gebäude und dem AT&T in Manhattan. Seit den zwanziger Jahren hatte sich kein amerikanisches Unternehmen mehr einen so grandiosen Sitz wie die Republic Bank errichten lassen – was Johnson, selbstredend, sehr zufrieden stimmt.

to tried and tested traditional materials, after some dramatic problems in the 1970s with new, cutting edge finishes that did not seem to work. Johnson probably was one of the architects in the U.S. who lead this return to traditional materials, both in this building and at AT&T, in Manhattan. Whatever the reason, American business has not built a corporate headquarters tower quite as grand as the Republic Bank since the 1920s; and Philip Johnson, needless to say, likes it a lot.

Progressive Architecture, February 1984
«The Tall Building Artistically Reconsidered», A. Huxtable, 1984
«Skyscrapers, Higher and Higher», Caroline Mierop, 1995

Innenansicht der Schalterhalle
Außenansicht der Schalterhalle

Interior view of banking hall
Exterior view of banking hall

53rd at Third – Lipstick Building

John Burgee Architects mit Philip Johnson
1984
New York, New York
Assoziierte Architekten: Emery Roth & Sons, P.C.
Statik: Office of Irwin G. Kantor, P.C.
Haustechnik: Cosentini Associates
Lichttechnik: Claude R. Engle

Ein Taxifahrer würde auf die Frage nach den bekanntesten Wolkenkratzern Manhattans wahrscheinlich das Empire State, das Chrysler, das Woolworth-Gebäude, das RCA-Gebäude im Rockefeller Center und das AT&T (mittlerweile Sony) aufzählen, sowie das «Lippenstift-Gebäude» Ecke 53. Straße und Third Avenue. Von diesen Bauten stammen zwei von Philip Johnson, und obwohl das Lipstick Building viele Jahrzehnte später entstand, wurde es alsbald zu einem ähnlichen Wahrzeichen wie das Empire State Building.

Ist es deswegen ein gutes Bauwerk? Nicht unbedingt – es hat aber als ein Stück Pop in der berühmten Skyline Manhattans durchaus seine Berechtigung. In seiner facettenreichen Karriere gibt Johnson hier eine weitere Kostprobe des architektonischen Spiels, das er nach der endgültigen Trennung von Mies van der Rohe so meisterhaft beherrschen lernte.

Dieses Spiel hat ihn von Schinkel bis Micky Maus geführt, mit zahllosen Probestücken nach Art von Claude-Nicolas Ledoux, Peter Behrens, Hermann Finsterlin, auch Le Corbusier, Alvar Aalto und Hans Scharoun, nicht zu vergessen Thomas Chippendale, Bertram Goodhue und Sir Charles Barry, selbst Jakow Tschernichow und viele und vieles mehr. Für jemand wie Johnson ist die Vorstellung absurd, daß die «Ideale Stadt» in Amerika wie ein Schema von Ludwig Hilberseimer auszusehen hätte. Amerika ist seinem ganzen Wesen nach vielschichtig – in kultureller, geographischer, ethnischer, linguistischer, wirtschaftlicher sowie politischer Hinsicht. Spätestens seit Ende der fünfziger Jahre muß die im architektonischen Sinne ideale amerikanische Stadt, laut Johnson, diese Vielschichtigkeit wiedergeben – wie entsetzlich langweilig wäre ein Hilberseimer nachempfundenes, ideales Manhattan. In seiner Idealvorstellung von der amerikanischen Stadt suchte Johnson nach der angemessenen Mischung aus Bauten und Typologien, Nutzern und Nutzungen sowie Volumen, Farbe, Form und Ausdruck. Mit der Abkehr von der Regelmäßigkeit eines Mies und seines Freunds Hilberseimer kam er erstaunlicherweise der Stadtbauvision von Jane Jacobs immer näher. In den sechziger Jahren rüttelte sie mit ihrem Buch «Tod und Leben großer amerikanischer Städte» die gesamte Architekten- und Planergemeinde

53rd At Third – Lipstick Building

John Burgee Architects with Philip Johnson
1984
New York, New York
Associate Architects: Emery Roth and Sons, P.C.
Structural Engineer: Office of Irwin G. Kantor, P.C.
Mechanical Engineer: Cosentini Associates
Lighting: Claude R. Engle

If you asked any New York cab driver to name the best known Manhattan skyscrapers, he would probably list the Empire State, the Chrysler, the Woolworth Building, the RCA Building in Rockefeller Center, the AT&T Building (now known as Sony) – and the Lipstick Building at East 53rd Street and Third Avenue. Two of those were designed by Philip Johnson, and even though the Lipstick Building was completed several decades later, it has become a «signature building» as recognizable as the Empire State. Does that make it a good building? Not necessarily – but it does make it a perfectly valid piece of pop on the best-known skyscraper skyline in the world. And in Johnson's many-faceted career, it is one more exercise in the architectural fun and games of which he came to be a master once he and Mies van der Rohe had separated and divorced.

This exercise has taken Johnson from Schinkel to Mickey Mouse, with dozens of stops in between: he has done buildings in the manner of Claude-Nicolas Ledoux, in the manner of Peter Behrens, in the manner of Herman Finsterlin, in the manner of Le Corbusier, in the manner of Alvar Aalto, in the manner of Hans Scharoun, in the manner of Thomas Chippendale, of Bertram Goodhue, of Sir Charles Barry, of Iakov Chernikhov – to mention only a few. To Johnson, the idea that an «Ideal City», in America, should look roughly like a diagram by Ludwig Hilberseimer seems absurd; the very nature of America is multi-faceted – culturally, geographically, ethnically, linguistically, economically, and politically. The architecturally ideal American city, to Johnson – at least after the 1950s – was just as multifaceted; and an Ideal Manhattan, as it might have been designed by Hilberseimer, would have been a crashing bore.

Johnson's vision of an appropriate American city became something very different – a mixture of buildings and building types, a mixture of images, a mixture of people and uses, a mixture of shapes and forms and colors. Oddly enough, as he drifted away from the regularity of Mies and his friend, Hilbs, Johnson came closer and closer to the vision first spelled out, in 1960, by Jane Jacobs, in «Life and Death of Great American Cities» – a book that stunned the community of modern architects and plan-

auf und legte damit womöglich den Grundstein für die Art von Postmoderne, die Robert Venturi und andere später propagierten.

Obwohl der erste (und zweite und dritte) Blick auf das Lipstick Building ein Schock ist, war es eigentlich keine Überraschung. Es sollte schockieren, und es sollte sich einprägen. Obwohl als reines Investitionsobjekt ohne bestimmte Zielgruppe entworfen, sieht es (schon fast zu) offensichtlich nach einer Rotunde für Revlon aus. In New York weiß sicher niemand, wo das Gebäude der American Bible Society steht (um ein beliebiges Beispiel zu nennen), ein gut geplantes, anonymes Bürohaus am Broadway von Skidmore, Owings & Merrill – das Lipstick Building hingegen kennt jeder, und das wird sich erst ändern, falls Johnson an der nächsten Ecke einen Wolkenkratzer in Form einer Colaflasche hinstellen sollte.

Das Lipstick weist über seine 34 elliptischen Stockwerke hinweg drei Rücksprünge auf, die der Bebauungsplan verlangte. Diese Vorschrift führt sonst zu den typischen Hochzeitstorten, die man mit New Yorker Spekulationsobjekten verbindet. Im Vergleich dazu wirken die Rücksprünge des Lipstick-Gebäudes aufgrund der elliptischen Grundform wesentlich eleganter. Der Zuschnitt der Geschoßflächen sorgt für ansprechende – und wohl auch funktionalere – Büroräume mit Aussicht.

Bänder aus rotem (geschliffenem) und rosa (geflammtem) schwedischem Granit fassen den Turm ein. Abwechselnd schmale und breite Edelstahlbänder trennen die unterschiedlichen Steinbänder und die graugetönten Fensterbänder. Die Technikaufbauten auf dem Dach sind ebenfalls mit Granit verkleidet.

Granit und Edelstahl kommen bei der Innenverkleidung der Lobby, die zu einem Drittel von einem hübschen Straßencafé genutzt wird, in ähnlicher Weise zum Einsatz, wobei die Oberflächen der Wände, Fußböden und Stützen eine individuelle Behandlung erfahren. Der erste, etwas grelle Eindruck, den das Gebäude macht, wird bei näherem Hinsehen durch die Material- und Oberflächenqualität gemildert. Es sticht zwar aus seiner Umgebung heraus, ist im Vergleich aber auch wesentlich eleganter. Die Architekten selbst richteten sich im 2. Stockwerk des Gebäudes ihr Büro ein (mittlerweile umgebaut), nach Johnsons Umzug aus dem obersten Geschoß des Seagram-Gebäudes.

ners, and probably laid the foundations for Robert Venturi's postmodernism, and that of others.

And so the Lipstick Building, though it shocked everyone the first or second or third time they saw it, should not have come as any kind of surprise. It was meant to shock, and it was meant to be remembered. Although it was designed as a commercial skyscraper without any specific tenant in mind, it obviously should have been the Revlon Rotunda, although that might have been a trifle obvious. While nobody in New York remembers the American Bible Society Building (for example) – a perfectly nice and anonymous office building on Broadway by Skidmore, Owings & Merrill – nobody is likely to forget the Lipstick Building, at least not until Johnson builds a skyscraper in the shape of a Coca Cola bottle somewhere down the street.

The Lipstick Building is 34 stories tall, and its elliptical floors are set back from Third Avenue in three steps to meet zoning requirements that usually produce the «wedding cake» profiles characteristic of speculative office buildings in New York. Because of the elliptical floor plans of the Lipstick Building, the setbacks are much more graceful than those found in routine commercial buildings. Moreover, the configuration of each floor makes for more interesting (and apparently much more efficient) office layouts and views out of the offices.

The tower is sheathed in rings of Swedish Imperial granite, red where it is polished, pink where it is flame-finished. There are also wide and narrow bands of brushed stainless steel, and gray-tinged ribbon windows. The mechanical tower on the top of the building is sheathed in granite too.

The lobby (a third of which is occupied by a very pleasant «sidewalk restaurant») is finished in a similar way, using granite and stainless steel in different finishes on floors, walls and columns. The slightly strident initial impression of the building is somehow overcome by the quality of materials and finishes at close quarters. It not only stands out from its neighbors – it is distinctly more elegant by comparison. The firm designed the building's 3rd floor for their own office (now demolished), after Johnson's move from the top floor of the nearby Seagram Building.

Architectural Record, September 1986
«American Architecture and Urbanism», revised edition, Vincent Scully, 1988

Seite 187: Außenansicht
Grundriß Erdgeschoß, 1:1000
Grundriß 2. Obergeschoß,
1:1000, Architekturbüro
Johnson/Burgee
Blick in die Lobby

Page 187: Exterior view
Ground floor plan, 1:1000
Third floor plan, 1:1000,
Johnson/Burgee offices
Lobby view

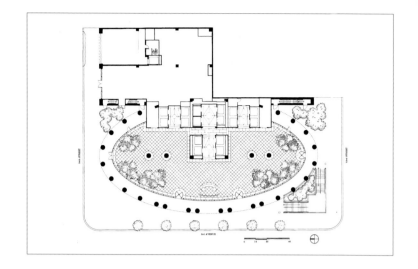

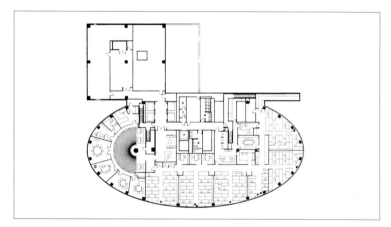

Dade County Kulturzentrum

Johnson/Burgee Architects
1977–1984
Miami, Florida
Assoziierte Architekten, Statik, Haustechnik:
Connell, Metcalf & Eddy
Landschaftsplanung: Stresau, Smith & Stresau
Lichttechnik: Claude R. Engle

Das Kulturzentrum nimmt eine Fläche von ca. 13.300 m²
ein und liegt im Verwaltungsviertel in der Innenstadt von
Miami. Es besteht aus drei Gebäuden – der Miami-Dade-
Stadtbibliothek, dem Zentrum der schönen Künste sowie
dem Historischen Museum von Südflorida – , die auf
einem 4,30 m hohen Sockel um einen ca. 3.000 m²
großen Platz angeordnet sind.
Aufgrund des hohen Grundwasserspiegels der Stadt sind
Parkplätze und Versorgungseinrichtungen ebenerdig in
dem Gebäudesockel untergebracht; die Gebäude und der
Platz liegen auf dem Sockel.
Die Anlage nimmt in ihrem Erscheinungsbild Bezug auf
Floridas erste Bauwerke im spanischen Kolonialstil, die
sich an Bauten der Mittelmeerregion anlehnten. Jedes
Gebäude weist einen abgeschrägten Steinsockel aus
Texas Cordova Muschelkalk auf, der mit verputzten Wän-
den und geneigten Ziegeldächern das Gesamtbild prägt.
Ein getreppter, schattiger Arkadengang neben einer Was-
serkaskade ist Teil der Erschließung.

Dade County Cultural Center

Johnson/Burgee Architects
1977–1984
Miami, Florida
Associate Architects, Structural Engineer, Mechanical
Engineer: Connell, Metcalf & Eddy
Landscape Architect: Stresau, Smith & Stresau
Lighting: Claude R. Engle

This 3.3 acre cultural center is located in Miami's downtown government center. The Cultural Center is divided into
four parts: The «Miami-Dade Public Library», the «Center
for the Fine Arts», the «Historical Museum of Southern
Florida» and a continuous 14 foot tall base for all parts.
Because of the city's high water table all parking and service functions are located at grade. Therefore, the buildings rest on top of the continuous base and are grouped
around a 33,000 square foot plaza.
The image of the complex relates to the Mediterranean
style in Florida's early Spanish colonial beginnings. All
buildings in the new Center have a canted masonry base
of Texas Cordova shell limestone with stucco walls and
terra cotta tile covered hip and gable roofs.
The buildings are linked by an arcaded and sloping ramp
with a parallel and gently cascading water pool.

Architectural Record, July 1978
«Philip Johnson/John Burgee Architecture 1979–1985»,
Carleton Knight, 1985
New York Times, January 12, 1984

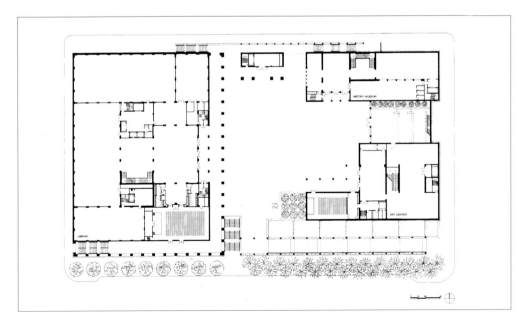

Grundriß der Platzebene, 1:1500
Blick auf die Bibliothek
Arkadengang und Wasserkaskade
führen zur Straße hinab

Plaza level floor plan, 1:1500
Exterior view of library
Water pool and arcaded ramp to
sidewalk level

AT&T Hauptsitz (Sony Gebäude)

Johnson/Burgee Architects
1979–1984
New York, New York
Assoziierte Architekten: Simmons Architects
Statik: Skilling, Helle,
Christiansen & Robertson Inc.
Haustechnik: Cosentini Associates
Lichttechnik: Claude R. Engle

Außer seinem Glashaus in New Canaan gibt es kaum etwas, das Philip Johnson bekannter gemacht hätte, als das Gebäude für die amerikanische Telefongesellschaft AT&T an der Madison Avenue in Manhattan. Es war auf dem Titelblatt so ziemlich jeder Illustrierten, von Time bis zum New Yorker, abgebildet und war überall Gegenstand zahlloser Debatten (und gewissen Spotts) unter Kritikern und Architekten, selbst in Singapur und weiß-Gott-wo.

Das Bauwerk ist aus mancherlei Gründen berühmt und berüchtigt. Erstens war es die augenfälligste «Unabhängigkeitserklärung», die Johnson Mies van der Rohe gegenüber machen und bauen konnte; es befindet sich ganz in der Nähe des 1957 entstandenen Seagam Building, an dem Johnson nicht unwesentlich beteiligt war, und könnte doch nicht weiter davon entfernt sein. Zweitens ist das AT&T mit seinem durchbrochenen Giebel einer der auffälligsten New Yorker Wolkenkratzer seit dem Empire State und dem Chrysler. Drittens erhebt sich das Bauwerk auf 18,30 m hohen Stützen, die einen grandiosen Arkadengang entlang des Bürgersteigs bilden (besser: bildeten – der neue Besitzer sah eine Ladennutzung vor und ließ die Arkade 1994 verglasen). Ein Arkadengang dieser Größenordnung in Verbindung mit einem 35,40 m hohen Bogen über dem Eingang – das hatte es seit Erfindung des Wolkenkratzers noch nicht gegeben, nicht einmal in New York. (Das Seagram-Gebäude steht auf ca. 7,30 m hohen Stützen und über einer Lobby mit ähnlicher Raumhöhe.) Viertens und letztens ließ man beim Bau des AT&T die Verwendung traditioneller Steinverkleidungen – in diesem Fall 13.000 Tonnen Granit – bei Bürohochhäusern wieder aufleben. Dies nach dem jahrzehntelangen Einsatz von Vorhangfassaden aus Glas und Metall, die, wie sich zeigte, in der Regel nicht gut alterten – die rühmliche Ausnahme bleibt Saarinens CBS-Gebäude an der Sixth Avenue.

Im wesentlichen gab es zwei Beweggründe für das Erscheinungsbild des AT&T. Zum einen war es der entschiedene Wunsch des Bauherrn, nicht noch eine Glaskiste entstehen zu lassen, und zum zweiten sproß eine historisierende Postmoderne in ganz Amerika pilzartig aus dem Boden, und Johnson hatte diese Entwicklung genaue-

AT&T Corporate Headquarters (Sony Building)

Johnson/Burgee Architects
1979–1984
New York, New York
Associate Architects: Simmons Architects
Structural Engineer: Skilling, Helle,
Christiansen & Robertson Inc.
Mechanical Engineer: Cosentini Associates
Lighting: Claude R. Engle

Few buildings other than his own glass house in Connecticut have made Philip Johnson's name as widely known as did the AT&T Building on Madison Avenue in Manhattan. Its image has been on the cover of just about every popular magazine from Time to the New Yorker; and it has been discussed (and sometimes derided) by critics and Johnson's fellow architects from New York to Singapore and beyond.

What has made the building so famous or so notorious is a number of facts: first, it was the most visible «Declaration of Independence» from Mies van der Rohe that Johnson had built. Located only a few hundred feet from Mies' 1957 Seagram Building (on which Johnson had significantly collaborated) it is about as different from Seagram as you could get without going underground. Secondly, AT&T, being topped by a broken apex pediment, is clearly the most identifiable skyscraper on the New York skyline since the Chrysler Building and the Empire State. Third, the building stands on 60 foot tall columns that form a majestic loggia at sidewalk level (or did so until filled in with shops by a new owner in 1994). A loggia of that dimension, flanking an entrance archway 116 feet tall, had been unheard of in New York or anywhere else since skyscrapers were invented. (The Seagram Building stands on 24 foot high columns, and over a lobby of similar height.) And, fourth, the AT&T Building resurrected the use of traditional masonry finishes in tall office buildings – in this case, 13,000 tons of granite – after decades of thin glass and metal curtain walls that did not always wear very well. (A significant exception in recent decades, was Saarinen's CBS Building on Sixth Avenue.)

The reason Johnson designed what he did at AT&T was twofold: first, his client had made it clear that he simply did not want «another glass box!» And, second, Johnson had been watching (and occasionally emulating) postmodern historicists popping up all over America, and decided that he could easily do as well as they, and possibly as well as McKim, Mead & White or Raymond Hood.

The AT&T Building may not be the best postmodern exercise built in the United States; but it is clearly the biggest and most visible. To understand the design of its principal

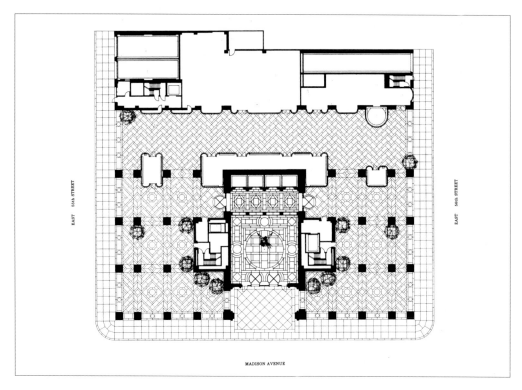

Grundriß Erdgeschoß, 1:750

Ground floor plan, 1:750

stens verfolgt (und ihr gelegentlich nachgeeifert). Er war überzeugt davon, daß er damit leicht mithalten und vielleicht sogar so gut wie Raymond Hood oder McKim, Mead & White werden könne.

Das AT&T-Gebäude ist nicht unbedingt das beste postmoderne Bauwerk Amerikas, mit Sicherheit ist es aber das größte und auffälligste. Die Gliederung der Hauptfassade wird von ihrem Standort an der Madison Avenue her verständlich. Die Straße ist zu schmal, um das Gebäude in voller Höhe betrachten zu können, es besteht deshalb konzeptionell aus drei Bauteilen – dem stattlichen, ca. 1350 m² umfassenden Arkaden- und Eingangsbereich im Blickfeld des Fußgängers, dem weithin sichtbaren Giebel und der dem Blick eher entzogenen Vorhangfassade.

Sowohl der Arkaden- und Eingangsbereich als auch der aufgebrochene Giebel sind als eigenständige, weithin sichtbare dramatische Elemente gelungen. Die Fassade ist weniger aufsehenerregend. Dem Gesamtentwurf wurde offensichtlich viel Überlegung gewidmet – es wäre interessant zu wissen, welche Alternativentwürfe Johnson erwogen haben mag.

Der Ausarbeitungsgrad der Details und Oberflächen ist,

facade, one must realize that Madison Avenue is quite narrow, so that one cannot really see the entire building from the sidewalk level. So it may have been designed to be three buildings: a stately 14,400 square foot loggia and entrance visible to pedestrians; a pediment to be visible from far away; and a curtain wall to be visible to almost nobody.

Both the loggia and the entrance, and the broken-apex pediment, are successful in their own ways: dramatic, and highly visible. The curtain wall is not especially interesting. Obviously a great deal of thought went into the design, and one wonders what alternatives Johnson considered.

As in most of Johnson's buildings, the finishes and details are admirably worked out. The pink granite used inside and out is from the Stony Creek Quarry in Connecticut; it has been given a polished finish in some areas. The «sky lobby» on the second floor is finished in a bright, white Breccia Strazzema marble. And elevator doors and similar details are of polished bronze.

But the most important contributions of the AT&T Building, curiously enough, are not the ones most immediately visible; here as in many other buildings in the

Grundriß 33. Obergeschoß (Chefetage), 1:750
Außenansicht
Aufzugstür im Foyer
Foyer mit Skulptur «Spirit of Electricity»

34th floor (executive floor) plan, 1:750
Exterior view
Lobby view with elevator
Lobby view with sculpture «Spirit of Electricity»

wie in vielen Bauten Johnsons, bewundernswert. Der rosafarbene Granit im Innen- und Außenbereich stammt aus dem Stony Creek Steinbruch in Connecticut, er wurde an ausgewählten Stellen in polierter Form verwendet. Die Oberflächen der «Sky Lobby» im ersten Obergeschoß bestehen aus Breccia Strazzema-Marmor. Aufzugstüren und verwandte Elemente wurden in polierter Bronzeverkleidung ausgeführt.

Das AT&T hat aber weitere Vorzüge, die nicht sogleich ins Auge fallen. Wie schon in einigen der früher entstandenen Bauten bemühte sich Johnson auch hier, Raum für den Fußgänger zu schaffen. Der Arkadengang entlang des Bürgersteigs stellte einen ungewöhnlich großzügigen, mit Stühlen, Tischen und Bänken möblierten Bereich von beinahe 1350 m^2 bereit. Auf der Gebäuderückseite befindet sich eine glasüberdachte, von Ladenbereichen gesäumte Passage, die als Querverbindung zwischen der 55. und 56. Straße dient. Diese nimmt eine Fläche von ca. 540 m^2 ein und ist 30,50 m hoch. Der Raum hat das angenehme Flair einer alten Londoner Passage.

Bemerkenswerterweise schenken weder die Architekturkritiker noch Johnson selbst dieser städtebaulichen Errungenschaft viel Aufmerksamkeit. Johnsons erfolgreicher Umgang mit Themen wie dem öffentlichen Innen- und Außenraum und der Fußgängererschließung ist mittlerweile, nach etlichen Aufträgen von städtebaulichem Ausmaß, schon fast so eindrucksvoll wie seine Architektur. Auch diesbezüglich gehört das AT&T womöglich zu den anregendsten Beiträgen zum New Yorker Geschehen.

later years of his career, Johnson created a series of pedestrian spaces. There is (or was) not only the extraordinarily generous space created by the loggia at sidewalk level – almost a third of an acre of pedestrian space, furnished with chairs, tables, and benches; there is also a «galleria» or arcade in the back of the office tower that links East 55th and 56th Streets, it is glass-roofed, and has stores lining it on both sides. This «galleria» is 5,800 square feet in area, and 100 feet high to the underside of the skylight; and it is as nice a pedestrian shopping street as any London arcade.

What makes these urbanistic accomplishments so remarkable is that neither Johnson nor the architecture critics reviewing his work ever pay much attention to them. Yet as Philip Johnson has become more and more involved in large-scale urban projects, his successes in dealing with such issues as pedestrian circulation and public outdoor and indoor spaces have become almost as impressive as his accomplishments in making architectural forms. The «footprint» of the AT&T Building may be one of its most interesting contributions to the New York scene.

Time, January 8, 1979
New York Times, March 31, 1979
New York Magazine, November 15, 1979
Architectural Record, October 1980
«Philip Johnson/John Burgee Architecture 1979–1985»,
Carleton Knight, 1985
Art in America, September 1984

580 California Street

Johnson/Burgee Architects
1983–1984
San Francisco, Kalifornien
Assoziierte Architekten: Kendall Heaton Associates Inc.
Statik: Skilling, Helle, Christiansen & Robertson Inc.
Haustechnik: I.A. Naman & Associates Inc.
Skulpturen: Muriel Costanis
Aluminiumelemente: S. Baird

Das von einem Investor errichtete Bürohaus aus 23 Geschossen hat einen klassischen dreiteiligen Aufbau. Ein offener, 9,10 m hoher und ca. 38 m langer Arkadengang entlang der Straße bildet den Sockel. Der «Schaft» mit massiv wirkenden Gebäudeecken ist eine granitverkleidete Lochfassade, die sich aus vertikal durchlaufenden Rundsäulen im Wechsel mit ausgebuchteten Elementen zusammensetzt.
Die quadratischen Geschoßflächen sind jeweils ca. 1450 m² groß. Das ca. 99 m hohe Gebäude endet in einer dreigeschossigen verglasten Schrägfassade, gefolgt von einem zurückgesetzten Technikgeschoß. Jede Fassadensäule trägt eine der drei 3,65 m hohen Statuen, die in einem Glasfasergußverfahren hergestellt wurden. Fialen aus Aluminium bekrönen das Dachgesims.

580 California Street

Johnson/Burgee Architects
1983–1984
San Francisco, California
Associate Architects: Kendall Heaton Associates Inc.
Structural Engineer:
Skilling, Helle, Christiansen & Robertson Inc.
Mechanical Engineer: I.A. Naman & Associates Inc.
Artist: Muriel Costanis
Aluminum Designs: S. Baird

This 23-story speculative office building organizes itself in a classic three part composition. The base is articulated as a continuous open colonnade 30 feet in height along its 125 foot street frontage. The shaft is a set of articulated heavy corner piers with punched windows in a granite-clad curtain wall, with the center an alternating series of cylindrical columns and curved bay windows.
The building is square in plan, with 15,500 square feet per floor. The top of the 325 foot tower is a 3 story canted glass curtain wall stepped back at the top (mechanical) floor. The top of the column carries 12 foot tall statues cast in fiberglass, and the edge of the cornice is decorated with aluminum finials.

Philip Johnson – A+U 1979
Architectural Design, 18–9/1979
«Philip Johnson/John Burgee Architecture 1979–1985»,
Carleton Knight, 1985

Grundriß Erdgeschoß, 1:1000
Grundriß Normalgeschoß, 1:1000
Außenansicht

Ground floor plan, 1:1000
Typical floor plan, 1:1000
Exterior view

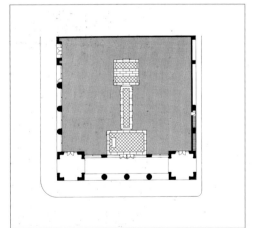
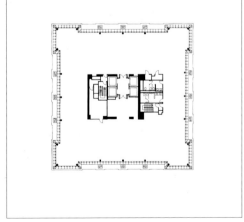

Geisterhaus

Philip Johnson
1984
New Canaan, Connecticut

Auf demselben Grund und Boden, auf dem auch das Glashaus steht, wurde diese Hülle errichtet, die die Form eines herkömmlichen Hauses hat, aber lediglich aus Stahl und Maschendraht besteht. Das Gebilde ist in gewisser Weise eine Hommage an einen Freund Johnsons, den Architekten Frank Gehry, der den Maschendraht zum bevorzugten Material der architektonischen Avantgarde erkor. Das 5 m x 6,40 m große «Haus» hat die Aufgabe, eine Blumenaussaat vor Verbiß durch umherstreifendes Rotwild zu schützen. Entlang seiner Mittelachse klafft eine Öffnung. Es ruht auf einem alten Fundamentstreifen, dem letzten Überrest des Farmhauses, das ursprünglich auf dem Grundstück stand.

Ghost House

Philip Johnson
1984
New Canaan, Connecticut

This enclosure on the grounds of the Glass House is built in the shape of a gabled house, but made of chain link and steel. The structure is a tribute to Johnson's friend, the architect Frank Gehry, who elevated chain link fencing to the status of avant-garde architecture. The function of this 16.5 x 21 feet «house» was to protect the flower garden within from roaming deer. It is split down the middle, and rests on foundations left from the original farm house on the property.

«Philip Johnson, The Glass House», David Whitney 1993
«Light Architecture», Terence Riley, 1995

Ansicht der Ostseite

East elevation

Lincoln Kirstein Turm
Philip Johnson
1985
New Canaan, Connecticut

Mit diesem Turm von 9,30 m Höhe, der sich unterhalb des Glashauses in der Nähe des Teiches befindet, zollt Johnson seinem verstorbenen Freund, dem Dichter und Gründer des New York City Ballets, Lincoln Kirstein, Tribut. Johnson hatte für ihn das New York State Theater am Lincoln Center gebaut. Als Vorlage für den Turm diente ihm ein eigener Entwurf aus dem Jahre 1955 – eine freistehende Treppe am Meteorkrater in Arizona, die als Aussichtsplattform genutzt wird. Die willkürlich plazierten, künstlichen Ruinen romantischer englischer Landschaftsgärten aus dem 18. Jahrhundert mögen eine zusätzliche Bezugsquelle gewesen sein.

Lincoln Kirstein Tower
Philip Johnson
1985
New Canaan, Connecticut

This 30 feet tower near the pond of the Glass House is a tribute to Johnson's friend, the late Lincoln Kirstein, the poet and founder of the New York City Ballet, for whom Johnson built the New York State Theater at Lincoln Center. The precedent for this design is the free standing stair at meteor crater in Arizona, used as an observation platform, and designed by Johnson in 1955. The other inspirations are the artificial eighteenth century ruins which dotted the romantic English landscape gardens.

House & Garden, June 1986
«Philip Johnson – The Glass House», D. Whitney, 1993

Lincoln Kirstein Turm mit Glashaus im Hintergrund

Exterior view with Glass House in background

500 Boylston Street
Johnson/Burgee Architects
1983–1985
Boston, Massachusetts
Statik: LeMessurier Associates/SCI
Haustechnik: Cosentini Associates
Landschaftsplanung: Zion & Breen
Lichttechnik: Claude R. Engle

Der sechsgeschossige Sockelbau dieses Bürokomplexes nimmt die gesamte Grundstücksfläche ein, in dessen rückwärtigem Bereich sich ein Bürohochhaus mit 25 Stockwerken erhebt. Am Haupteingang weist der Sockel einen ca.1150 m² großen Einschnitt in Form einer Arena auf, der als Eingangshof dient.
Ursprünglich sah der Entwurf zwei parallele Türme vor. Das postmodern-klassizistische Erscheinungsbild war aber so umstritten, daß der Auftrag für den zweiten Turm an Robert A.M. Stern Architects weitergegeben wurde.
Die neo-klassizistische Hülle spannt sich zwischen regelmäßigen Stützfeldern im Abstand ca. 4,90 m auf. Die Stützen sind mit Pilastern aus Stein verkleidet und die Zwischenfelder bestehen aus zweigeschossigen Fassadenelementen, die die Vertikale betonen und für einen Maßstabswechsel sorgen. Die Gliederung der Hauptfassade wird von einem mittig angeordneten, vertikal durchlaufenden Fassadenelement aus Glas bestimmt, das ein Bogen mit ca. 18,30 m Durchmesser nach oben abschließt. Er bildet gleichzeitig die Stirnseite eines Tonnengewölbes, das die Haustechnik beherbergt.

500 Boylston Street
Johnson/Burgee Architects
1983–1985
Boston, Massachusetts
Structural Engineer: LeMessurier Associates/SCI
Mechanical Engineer: Cosentini Associates
Landscape Architect: Zion & Breen
Lighting: Claude R. Engle

A 25 story speculative office building with a 6 floor base that continues to the edges of the site and is then cut away at the main entry for a 12,500 square feet encircled hemicycle plaza.
It was a originally planned as a pair of parallel towers, but due to intense controversy about its post-modern classical image, the second tower was finished by Robert A.M. Stern Architects.
The building uses a neo-classical vocabulary based on a 16 foot column bay system. Between pilasters on this system is a curtain wall infill articulated as a two-story system for a vertical emphasis and scale change. The entire composition is centered by a vertically continuous central curtain wall bay ending in a 60 foot diameter vaulted mechanical penthouse.

«Boston Architecture 1975–1990»,
Miller & Morgan, 1990
«Johnson/Burgee Architecture 1979–1985»,
Carleton Knight, 1985

Grundriß Normalgeschoß
des Bürohochhauses,
1:1000
Grundriß Erdgeschoß,
1:1000

Typical floor plan of tower,
1:1000
Ground floor plan, 1:1000

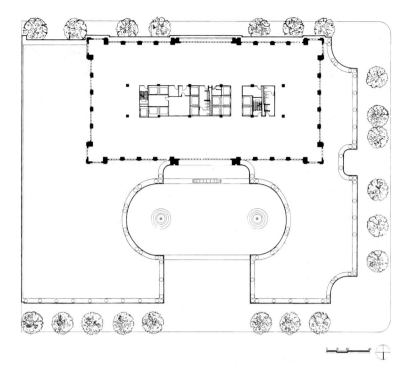

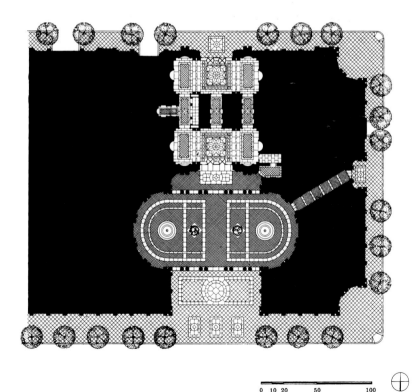

0 10 20   50   100

Außenansicht mit der Trinitäts-Kirche im Vordergrund

Exterior view, Trinity Church in foreground

Blick in den Eingangshof

Exterior view of entry and plaza

Architekturfakultät der Universität Houston

Johnson/Burgee Architects
1985
Houston, Texas
Assoziierte Architekten: Morris * Aubry Architects
Statik: CBM Engineers,Inc.
Haustechnik: Cook & Holle Inc.
Lichttechnik: Claude R. Engle

Das vernünftigste, was ein Architekt mit einem Auftrag für eine Architekturfakultät machen kann, ist, ihn nicht anzunehmen. Die Nutzer verreißen das Resultat so oder so, wenn sie es nicht gar anzuzünden versuchen. Die Professoren, von denen jeder einzelne von seiner weitaus besseren Qualifikation überzeugt ist, kümmern sich darum, daß das Bauwerk als Fehlschlag in Verruf kommt und daß der Ruf des Architekten damit ruiniert wird. Generationen von Studenten schließen die Reihen mit der zur Lynchjustiz wild entschlossenen Lehrerschaft und verspritzen noch ein wenig eigenes Gift.

Philip Johnson wandte eine brillante Strategie an, um vorhersehbaren Auseinandersetzungen mit der Fakultät und den Studenten aus dem Weg zu gehen. Anstatt zum Bau eines Johnson-Gebäudes entschloß er sich zum Nachbau eines der großen Entwürfe vergangener Zeiten – um genau zu sein, dem Haus der Erziehung, das Claude-Nicolas Ledoux um 1770 herum im Zuge seiner Idealen Stadt von Chaux entworfen, aber nie gebaut hatte. Johnson baute es nun, zweihundert Jahre später, aus Ziegel, Kalksandstein und Granit, versah es mit einem kupferge-

School of Architecture, University of Houston

Johnson/Burgee Architects
1985
Houston, Texas
Associate Architects: Morris * Aubry Architects
Structural Engineer: CBM Engineers, Inc.
Mechanical Engineer: Cook & Holle Inc.
Lighting: Claude R. Engle

Any time an architect is commissioned to design a building for a School of Architecture, the smartest thing to do is to turn down the opportunity. Whatever you do, the users are going to shred what you have done and probably try to burn it down: the faculty members (each of whom thinks he or she could have done a better job) will make sure your building will fail, and demolish your reputation in the process; and the students – several generations of them – will join the faculty lynch mob and add their own brand of venom to that of the faculty.

When Philip Johnson was asked to design the new School of Architecture at the University of Houston, he was not a faculty member, and was not likely to be one. Still, to avoid predictable problems with faculty and students, he decided on a brilliant strategy: instead of designing a Johnson building, he decided to build a replica of a great design of the past – specifically, Claude-Nicolas Ledoux' House of Education designed, in the 1770s, for his Ideal City of Chaux. Ledoux's House of Education was never built, but the Johnson replica was constructed more than two hundred years later, of brick, Indiana limestone, and

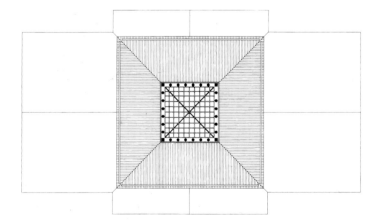

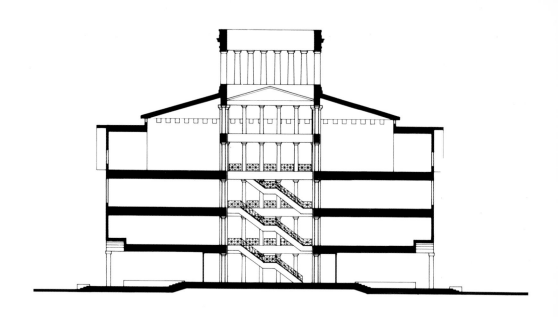

Normalgeschoß, 1:1000
Schnitt, 1:1000
Außenansicht

Typical floor plan, 1:1000
Building section, 1:1000
Exterior view

deckten Dach, einer Aufzugsanlage, einem Computerzentrum und noch so einigem mehr.

Ledoux' Entwurf eignet sich für eine Architekturschule besonders gut. Am Schnittpunkt des kreuzförmigen Grundrisses befindet sich ein viergeschossiger, von Galerien gesäumter Innenhof, von dem aus Unterrichts-, Atelier- und Büroräume erschlossen werden. Einige Atelierräume sind zum Hof hin offen. Ein Arkadengang umgibt diesen zentralen Innenhof, der Lehrern und Studenten als Treffpunkt dient. Ein großes Oberlicht sorgt für die Ausleuchtung des Raumes.

Johnsons Fassung des Ledoux'schen Projekts weicht in zwei wesentlichen Punkten von der Vorlage ab. Im Vergleich zum Originalentwurf steht das Bauwerk zum einen nicht auf einem Podium, sondern sitzt direkt auf dem Erdboden auf. Zum anderen wurde die offene Säulenhalle, die das Gebäude bekrönt, quadratisch und nicht rund ausgeführt. Weitere Unterschiede finden sich im Maßstab und vor allem in der Befensterung. Abweichungen dieser Art wirken sich nicht immer vorteilhaft aus. Im großen und ganzen gibt das Gebäude im Erscheinungsbild jedoch eine vornehme Architekturschule ab. Und da Ledoux schon lange nicht mehr unter uns weilt, hat er von den Architekturkritikern unserer Zeit nichts zu befürchten.

granite, with a copper roof, elevators, a computer center, and much, much more.

Ledoux's scheme seems to work very well for a School of Architecture: it is cruciform in plan, and has a four-story high atrium at its center, where the wings intersect. All the classrooms, studios and offices are accessible from galleries that ring the atrium. Some of the studios are open to the central atrium; and the latter is an arcaded public space that brings all the students and teachers together. It is lit through a tall skylight, and works very well as a central plaza.

Johnson's version of Ledoux's project differs from the original in two significant respects: unlike the original sketch, it has no podium, and so the building sits directly on the ground. And unlike the original, Johnson's building is crowned with a square instead of a circular colonnade. There are other differences in scale and especially in fenestration; and these departures from the original are not always improvements. Still, the resulting building is a fine School of Architecture; and since Ledoux has been dead for some time, he has little to fear from today's architecture critics.

Architecture, March 1986
Architectural Record, September 1986

Innenhof mit Treppenanlage

Interior view of atrium and stairs

190 South LaSalle Street

John Burgee Architects mit Philip Johnson
1985–1986
Chicago, Illinois
Assoziierte Architekten: Shaw & Associates, Inc.
Statik: Cohen, Barreto, Marchertas, Inc.
Haustechnik: Cosentini Associates, Inc.
Lichttechnik: Claude R. Engle

Der Freimaurertempel von Burnham and Root, der im Jahre 1892 zerstört wurde, bildet die Vorlage für dieses 42-geschossige Bürohochhaus. Das Gebäude hat einen rechteckigen Grundriß mit einer Geschoßfläche von jeweils 2070 m². Die Verkleidung des fünfgeschossigen Gebäudesockels besteht aus poliertem, rosafarbenem Granit und nimmt auf die Gesimshöhen an der LaSalle Street Bezug. Der Bogen über dem Eingang ist 15,20 m hoch und öffnet sich auf eine 16,80 m hohe, 12,20 m breite und 54,90 m lange Lobby hin, deren Gewölbedecke mit Blattgold belegt ist. Die Oberflächen der Wände und Fußböden bestehen aus poliertem Marmor. Die Raumachse der Lobby wird am Nordende von einer Nische begrenzt, in der eine Bronzeskulptur von Anthony Caro steht.

Der Fassadenrhythmus wird vom Wechsel zwischen den Teilen mit geflammter Granitverkleidung und Lochfenstern und den zweigeschossig verglasten Elementen, die die vertikale Proportionierung betonen, bestimmt. Der vier Geschosse hohe obere Abschluß des Gebäudes besteht aus ineinander verschnittenen, kupfergedeckten Satteldächern.

Im dem nach Süden ausgerichteten Giebel befindet sich, unter einer Gewölbedecke, eine juristische Bibliothek, die für einen der Hauptmieter des Gebäudes eingerichtet wurde.

190 South LaSalle Street

John Burgee Architects with Philip Johnson
1985–1986
Chicago, Illinois
Associate Architects: Shaw & Associates, Inc.
Structural Engineer: Cohen, Barreto, Marchertas, Inc.
Mechanical Engineer: Cosentini Associates, Inc.
Lighting: Claude R. Engle

This 42 story office building was inspired by the destroyed 1892 Masonic Temple designed by Burnham and Root. The building is rectangular in plan, a typical floor containing 22,200 square feet. The five-story base of the building is faced with polished pink granite to match intermediate cornice lines along LaSalle Street. The entrance is an arched doorway 50 feet high opening into a gold leafed vaulted lobby 55 feet high, 40 feet wide and 180 feet long. Floors and walls are finished in polished marble. A bronze sculpture by Anthony Caro ends the north axis and niche of the lobby.

The facade alternates between a punched window pattern in a flamed granite curtain wall, and a glass curtain wall in two story modules to give a greater verticality to its proportions. The four story top is a series of intersecting gable roofs clad in copper. Inside the south gable, there is a vaulted law library designed for a major tenant.

Award: Structural Engineers Association of Illinois, Certificate of Honor, 1986

Architecture, May 1988
Metropolitan Review, November/December 1988

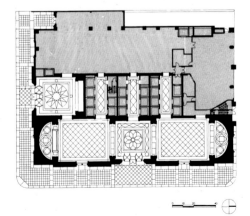

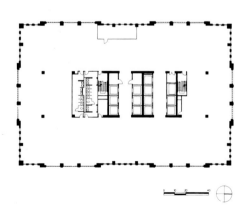

Grundriß Erdgeschoß, 1:1000
Grundriß Normalgeschoß, 1:1000
Grundriß Dachgeschoß
mit Bibliothek, 1:1000
Innenansicht der Lobby

Ground floor plan, 1:1000
Typical floor plan, 1:1000
Top floor plan with law library, 1:1000
Lobby view

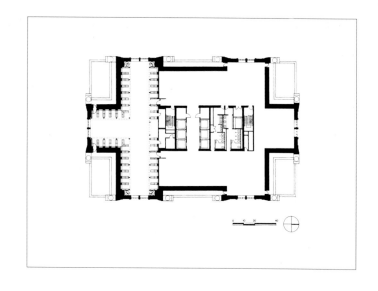

Außenansicht

Exterior view

One Atlantic Center (IBM Tower)
John Burgee Architects mit Philip Johnson
1985–1987
Atlanta, Georgia
Assoziierte Architekten: Heery Architects & Engineers, Inc.
Statik: Datum/Moore Partnership
Haustechnik: Blum Consulting Engineers
Lichttechnik: Claude R. Engle

Das 50-geschossige Hochhaus ähnelt in seinem Erscheinungsbild den neogotischen Wolkenkratzern aus dem New York der zwanziger Jahre. Der quadratische Grundriß nimmt pro Regelgeschoß eine Fläche von ca. 2250 m² ein. Die optische Gliederung der Fassade nach jeweils drei Geschossen betont die Vertikale, wirkt großzügiger im Maßstab und erzielt einen hohen Glasanteil. Ein insgesamt 30,50 m hohes kupfergedecktes Dach, das von einer Laterne bekrönt wird, bildet den oberen Gebäudeabschluß. Die Gesamthöhe des Gebäudes beträgt ca. 250 m.
Ein ca. 12200 m² großer Grünbereich mit Brunnen umgibt das Bauwerk. Der Brunnen dient gleichzeitig als Vorführbühne und Amphitheater. Das zugehörige Parkhaus liegt auf der gegenüberliegenden Straßenseite und bietet Raum für 2000 Kraftfahrzeuge, verteilt über zehn Geschosse.

One Atlantic Center (IBM Tower)
John Burgee Architects with Philip Johnson
1985–1987
Atlanta, Georgia
Associate Architects: Heery Architects & Engineers, Inc.
Structural Engineer: Datum/Moore Partnership
Mechanical Engineer: Blum Consulting Engineers
Lighting: Claude R. Engle

This 50-story office building is similar in composition to the New York neo-gothic skyscrapers of the 1920s. Its plan is square, and a typical floor contains 24,000 square feet. The placement of the windows into three story modules gives the facade a vertical emphasis and a larger scale, while providing an abundance of glass. The 100 foot tall copper roof with its lantern, completes the building. The overall height is 825 feet.
Next to the building is a three-acre green park with a fountain which also serves as a performance platform and amphitheater. The parking garage for the project is located across the street from the tower and can hold 2,000 cars in ten stories.

Architecture, January 1988
Paul Goldberger, New York Times, May 8, 1988

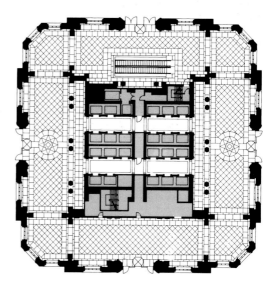

Grundriß Erdgeschoß, 1:1000

Ground floor plan, 1:1000

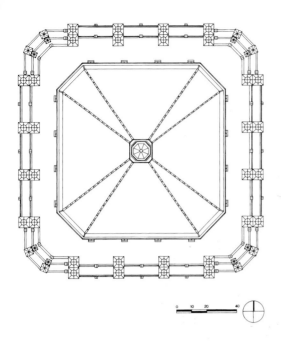

Dachaufsicht, 1:750
Grundriß Normalgeschoß, 1:750

Roof plan, 1:750
Typical floor plan, 1:750

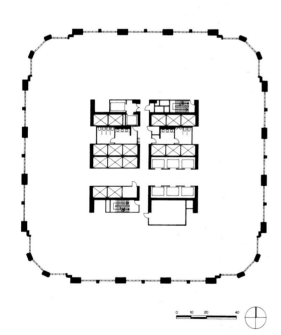

One und Two International Place
am Fort Hill Square

John Burgee Architects mit Philip Johnson
1983–1988 (One International Place)
1988–1992 (Two International Place)
Boston, Massachusetts
Statik: McNamara/Salvia Inc.
Haustechnik: Cosentini Associates
Lichttechnik: Claude R. Engle

Der Bürokomplex International Place besteht aus sechs deutlich ablesbaren Volumina, darunter zwei Hochhäusern, und paßt sich der unregelmäßigen Topographie der Umgebung an. Das Gebäudeensemble umschließt einen zentralen Innenhof und wirkt wie eine «dorfähnliche» Anordnung. Die zylindrischen und rechteckigen Baukörper scheinen einander in verschiedenen Winkeln zu durchdringen, was den Maßstab der Gesamtanlage auflockert und mit dem unregelmäßigen Straßenraster der Innenstadt Bostons korrespondiert.

Drei deutlich voneinander verschiedene Muster prägen das Fassadenbild des ersten Bauabschnitts – die Oberflächen der Kreisbauten erhielten einen großmaßstäblichen Raster aus Granit und Glas, im Übergangsbereich der zylindrischen Türme wurde ein kleinteiligerer Raster aus Spiegelglas eingesetzt, und den rechteckigen, massiven Gebäudesockel kennzeichnen Lochfenster im Palladio-Stil. Letztere waren aufgrund ihrer seriellen Verwendung heftigst umstritten, bildeten sie doch einen krassen Gegensatz zur Standardtapete der Nachbarbauten.

Im Innenbereich der Lobbies kommen neoklassizistische Details unter Verwendung diverser Marmorarten zum Einsatz. Im Innenhof steht ein Brunnen, der von einem konisch zulaufenden Glasdach überdeckt wird.

One and Two International Place
at Fort Hill Square

John Burgee Architects with Philip Johnson
1983–1988 (One International Place)
1988–1992 (Two International Place)
Boston, Massachusetts
Structural Engineer: McNamara/Salvia Inc.
Mechanical Engineer: Cosentini Associates
Lighting: Claude R. Engle

International Place consists of two office towers broken into six distinct volumes that follow the irregular perimeter of the site. The buildings enclose a central atrium space between them, establishing a «village-like» assembly of office towers. The volumes of the towers are either cylinders or rectangles that appear to intersect each other in various different angles with the objective of breaking down the scale of the complex.

The facades for Part I were three distinct patterns: (1) a large scale grid of granite and glass at the cylindrical face, (2) a smaller grid of mirrored glass where «cut-outs» of the cylinder occur and (3) at the base is a solid block with punched windows of Palladian motifs. The latter window in its repetitive figures across the building was quite controversial for it departed from the typical «wallpaper» cladding of nearby office buildings.

The interior lobbies are articulated in neo-classical detailing using various marbles. The central atrium space is a conical glass skylight above a central fountain.

«Three New Skyscrapers», Arthur Drexler,
Museum of Modern Art, 1983
Robert Campbell, Boston Globe, November 6, 1992

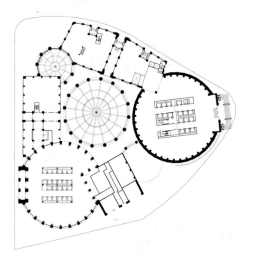

Grundriß Erdgeschoß, 1:2000

Ground floor plan, 1:2000

Außenansicht One International Place
Ansicht aus der Gegenrichtung
Blick in den Innenhof

Exterior view of One International Place
Exterior view from opposite direction
Interior view of central atrium

191 Peachtree Tower

John Burgee Architects mit
Philip Johnson (Beratung)
1987–1991
Atlanta, Georgia
Assoziierte Architekten: Kendall/Heaton Associates
Statik: CBM Engineers Inc.
Haustechnik: I.A. Naman & Associates, Inc.
Lichttechnik: Claude R. Engle

Eingehüllt in Granit und Glas ragt das 50-geschossige
Bürohochhaus mit ca. 112.000 m² Gesamtgeschoßfläche
235 m hoch in den Himmel über Atlanta. Die Gebäudeecken sind symmetrisch zurückversetzt, und die Gebäudemitte erhielt im Grundriß eine Einschnürung, um die
Gebäudemasse optisch leichter und wie zwei getrennte
Türme erscheinen zu lassen. Beide Türme werden jeweils
von einem Tempel in der Manier von Hawksmoore bekrönt. Das 18,30 m hohe, 30,50 m breite quadratische
Atrium in der Sockelzone des Turms dient als Eingangsbereich und wird durch ein Oberlicht ausgeleuchtet. Ein
für 1600 Kraftwagen ausgelegtes Parkhaus wurde an den
Komplex angeschlossen und erhielt eine Fassade aus Ortbeton.

191 Peachtree Tower

John Burgee Architects,
Philip Johnson Consultant
1987–1991
Atlanta, Georgia
Associate Architects: Kendall/Heaton Associates
Structural Engineer: CBM Engineers Inc.
Mechanical Engineer: I.A. Naman & Associates, Inc.
Lighting: Claude R. Engle

Clad in granite and glass, this 1.2 million square foot, 50-
story office tower in Atlanta rises 770 feet, and is crowned
by twin temple forms in the manner of Hawksmoore. In
plan the building sets back symmetrically on the corners,
to reduce its visual mass and to create the appearance of
two adjacent towers. The base of the tower has a 60-foot
tall skylit atrium entrance measuring 100 feet square in
plan. A parking garage for 1,600 cars with a precast concrete facade was built on an adjoining site.

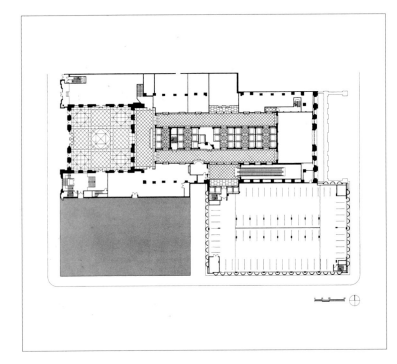

Grundriß Erdgeschoß, 1:1500,
mit dem angeschlossenen
Parkhaus

Ground floor plan showing
through-block site with adjacent
parking garage, 1:1500

Außenansicht
Innenansicht des Atriums
Dachaufsicht, 1:1500
Grundriß Normalgeschoß, 1:1500

Exterior view
Interior view of atrium
Roof plan, 1:1500
Typical floor plan, 1:1500

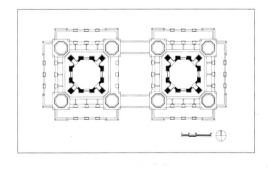

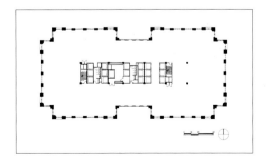

Kanadisches Rundfunk- und Fernsehzentrum

John Burgee Architects mit
Philip Johnson (Beratung)
1989–1992
Toronto, Kanada
Assoziierte Architekten: Scott Associates Architects
Statik: Quinn and Dressel Associates
Haustechnik:
Smith and Anderson Consulting Engineers

Das 10 Geschosse hohe Kanadische Rundfunk- und Fernsehzentrum (Geschoßfläche ca. 149.000 m²) dient der Canadian Broadcasting Corporation als Hauptsitz mit Büro- und Studionutzung. Die Büroräume liegen an einem großzügigen Atrium mit Glasdach, in dem ein Treppenturm steht, der mit Stahlpaneelen ummantelt ist. Die einzelnen Studios sind von außen sichtbar und werden vom rot-weißen Raster der Fassade durchkreuzt. Das Gebäude hat öffentlich zugängliche Zuschauerräume im Erdgeschoß.

Canadian Broadcasting Center

John Burgee Architects,
Philip Johnson Consultant
1987–1992
Toronto, Ontario
Associate Architects: Scott Associates Architects
Structural Engineer: Quinn and Dressel Associates
Mechanical Engineer:
Smith and Anderson Consulting Engineers

The Canadian Broadcasting Center serves as a headquarters for the 10-story (1,600,000 square feet) Canadian Broadcasting Corporation, and integrates office space with broadcast studios. The offices are grouped around a large, skylit atrium with a steel panelled stairtower. On the exterior, the broadcast studios are treated as discrete elements intersecting the white and red grid of the building. The building operates as a civic center as well, with ground floor viewing galleries for the public.

The Globe and Mail, April 25, 1992
The Globe and Mail, September 10, 1993

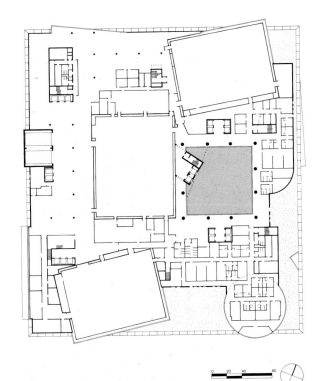

Grundriß 8. Obergeschoß mit
Hauptstudioräumen und Atrium, 1:1500

Floor 9 plan showing major studios and
atrium, 1:1500

Schnitt durch Atrium, 1:500
Außenansicht mit Haupteingang

Section at atrium, 1:500
Exterior view at main entry

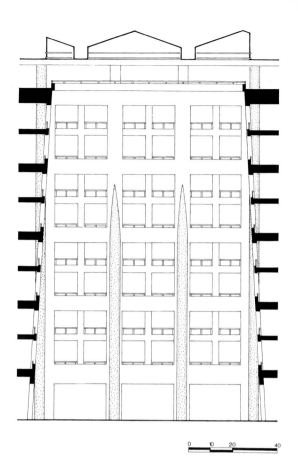

0   10   20   40

Wissenschaftsbibliothek der Ohio State Universität

John Burgee Architects
mit Philip Johnson (Beratung)
1987–1992
Columbus, Ohio
Assoziierte Architekten: Collins, Reimer and
Gordon Architects, Inc.
Statik: Korda Nemeth Engineering, Inc.
Haustechnik: M-E Engineering, Inc.

Die Gesamtanlage besteht aus dem siebengeschossigen Mathematikgebäude, einem benachbarten zweigeschossigen Unterrichtsgebäude und der viergeschossigen Wissenschaftsbibliothek. Die Fassade besteht aus einer roten Ziegelschale mit in Schichtbauweise aufgesetzten römischen Bogen, ähnlich der kunstvollen Mauerwerkstechnik, die von der englischen Arts and Crafts-Bewegung zu Beginn des 20. Jahrhunderts verwendet wurde. Abdeckungen und Einfassungen sind mit Granit abgesetzt, Fensterrahmen und Eingangstüren bestehen aus Edelstahl.

Ohio State University Science Library

John Burgee Architects,
Philip Johnson Consultant
1987–1992
Columbus, Ohio
Associate Architects: Collins, Reimer, and
Gordon Architects, Inc.
Structural Engineer: Korda Nemeth Engineering, Inc.
Mechanical Engineer: M-E Engineering, Inc.

This complex, also called Brown Hall Annex, consists of a seven story mathematics building, with an adjacent two story classroom building and a four story science library. They are clad in red brick, with arches applied to the exterior in layers of brick work inspired by 20th century British Arts and Crafts decorative masonry work. Granite is used for copings and trim for a contrasting color, and window frames and entrance doors are stainless steel.

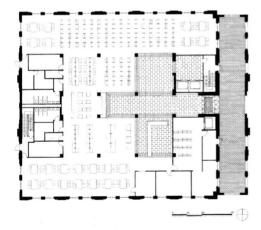

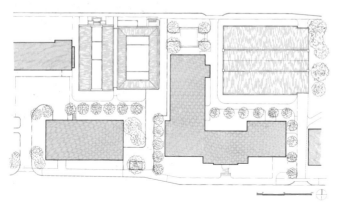

Grundriß Erdgeschoß der Wissenschafts-
bibliothek, 1:750
Lageplan, 1:2000, neue Gebäude in der
Dachaufsicht schraffiert angelegt

Ground floor plan of science library, 1:750
Site plan with new buildings' roofs rendered
in hatched, 1:2000

Außenansicht des Mathematikgebäudes mit dem
Unterrichtsgebäude im Vordergrund
Außenansicht der Wissenschaftsbibliothek

Exterior view of seven story math building with
classroom building in foreground
Exterior view of four story science library

Rundfunkmuseum

John Burgee Architects
mit Philip Johnson (Beratung)
1989–1992
New York, New York
Statik: Irwin Cantor P.C.
Haustechnik: Cosentini Associates
Lichttechnik: Claude R. Engle

Das Museum für Rundfunk und Fernsehen hat ein für ein Museum ungewöhnliches Raumprogramm. Es beherbergt nicht die üblichen, von Menschenhand geschaffenen Objekte verschiedener Kulturen, sondern Rundfunk- und Fernsehaufzeichnungen, die hier gelagert und gezeigt werden. Daher finden sich hier keine Ausstellungsräume. (Im Erdgeschoß wurden dennoch ein paar großzügigere Hallen zur Ausstellung von Schaubildern eingerichtet, in denen das Museum auch Veranstaltungen abhalten kann.) Das Gebäude nimmt 16 Geschosse ein, auf denen zum Teil auch Büroräume untergebracht sind, die an Stiftungen und ähnliche Gruppen vermietet werden. Die Rücksprünge des Baukörpers passen sich den benachbarten Stadthäusern und Geschäftsbauten an. Die Kalksandsteinfassade erinnert in den Details und der Oberflächenbehandlung an Goodhues State Capitol in Lincoln, Nebraska.

Museum of Broadcasting

John Burgee Architects,
Philip Johnson Consultant
1989–1992
New York, New York
Structural Engineer: Irwin Cantor P.C.
Mechanical Engineer: Cosentini Associates
Lighting: Claude R. Engle

The Museum of Broadcasting (or Museum of Television and Radio) has a unique program in that it does not house cultural artifacts, but stores and displays recordings of radio and television broadcasts. The interior of the museum, therefore, does not contain exhibit rooms (although the ground floor does have some monumentally scaled halls to display some images, and to accommodate the museum's social functions).

The 16 story building, which also contains offices rented by foundations and other special tenants, steps back in its mass to relate to the neighboring row of townhouses and commercial structures. The limestone exterior recalls some of the details and finishes of Goodhue's State Capitol in Lincoln, Nebraska.

Architecture and Urbanism, January 1993

Grundriß Untergeschoß mit Theater, 1:500
Grundriß Erdgeschoß mit Ausstellungshalle, 1:500

Plan lower level with theater, 1:500
Ground floor plan with exhibition hall, 1:500

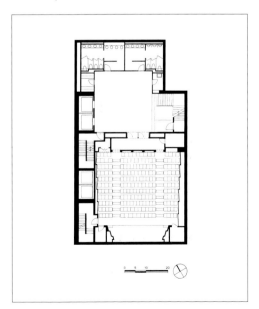

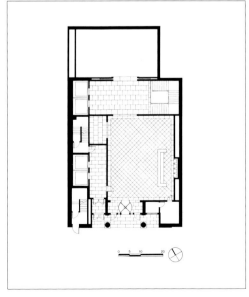

Haupteingang
Grundriß 1. Obergeschoß mit
Veranstaltungsräumen, 1:500
Grundriß 3. Obergeschoß mit
Bibliothek, 1:500

Main entrance
First floor plan with lecture halls,
1:500
Third floor plan with library, 1:500

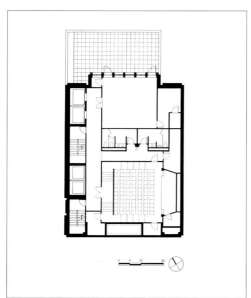

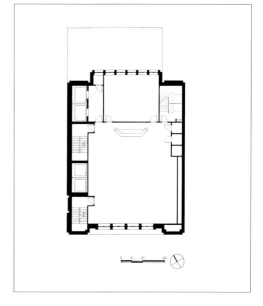

225

Puerta de Europa
John Burgee Architects
mit Philip Johnson (Beratung)
1991–1995
Madrid, Spanien
Assoziierter Architekt: Pedro Sentieri Cardillo
Statik: Leslie E. Robertson Associates
Haustechnik: Goymar Ingenieros Consultores, S.A.

Das Bürohausprojekt sitzt rittlings über der Paso de la
Castellana in Madrid. Der Entwurf, der an den Russischen
Konstruktivismus eines Lissitzky oder Melnikov (vielleicht
gar Tatlins Denkmal der Dritten Internationalen) anknüpft,
ist nicht willkürlich entstanden. Wie der Zufall so will, befindet sich unter einem der beiden Grundstücke, über
denen die Hochhäuser errichtet werden sollten, eine U-
Bahn-Kreuzung. Ein direkt darüber aufstrebender Turm
war damit unmöglich. So wenigstens lautet die Begrün-
dung – das sichtbare Resultat sind zwei Hochhäuser, die
sich um jeweils 15 Grad gegeneinander neigen und eine
Art Durchgangstor bilden. Die Vorhangfassade der Türme
besteht aus Edelstahlprofilen mit einer graugetönten Verglasung, über die sich eine zweite, außenliegende Tragstruktur legt, die einen roten Anstrich erhielt.

Puerta de Europa
John Burgee Architects,
Philip Johnson Consultant
1991–1995
Madrid, Spain
Associate Architects: Pedro Sentieri Cardillo
Structural Engineer: Leslie E. Robertson Associates
Mechanical Engineer: Goymar Ingenieros Consultores, S.A.

This office project stands astride the Paso de la Castellana
in Madrid. The «Russian Constructivist» composition, à la
Lissitzky or Melnikov (or possibly Tatlin's Monument to the
Third Internationale) is no arbitrary exercise: it so happens
that one of the two buildings had to be sited over a subway interchange, and this made a vertical tower standing
at the street intersection impossible. That, at least, is the
rationalization; the result is that there are two 25-story
towers built to lean 15 degrees toward each other over
their plazas, and forming a gateway. The curtain wall of
the towers is of gray glass, framed in stainless steel; there
is a secondary structural grid painted red and visible
through the glass.

Award: New York Association of Consulting Engineers,
1st Prize 1996 Engineering Excellence

El Pais, July 16, 1995
«Philip Johnson», J. Kipnis, 1996

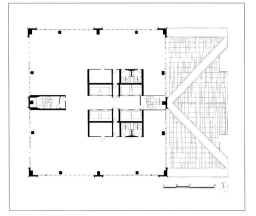

Normalgeschoß, 1:1000

Typical floor plan, 1:1000

Luftbild der beiden Hochhäuser

Aerial view of towers

Torhaus

Philip Johnson
1995
New Canaan, Connecticut
Statik: Ysrael Seinuk PC
Lichttechnik: Claude R. Engle

Nach der Fertigstellung des Torhauses am Zugang zu seinem Landsitz in New Canaan erklärte Johnson, daß dies das letzte Bauwerk sei, das dort zu seinen Lebzeiten errichtet würde. Dies ist aller Voraussicht nach ein leeres Versprechen – das Architekturkontor des 20. Jahrhunderts hält noch zu viele stilistische Mäntelchen zur Anprobe bereit, um dem Schaffensdrang bereits jetzt Einhalt zu gebieten. Bis dato gibt es beispielsweise weder ein konstruktivistisches, geschweige denn dekonstruktivistisches Gebäude von Johnson, noch einen postmodernen Schuppen – außer man betrachtet die Pergola unterhalb des Glashauses oder das Geisterhaus als postmodern. Es gibt keinen Entwurf im Stil des italienischen Futurismus, keine Wright'sche Utopie, keinen Krieg der Sterne à la Archigram und kein geodätisches Gebilde in der Manier eines Buckminster Fuller. Johnson will uns zum Zeitpunkt dieser Zeilen noch einige Jahre erhalten bleiben und hat zweifelsohne noch so einiges in der Hinterhand.

Eine Fantasie im Sinne Hermann Finsterlins hätte sicherlich niemand von ihm erwartet; zum einen, da fast niemand Finsterlin außerhalb der Grenzen Deutschlands und New Canaans kennt, und zum zweiten, da Finsterlin selbst nicht eines seiner Traumgebilde verwirklichen konnte. Für all jene, die weder aus Deutschland noch aus New Canaan stammen: Finsterlin war ein bayrischer Fantast, der zunächst Medizin, Physik und Chemie sowie Philosophie und Malerei studierte. Nachdem er damit fast alles durch hatte, wandte er sich der Architektur zu und wurde von Gropius «entdeckt», als jener 1919 eine Ausstellung «Unbekannter Architekten» zusammenstellte.

Gate House

Philip Johnson
1995
New Canaan, Connecticut
Structural Engineer: Ysrael Seinuk PC
Lighting: Claude R. Engle

When he completed the Gate House at the entrance to the New Canaan estate, Philip Johnson announced that it would be the last building to be constructed on the property during his lifetime. This promise is not likely to be kept, seeing that Johnson has not, as yet, explored several directions in 20th century architecture that he will probably want to explore before he decides that enough is enough: there is not, as yet, a constructivist building or, for that matter, a deconstructivist exercise; there is no postmodernist shed, unless you want to call the colonnaded gazebo below the Glass House, or the Ghost House, post-modernist; there is no Italian Futurist exercise so far, no Wrightian utopia, no Archigram Star Wars, and no Buckminster Fuller geodesia! But, then, Johnson plans to be with us for some more years, as this is written, so all of these exercises are, undoubtedly, in the wings.

But who would have expected him to do a Hermann Finsterlin fantasy, especially in view of the facts that (a) very few people, outside Germany and New Canaan, had ever heard of Finsterlin; and that (b) Finsterlin himself had never succeeded in building any of his dreams himself? For the information of non-Germans and non-New Canaanites, Finsterlin was a Bavarian fantasist who started out studying medicine, physics and chemistry, philosophy, and painting. Having thus exhausted almost everything else, he turned to architecture and was «discovered» by Walter Gropius when the latter put on an exhibition in 1919 of «Unknown Architects».

After the 1919 Exhibition, Finsterlin played with various architectural fantasies, including neo-plasticism, expres-

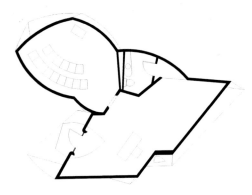

Grundriß Erdgeschoß, 1:250

Ground floor plan, 1:250

Blick auf den Eingang
Ansicht von Süden

Entry view
South elevation

Nach 1919 beschäftigte sich Finsterlin spielerisch mit verschiedenartigen Architekturfantasien, unter anderem mit neoplastizistischen, expressionistischen, geometrischen und biomorphen Ideen. Er fristete sein Dasein als Maler und Schriftsteller. Seine einzige indirekte architektonische Hinterlassenschaft blieb beschränkt auf ein Denkmal, das Walter Gropius 1921 in Weimar errichten ließ, eingedenk der Märzgefallenen, einer Gruppe von Arbeiterführern, die während des Kapp-Putsches den Rechtsradikalen zum Opfer fielen. Finsterlins Zeichnungen hatten offensichtlich erheblichen Einfluß auf das Denkmal aus Beton, das auch im Werk von Gropius die einzige Arbeit dieser Art bleiben sollte.

Das Bemerkenswerte an dem neuen Gebilde auf Philip Johnsons Landsitz ist nicht nur der Bezug auf einen relativ obskuren Expressionisten wie Finsterlin, sondern auch der Umstand, daß das Torhaus von keinem anderen als Walter Gropius inspiriert wurde. Es besteht jedoch kein Zweifel, daß Johnsons jüngstes Werk in New Canaan seinem bewundernswerten Gedächtnis und seiner eigenen Vorstellungskraft ebensoviel zu verdanken hat wie Finsterlin und Gropius.

Die Nutzung des Torhauses liegt auf der Hand. Es liegt direkt am Zugang des Anwesens und soll nach Johnsons Tod und der Übernahme der Gesamtanlage durch den National Trust als Empfangs- und Informationspavillon dienen.

Im Inneren finden sich zwei Räume, der eine ein Empfangs- und Warteraum, den die Besucher bei ihrer Ankunft betreten, der andere ein Raum zur Videovorführung, in denen Johnson sein Werk, seinen Landsitz und sich selbst erklärt.

Eine rot-schwarze Skulptur von scheinbar enormen Ausmaßen umhüllt das einfache und unkomplizierte Innere. Die Konstruktion der bewehrten Betonschale ähnelt der eines Schwimmbeckens, wobei auf einen Stahlmaschendraht zunächst Wärmedämmung aufgebracht, diese dann mit Beton besprüht und zum Schluß eine wasserdichte Acrylschicht aufgetragen wird. Das Konstruktionssystem ist ein italienisches Patent, mit dem Johnson von seinem Tragwerksplaner, Ysrael A. Seinuk vertraut gemacht wurde. Es kann während der Bauzeit noch verändert, die Flächen und Kanten der Schale können vor dem Erstarren in die gewünschte Form gebracht werden, wovon Johnson ausgiebig Gebrauch machte.

Das Torhaus wurde mit allen möglichen Bezeichnungen von «Monster» bis «Stealth Bomber» versehen. (Das Wort «finster» mag in Johnsons Unterbewußtsein mitgeschwungen haben.) Die düstere Hülle hat lediglich zwei Öffnungen, zum einen den verglasten Eingang, zum anderen ein kleines Fenster im Warteraum. Beide Öffnungen

sionism, global geo-metrics and biomorphics – concepts that probably lose (or win) something in the translation from the German. He ended up as a painter and writer, with his architectural legacy, oddly enough, limited to a Gropius-designed «Monument to the March Heroes» constructed in 1921, in Weimar, in honor of a group of left-wing workers murdered by rightists during the Kapp Putsch – a concrete monument quite obviously and profoundly influenced by Finsterlin's renderings, and the only structure in this manner ever completed by Walter Gropius himself.

What makes the new Gate House on Philip Johnson's estate so remarkable is not only that it was designed and built in the idiom of a rather odd expressionist like Finsterlin, but that the Gate House got to where it stands today via – of all people – Walter Gropius! There seems little doubt that the most recent work on the New Canaan estate owes as much to Finsterlin and to Gropius as it does, needless to say, to Johnson's own remarkable memory and imagination.

The function of the Gate House is obvious: it is located just inside the entrance to the estate, and it will serve to receive and to brief visitors once the place has been turned over to the National Trust for Historic Preservation after Johnson's death.

The building contains two rooms: one, a reception area and waiting room, which visitors will enter upon their arrival; and the second a Video Room, where visitors can watch films and videos of Johnson explaining his work, his estate and himself.

These simple and straightforward functions are enclosed in a seemingly enormous sculpture painted a bright red and black. The sculpture is a reinforced concrete shell formed much the way a swimming pool is constructed – a steel mesh, a layer of insulation, sprayed on concrete, and a waterproof finish of acrylic. The system – an Italian patent, introduced to Johnson by the structural engineer, Ysrael A. Seinuk – remains sufficiently flexible during construction that one can change the forms and edges of the shell before it settles into permanent shape. Which is what Johnson did.

The Gate House has been described, variously, as a «Monsta» and as a «Stealth Bomber», with other expletives in between. (The German word «Finster» translates into «gloomy» or «ominous», and that may have been in Johnson's subconscious!) There are only two openings in the ominous shell: one, a glassy entrance; the other a small window in the waiting area. Both openings are biomorphic in shape. The interior has white walls and a acrylic-coated plywood floor. At its lowest point, the building is 9 feet tall; at its highest, 21. There is no sense of

haben eine biomorphe Gestalt. Die Innenwände sind weiß gestrichen, und der Fußboden aus Sperrholz ist mit Acrylharz eingelassen. An der niedrigsten Stelle ist das Gebäude 2,70 m hoch, an seiner höchsten 6,40 m. Man verliert sowohl außen wie innen den Maßstab. Einzig das kleine Fenster gewährt Ausblick auf das Anwesen und einen flüchtigen Blick auf die kleine, weiße, kubistische Studierklause am Fuße des Hügels aus dem Jahr 1980.

Niemand weiß so recht, was er von Johnsons jüngstem Schocker halten soll, nur wenige Besucher können den Bezug zur Architekturgeschichte herstellen. Vielleicht nicht einmal Johnson selbst – seine Beziehung zu Gropius war alles andere als herzlich, was einerseits mit Johnsons Studienzeit in Harvard zu der Zeit, als Gropius der Architekturfakultät vorstand, zu tun haben mag und andererseits damit, daß er das Werk von Gropius nie besonders leiden konnte und daraus auch keinen Hehl machte.

Walter Gropius verstarb 25 Jahre vor Fertigstellung des «Monsta», hat es also nie zu Gesicht bekommen und konnte von diesem Vorhaben und dessen Verwirklichung keine Ahnung gehabt haben. Mit zunehmender Entschlüsselung der Geschichte kann es jedoch gut sein, daß das ungewöhnliche Torhaus eines Tages als «Walters Rache» berühmt und berüchtigt wird.

scale inside or out; the only view of the estate, in effect, is through the window which offers a glimpse of the small, white, cubist study built downhill in 1980.

Nobody quite knows what to make of Johnson's latest shocker, in part because not many of those who come to visit can make the connection to the recent past. And Johnson himself may not have made it either: there was no love lost between him and Walter Gropius – in part, because Johnson was a student at Harvard when Gropius ran the Graduate School of Design; and partly because Johnson never thought very much of Gropius' work, and made no secret of that.

Walter Gropius died 25 years before Johnson designed his «Monsta»; so Gropius never saw it, and never would have imagined that Johnson could or would build such a «Monsta». Yet, as history begins to unravel, this extraordinary Gate House may some day be known as «Walter's Revenge».

Award: Concrete Industry Board 1995

Architecture, November 1995
New York Times, September 17, 1995

Bürgerhaus in Celebration

Philip Johnson, Ritchie & Fiore Architects
1996
Celebration, Florida
Assoziierter Entwurfsarchitekt: Dennis Wedlick
Assoziierte Architekten: HKS, Inc.
Statik: HKS Structural
Haustechnik: Blum Consulting Engineers

Das Gebäude ist Teil einer neuen Stadt in Florida, die von Disneys Immobilienbereich geplant wurde. Es ist zugleich Verwaltungsbau, Versammlungsstätte und Zentrum für Aktivitäten aller Art. Sein ausladendes Walmdach ruht auf dünnen, eng gestellten Stützen. Diese Kolonnade wirkt wie ein Foyer im Freien und macht eine Aussage über die bürgerorientierte Nutzung und die Stellung des Bauwerks in der Gemeinde. Seine Verkleidung besteht aus rotem Virginia-Ziegel, der auch als Platzbelag um das Bürgerhaus Verwendung findet.

Celebration Town Hall

Philip Johnson, Ritchie & Fiore Architects
1996
Celebration, Florida
Associate Design Architect: Dennis Wedlick
Associate Architects: HKS, Inc.
Structural Engineer: HKS Structural
Mechanical Engineer: Blum Consulting Engineers

This is an administration building, meeting hall and activities center for the new Florida town planned by the Disney Development Company. The building will have a large hip roof supported on thin, closely spaced columns. This colonnade creates an outdoor «lobby», and proclaims the structure's civic purpose and place in the community. The building is clad in a red Virginia brick used also for pavers around the Town Hall.

Architectural Record, January 1996

Grundriß Erdgeschoß, 1:250
Ansichtszeichnung

Ground floor plan, 1:250
Perspective

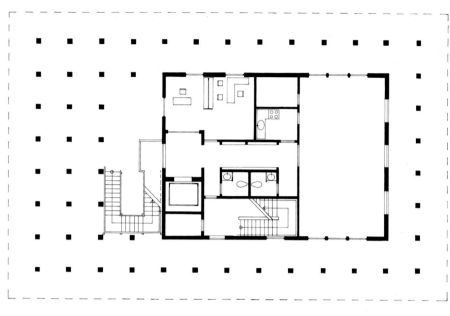

Millenia Walk Einkaufszentrum
John Burgee Architects
mit Philip Johnson (Beratung)
1993–1996
Singapur
Assoziierte Architekten: DP Architects PGE
Statik: Leslie E. Robertson
Haustechnik: Cosentini & Associates

Das Einkaufszentrum liegt im Geschäftsviertel von Singapur. Das äußere Erscheinungsbild wird von der roten
Granitverkleidung im Werksteinverband geprägt sowie
von einer Reihe pyramidenartiger Dächer, die in der
großen Pyramide über dem zentralen Innenhof kulminie-
ren. Bögen überspannen die Fenster, deren Einfassungen
wie in die Fassade eingeschnitten wirken. Der Innenraum
wird von einem großzügig und zentral angelegten Raum-
volumen bestimmt, dem ebenfalls mit rotem Granit aus-
gekleideten «Großen Innenhof». Die Begrenzungswände
des Innenhofs, die ein Oberlicht tragen, setzen sich aus
einer rhythmischen Abfolge von Stütze und Gebälk in
leuchtend grünem Anstrich zusammen. Der Raum ist allseitig von Läden gesäumt.

Millenia Walk
John Burgee Architects,
Philip Johnson Consultant
1993–1996
Singapore
Associate Architects: DP Architects PGE
Structural Engineer: Leslie E. Robertson
Mechanical Engineer: Cosentini & Associates

This is a retail mall in the business district of Singapore.
The exterior is red granite ashlar masonry, with a series of
overscaled pyramidal roofs of lead coated copper scales
that lead to the large pyramid over the central court. The
windows are arched and have surrounds recessed into
the facade. The interior has a large central space, a «Great
Court», also in red granite. The walls of the court are developed with a series of columns and entablatures,
painted bright green, and the whole is topped by a skylight. Shopping gallerias flank this space.

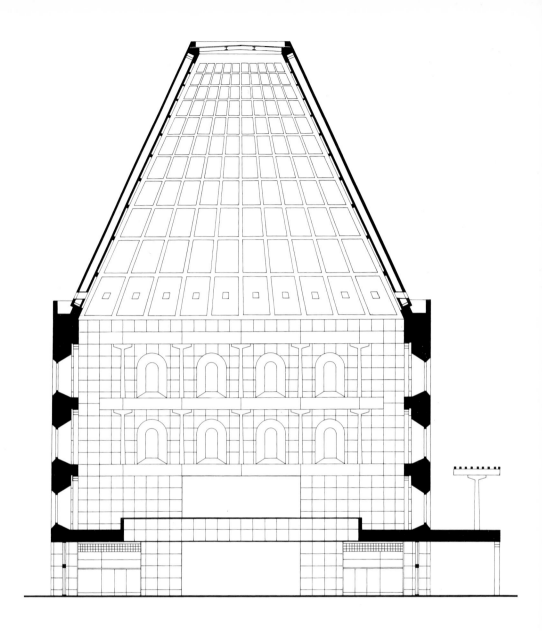

Schnitt durch den Großen Innenhof, 1:300

Section at Great Court, 1:300

Das Business Center am Checkpoint Charlie (Philip Johnson Haus)

Philip Johnson, Ritchie & Fiore Architects
1995–1997
Berlin
Assoziierte Architekten: Pysall, Stahrenberg & Partner
Statik: Leonhardt, Andrä und Partner
Haustechnik: Flack und Kurtz/Integ

Das Gebäude ist einer von mehreren Büro- und Geschäftsbauten, die von einer Investorengemeinschaft im wiedervereinten Berlin am ehemaligen Checkpoint Charlie, dem Grenzübergang im gespalteten Berlin, errichtet werden. Das Erscheinungsbild wird bestimmt vom vertikalen Wechsel verglaster Senkrecht- und Schrägfassaden mit granitverkleideten Lochfassaden und läßt das Gebäude, das den gesamten Block einnimmt, kleinmaßstäblicher wirken. Ein Gesims in 22,90 m Höhe nimmt die Gesimshöhen der Nachbarbebauung auf. Städtebaulichen Anforderungen gemäß wurden die beiden obersten Geschosse zurückgesetzt. Außenwände wie das Innere von Eingangsbereich und Lobby sind granitverkleidet. Der Hauptraum der Lobby erhebt sich bis in eine Höhe von 12,20 m und wird von einem Glasoberlicht mit abgehängter Lichtdecke überspannt. Dieses Atrium erinnert in Maßstab und Gestaltung an Heinrich Tessenows Innenraum für das Stadtbad Berlin-Mitte aus dem Jahr 1930.

Das Business Center am Checkpoint Charlie (Philip Johnson Haus)

Philip Johnson, Ritchie & Fiore Architects
1995–1997
Berlin, Germany
Associate Architects: Pysall, Stahrenberg & Partners
Structural Engineer: Leonhardt, Andrä und Partner
Mechanical Engineer: Flack and Kurtz/Integ

Near what was once Checkpoint Charlie in divided Berlin, this commercial and office building is part of a complex of speculative buildings in the newly united city. The facade alternates between vertical areas of curtain wall, and granite walls with punched windows to break down the scale of the full city block-sized structure. An intermediate cornice line is at the height of 75 feet to match that of neighboring buildings. The top two floors are stepped back in conformance with permitted zoning volume. The exterior granite «lila Gerais» continues into the entrance and main lobby. The lobby is a skylit atrium with laylite, and rises to a height of 40 feet inspired by the scale and pattern of Heinrich Tessenow's 1930 interior for the «Stadtbad Mitte» in Berlin.

«Philip Johnson, The Architect in His Own Words», Hilary Lewis, John O'Connor, 1994
Art in America, November 1995

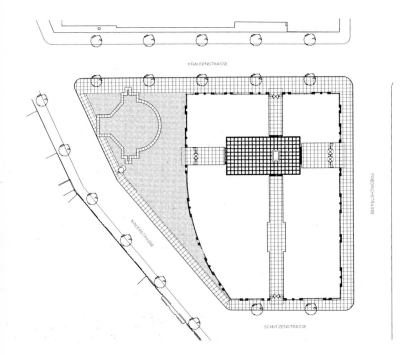

KRAUSENSTRASSE

MARKGRAFENSTRASSE

FRIEDRICHSTRASSE

SCHÜTZENSTRASSE

Lageplan mit Pflasterplan des Atriums, Aufzugspassage und Außenanlage mit dem Grundriß der ehemaligen Bethlehemkirche

Site plan with paving pattern of atrium, elevator passage, park with outline of destroyed church

Grundriß Normalgeschoß,
1:750
Ansicht von der
Friedrichstraße

Typical floor plan, 1:750
Building elevation at
Friedrichstrasse

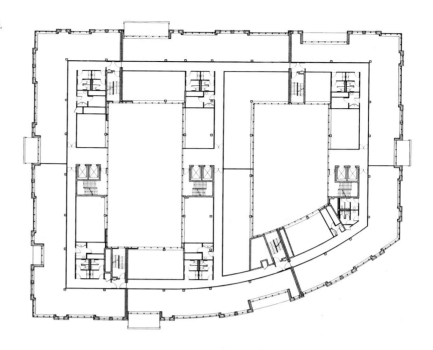

Kapelle des Heiligen Basilius an der St. Thomas Universität

Philip Johnson, Ritchie & Fiore Architects
1996–1997
Houston, Texas
Assoziierter Entwurfsarchitekt: John Manley
Assoziierte Architekten: Merriman Holt Architects
Statik: Cagley, Conti & Jumper
Haustechnik: CHP & Associates
Lichttechnik: Claude R. Engle

Das geometrische Konzept, das der Kapelle zugrunde-liegt, besteht aus einem Kubus, den eine senkrecht ste-hende Wandscheibe durchtrennt. Der weiß verputzte Kubus ist 15,20 m hoch und hält im Inneren 225 Sitz-plätze bereit. Die dem Innenhof zugekehrte Außenwand weist einen hohen Einschnitt auf, der sich wie eine Zelt-wand nach außen stülpt und den Haupteingang freigibt. Die senkrechte Wandscheibe besteht aus schwarzem Gra-nit und durchtrennt auch die Kuppel, die dem Kubus auf-sitzt. In die Schnittbereiche von Wand und Kuppel wurden Oberlichter eingefügt, zusätzliches Tageslicht dringt durch kleine Fenstereinschnitte in die Kapelle ein. Beide Enden der schwarzen Granitwand greifen in den umlaufenden Arkadengang ein, der die benachbarten, von Johnson in den fünfziger Jahren errichteten Universitätsbauten mit-einander verbindet.

St. Basil Chapel at University of St. Thomas

Philip Johnson, Ritchie & Fiore Architects
1996–1997
Houston, Texas
Associate Design Architects: John Manley
Associate Architect: Merriman Holt Architects
Structural Engineer: Cagley, Conti & Jumper
Mechanical Engineer: CHP & Associates
Lighting: Claude R. Engle

The basic geometry of this chapel is that of a cube split by a vertical plane. The white, stuccoed fifty foot cube con-tains a chapel with seating for 225. The front entrance wall is split and slightly warped like a tent flap to provide a front door. The cube itself is topped by a dome, and both the dome and the cube are divided by a large black gran-ite wall. Skylights are set where the wall intersects the dome, and there are smaller openings for light in the chapel. The black wall extends out to the colonnade that links the adjacent university buildings which Johnson completed in the 1950s.

Architecture and Urbanism, April 1992
«Philip Johnson», Jeffrey Kipnis, 1996

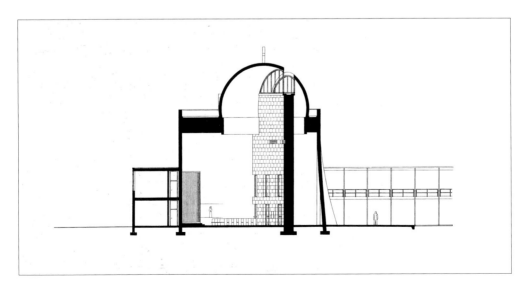

Schnitt mit Blick nach Osten,
1:500
Grundriß Erdgeschoß, 1:500
Modellansicht mit Blick aus
dem Innenhof nach Norden

Section looking east, 1:500
Ground floor plan, 1:500
View of model looking north
from courtyard

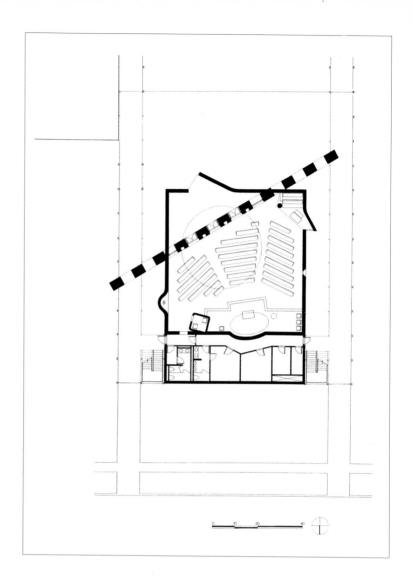

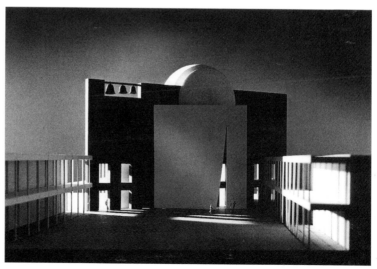

Philip Johnson im Rohbau seines Torhauses in New Canaan

Philip Johnson with Gate House in New Canaan under construction

Nachwort

Postscript

Die Kritiker Philip Johnsons werfen ihm, wie in der Einführung zu diesem Buch erwähnt, häufig Unbeständigkeit in seinem Werk vor. Sie sagen, daß kein wirklich seriöser Architekt derart herumspringen könne, wie Johnson es getan hat und immer noch tut: von einem Stil zum anderen, von einem historischen Bezug zum anderen, von einem Erscheinungsbild zum anderen. Sie beschuldigen ihn, keine festen Überzeugungen und in seinem Werk keine einheitliche, unverwechselbare Handschrift zu vertreten. Sie werfen ihm auch vor, daß er alles nur mögliche tue, um sich einen Bauherrn zu angeln oder um Aufsehen in der Öffentlichkeit zu erregen.

Manches davon trifft sicherlich zu. Aber was ist eigentlich daran so falsch?

Fast alle Architekten dieses Jahrhunderts würden akzeptieren, daß zwei Gebäude sich niemals exakt gleichen können, schon aufgrund der Tatsache, daß auch zweierlei Bauplätze und zweierlei Umweltbedingungen nicht genau gleich sein können. Und wie kann ein Architekt angesichts dieser und vieler anderer Tatsachen überhaupt einen persönlichen Stil oder eine Handschrift vertreten, bei dem alle Gebäude sich in Farbe, Form, Detail, Komposition und, und, und gleichen? Wie lassen sich überhaupt die einseitigen Stile und Handschriften vieler moderner Architekten rechtfertigen, es sei denn durch die Erklärung, daß er oder sie am Namen erkannt werden wolle – diese «Namens-Architektur» ist das eigentliche Ziel, und man schert sich den Teufel um den Bauherrn, den Bauplatz, den Etat und alles andere, was einem spezifischen Gebäude seine spezifische Identität verleihen könnte!

Philip Johnson hat einige sehr interessante Bauherren gehabt, von denen manche entscheidend zur Qualität seiner Bauten und zu den vielen unterschiedlichen Erscheinungsbildern beigetragen haben, die er für sie projektierte. Vor vielen Jahren erklärte der britische Architekturhistoriker Nikolaus Pevsner, das Problem der Architektur unserer Zeit sei nicht, daß die Qualität der Architekten nachgelassen habe, sondern daß unsere Bauherren nicht mehr so kultiviert und gebildet seien wie die der Vergangenheit. Mit anderen Worten, es ist zum wichtigen Bestandteil der Leistung jedes Architekten geworden, seine oder ihre potentiellen Bauherren zu erziehen – was ein Grund dafür ist, weshalb Johnson als «persona publica»

Philip Johnson's critics, as suggested in the introduction to this book, often accuse him of being inconsistent in his work. They say that no really serious architect can possibly bounce around as Johnson has done, and continues to do, from one style to another, from one historic reference to another, from one image to another. They accuse him of having no firm convictions, no single, unmistakable signature in his work. They accuse him of doing almost anything to snare a client, or to make a splash in terms of publicity.

Some of this is probably true. But what, exactly, is wrong with any of it?

Almost all architects in this century would agree that no two buildings can be exactly alike, given the fact that no two sites are alike, and no two environmental conditions are exactly alike. And given those facts, and many more, how can an architect possibly defend a personal style or signature in which every building is alike in color, form, detail, composition, and much, much more? How can one possibly defend the single-minded styles and signatures of many modern architects, except by saying that he or she clearly wants to be recognized by name – that «name architecture» is the underlying objective, and to hell with client, site, budget, and anything else that might give a specific building its specific identity.

Philip Johnson has had some very interesting clients, and some of them have significantly contributed to the quality of his buildings, and to the many different images he projected by them. Several years ago, the British architecture historian, Nikolaus Pevsner, suggested that the problem with architecture in our time was not that the quality of architects had gone downhill, but that our clients were no longer as civilized and as well educated as the clients of the past. In other words, it has become an important part of any architect's performance to educate his or her potential clients – which is one reason why Johnson's public persona has become so well known. He has spent a good part of his career identifying (and educating) exceptional clients – and so his best buildings may be the result of a fairly intensive dialogue between architect and user. Which is, of course, one more reason why no two buildings by Philip Johnson are ever very much alike. Those who criticize him and his work in those terms sim-

so bekannt geworden ist. Er hat einen beachtlichen Teil seiner Laufbahn darauf verwendet, exzeptionelle Bauherren ausfindig zu machen (und sie zu erziehen), und daher resultieren seine besten Bauwerke vermutlich aus einem intensiven Dialog zwischen Architekt und Nutzer. Und das ist natürlich ein weiterer Grund dafür, daß zwei Bauten von Philip Johnson sich nie sehr ähnlich sind. Diejenigen, die ihn und sein Werk unter diesem Aspekt kritisieren, haben schlicht keine Ahnung, wie Bauten entstehen, besonders in einer partizipatorischen Demokratie.

Tatsächlich haben einige der besten Architekten des letzten Jahrhunderts auf Unterschiede von Baugelände, Programm, Bauherr und Umgebung in durchaus ähnlicher Weise reagiert wie Johnson: Nur wenige Bewunderer von Le Corbusiers weiß-in-weißen kubistischen Bauten der zwanziger Jahre hätten voraussagen können, daß er eines Tages die Kapelle von Ronchamp planen und bauen würde. Sehr wenigen Bewunderern von Peter Behrens' neoklassizistischer Deutscher Botschaft in St. Petersburg war bewußt, daß er die hochfunktionalen AEG-Bauten in Berlin fast zur gleichen Zeit plante, oder daß er für sich selbst ein romantisches Jugendstilhaus und ähnliche Häuser für seine Freunde entwerfen würde, während er «Maschinenkunst»-Gebäude in Berlin baute. Sehr wenige Menschen warfen Eero Saarinen jemals Leichtfertigkeit in seiner Architektur vor, obgleich keine zwei seiner Projekte sich auch nur im entferntesten ähnlich waren, da jedes als besondere Entsprechung einer besonderen Situation geplant wurde.

Und nur wenige, die Frank Lloyd Wrights symmetrische Bauten der ersten dreißig Jahre seiner Laufbahn bewunderten – das Larkin Building, die Unity Church, das Imperial Hotel in Tokio und viele, viele andere –, hätten ihn für fähig gehalten, nur dreißig Jahre später das Guggenheim Museum zu entwerfen.

Kurz, es ist schwer zu verstehen, warum man Philip Johnson manchmal Leichtfertigkeit vorwirft, weil er es ablehnt, an der gleichen und engen, dogmatischen Linie der Moderne festzuhalten. Der wahre Grund, warum Johnson häufig der Frivolität seiner Architektur bezichtigt wird – als fähig, in jedem Idiom, jedem Stil zu arbeiten, der ihn zufällig gerade fasziniert –, ist in Wirklichkeit ein ganz einfacher: Viele seiner Architektenkollegen wissen nur sehr wenig über die Geschichte der Architektur, und sie ärgern sich darüber, daß Johnson sich in allen ihren Bereichen unglaublich gut auskennt. In der Tat gibt es heute kaum Architekten in Europa oder in den USA, die soviel wie er über das reiche Erbe wissen, das uns aus vergangenen Jahrhunderten überliefert wurde. Und so ist es für Architekturkritiker zweifellos ärgerlich festzustellen, daß Johnson auf ein gewaltiges Potential von Vorgängern

ply don't know how buildings are created, especially in a participatory democracy...

As a matter of fact, some of the finest architects of the past hundred years or so have responded to differences in site, program, client, environment, and so on in much the way Johnson has: few people who admired Le Corbusier's white on white cubist work of the 1920s could have predicted that he would, some day, design and build the chapel at Ronchamp. Very few people who admired Peter Behrens' neo-classical German Embassy in St. Petersburg realized that he had designed the highly functional AEG structures in Berlin at almost the same time when his Embassy was going up in Russia, or that he would design a romantic, Art Nouveau house for himself and similar houses for his friends while doing «Machine Art» structures in Berlin. Very few people ever accused Eero Saarinen of being frivolous about architecture, although no two of his projects were ever remotely alike – each being designed specifically in response to a specific situation.

And very few people who admired Frank Lloyd Wright's symmetrical compositions of the first thirty years of his career – including the Larkin Building, Unity Church, the Imperial Hotel in Tokyo, and many, many more – would have thought him capable of designing the Guggenheim Museum a mere thirty years later.

In short, it is hard to understand why Philip Johnson is sometimes accused of frivolity because he refuses to stick to the straight and narrow line of modern dogma. The real reason Philip Johnson is often denounced as being frivolous about architecture – as being capable of working in any idiom, any style that happens to intrigue him at the moment – is really quite simple: many of his fellow architects know very little about the history of architecture, and they resent the fact that Johnson is incredibly knowledgeable about all aspects of it. In fact, there are no architects in Europe or in the U.S. today who know as much as he does about the rich heritage passed on to us from past centuries. And so it is undoubtedly irritating to architecture critics to discover that Johnson can reach back to a huge wealth of precedents that are beyond the ken of any of his contemporaries. What architect, practicing today, would be capable of referring to a Rathaus and to the Stadtweinhaus in Münster, in northwest Germany (built in the 14th and 16th centuries, respectively) while designing an office skyscraper for a Texas bank? And what architect, practicing today, would think of a 1780 project by Ledoux while designing a new School of Architecture for the University of Houston?

How many architects would have any knowledge of those or many other historic precedents? An interesting byproduct of Johnson's wide knowledge of architectural history

zurückgreifen kann, das sich der Kenntnis seiner Zeitgenossen entzieht. Welcher praktizierende Architekt von heute wäre in der Lage, auf das Rathaus und das Stadtweinhaus in Münster (erbaut im 14. bzw. 16. Jahrhundert) Bezug zu nehmen, wenn er ein Bürohochhaus für eine Bank in Texas entwirft? Und welcher Architekt würde an ein Projekt von Ledoux aus dem Jahre 1780 denken, wenn er eine neue Architekturhochschule für die Universität Houston plant?

Wie viele Architekten haben überhaupt Kenntnis von diesen oder vielen anderen historischen Vorläufern? Ein interessantes Nebenprodukt von Johnsons umfassendem Wissen über die Architekturgeschichte ist die große Aufmerksamkeit, die er zum Beispiel der Qualität des Materials, den Details und der Ausführung widmet. Dies ist wohl eine der Lehren von Mies, die Johnson nie vergessen hat: Es läßt sich kaum ein einziges von Johnson geplantes Bauwerk finden, das heute nicht fast genauso gut aussieht wie am Tag seiner Eröffnung, wenn nicht besser. Das ist erheblich mehr, als von den meisten modernen Gebäuden gesagt werden kann – mit Ausnahme vielleicht jener bemerkenswerten Hinterlassenschaften von Peter Behrens oder Mies van der Rohe, von denen einige die Bomben und Granaten des Zweiten Weltkriegs ohne ernsthaften Schaden überstehen konnten.

Zugegebenermaßen mag das zum Teil auf die große Sorgfalt zurückzuführen sein, die einige von Johnsons Partnern, wie Landis Gores, Richard Foster und John Burgee, auf diese Aspekte verwendeten, und einiges resultiert auch aus der Tatsache, daß die meisten Bauherren Johnsons es sich leisten konnten, gut zu bauen. Und ein wenig liegt es auch daran, daß Johnson gern traditionelle Materialien wie Granit, Marmor, Backstein und Bronze verwendet anstelle der «brandneuen» Produkte, die den Test der Alterung noch zu bestehen haben und es vielleicht nie schaffen werden – Materialien und Produkte, die der Reputation einiger Kollegen Johnsons den Todesstoß versetzt haben.

Was jedoch Johnsons Platz in der Architektur des 20. Jahrhunderts wirklich bedeutend macht, sind nicht nur seine Kenntnis der Vergangenheit und seine Bereitschaft, daraus zu zitieren, auch nicht seine Vertrautheit mit der Tradition des Bauens; was seinen Beitrag so wertvoll macht, ist, daß er für viele alte wie neue Ideen die Türen aufgestoßen hat, die von seinen dogmatischeren Vorgängern versperrt worden waren.

Während die meisten Dogmatiker daran festhielten, daß die Form der Funktion folgen müsse, wies Johnson darauf hin, daß die meisten Gebäude ihre Funktionen wiederholt ändern, bis sie abgerissen werden – was ist also mit der Frage des Funktionalismus? Während die Dogmatiker dar-

is his careful attention to such things as quality of materials, of details, and of workmanship. This may be one of the Miesian lessons Johnson never forgot: it is hard to recall a single building designed by Philip Johnson that does not look almost as well today as it did on opening day or better. That is a great deal more than can be said about most modern buildings – except, perhaps, for those remarkable survivors done by Peter Behrens or Mies van der Rohe, some of which managed to stand up through the bombs and shells of World War II without very serious damage.

Admittedly, some of this may be due to the careful attention paid by some of Johnson's collaborators, like Landis Gores, Richard Foster and John Burgee; and some of it is clearly due to the fact that most of Johnson's clients could afford to build well. And some of it is due to the fact that Johnson likes to use traditional materials like granite, marble, brick and bronze – rather than «cutting edge» materials that have yet to stand the test of time, and may never do so – materials and products that have been the kiss of death to the reputations of some of Johnson's contemporaries.

But what really makes Johnson's place in 20th century architecture important is not only his knowledge of the past and his willingness to refer to it, or his familiarity with the traditions of building; what makes his place so valuable is that he opened up a great many doors to old as well as new ideas that had been closed by his more dogmatic predecessors.

When most dogmatists insisted that form must follow function, Johnson pointed out that most buildings changed their functions repeatedly before being torn down – so what was the point of functionalism? When dogmatists insisted that everything should be «honestly expressed,» Johnson asked «why?» When dogmatists insisted that repetitive, modular uniformity was the image of our time, Johnson thought that architecture ought to be a little more interesting than that. When dogmatists said that new materials and new technologies were the only proper tools of our time, Johnson wondered whether anyone had checked them out. And when dogmatists said that cubist boxes, flat roofs, glass walls and pilotis were the things that made architecture modern, Johnson dared to disagree – and proceeded to design whatever seemed most beautiful to him in a given place and time.

Did he miss out now and then? Of course he did. But this book, which documents fewer than one hundred of Johnson's completed works, out of almost twice that number, suggests that he may have built more than almost any of his contemporaries over the past half century; and he probably designed another hundred projects that

auf beharrten, daß alles «ehrlich ausgedrückt» werden müsse, fragte Johnson: «Warum»? Während die Dogmatiker daran festhielten, daß die repetitive modulare Einheitlichkeit das Abbild unserer Zeit sei, meinte Johnson, daß die Architektur etwas interessanter sein sollte. Während die Dogmatiker erklärten, daß neue Materialien und neue Technologien die einzigen geeigneten Mittel unserer Zeit seien, überlegte Johnson, ob jemand sie auch ausprobiert hätte. Und während die Dogmatiker behaupteten, daß kubistische Kisten, Flachdächer, Glaswände und Pilotis die Dinge seien, welche die Architektur modern machten, wagte Johnson zu widersprechen und fuhr fort zu entwerfen, was ihm für einen gegebenen Ort und eine bestimmte Zeit als schön erschien.

Ist ihm manchmal etwas fehlgeschlagen? Natürlich ist das auch passiert. Aber dieses Buch, das nahezu einhundert ausgeführte Bauten Johnsons von etwa doppelt so vielen vorstellt, läßt darauf schließen, daß er wohl mehr gebaut hat als fast alle seiner Zeitgenossen der zweiten Jahrhunderthälfte. Und er hat vermutlich weitere hundert Projekte geplant, die nicht realisiert wurden. Von dieser eindrucksvollen Zahl waren und sind etwa zwanzig erstklassig – ein Ergebnis, mit dem nur sehr wenige seiner Kollegen gleichziehen können.

Obgleich Philip Johnson dazu neigt, sein eigenes Werk oder sein Interesse an alltäglicheren Aufgaben der Architektur und Stadtplanung herunterzuspielen, hat er einige seiner wichtigsten Beiträge tatsächlich in genau diesen Bereichen geleistet.

In einem Entwurf nach dem anderen hat er Systeme des Fußgängerverkehrs in Städten erforscht oder wiederentdeckt, die anscheinend von fast allen übersehen worden sind. Seit der massenhaften Verbreitung des Automobils hat Johnson in einer städtischen Struktur nach der anderen Arkadengänge und Stadtplätze geschaffen, die auf Jeffersons Campus der University of Virginia zurückgehen, auf das alte Bologna und auf die früheren Prototypen aus der Zeit, als Städte noch vorwiegend für Fußgänger geplant und gebaut wurden. Seine Planungen für Houston, Pittsburgh, New York und andere Städte werden deren Bedürfnissen häufig auf sensiblere Weise gerecht als alles, was Wright, Mies oder Le Corbusier geplant oder gebaut haben. Johnson meint offenbar nicht, daß seine Beiträge in jenen Bereichen wichtig seien, aber sie sind möglicherweise wichtiger als diejenigen, welche mehr Schlagzeilen gemacht haben.

In zahlreichen Einzelbauten ebenso wie in städtebaulichen Projekten hat er auch den zentralen städtischen Platz wiederentdeckt – vermutlich den perfekten Platz, der städtisches Leben und städtische Aktionen erzeugen und stimulieren kann. Bei Individualbauten wie der Stadt-

were never realized. Out of this very impressive number, some twenty or thirty were and are first rate – a record that very few of his contemporaries can match.

Although Philip Johnson tends to belittle his own work or interest in some of the more commonplace issues of architecture and urban design, the fact is that some of his most significant contributions have been in precisely those areas.

In project after project, he has explored or rediscovered patterns of pedestrian circulation in cities that seem to have been neglected by just about everyone. In response to the massive automobilization, Johnson has created arcaded sidewalks and city squares that went back to Jefferson's campus at the University of Virginia, to the ancient city of Bologna, and the earlier prototypes from times when cities were still being designed and built largely for pedestrians. His projects in Houston, in Pittsburgh, in New York and elsewhere are often much more sensitive to those needs than anything designed and built by Wright or Mies or Le Corbusier. Johnson doesn't seem to think his contributions in those areas are important, but they may be more important than some of those that have made more headlines.

In numerous individual buildings as well as urban examples, the has also rediscovered the central urban square – probably he perfect place for urban life and action to be generated and made exciting. In individual buildings, like the Boston Public Library, the IDS complex in Minneapolis, and even in some of his larger houses, a central, indoor space makes everything and everyone come together; and where he has had a chance to work at a larger scale, in such outdoor spaces as the PPG complex in Pittsburgh and the MoMA garden in Manhattan, he has resurrected the urban square or piazza and made it more beautiful than many of his celebrated contemporaries were able to do.

Finally, and more surprisingly, Johnson has done some remarkably successful «functional» buildings: his high-rise laboratories work much better – and often look much better – than those that are more famous; his museums are the work of someone who understands how art can and should be displayed, lit, and experienced; his theaters, even when a little on the pretentious side, are designed by someone who understands what can make the experience of a theatrical performance memorable – for the audience as well as the actors; and his public memorials, even when just this side of kitsch, are very memorable.

Johnson is not often given credit for being a functionalist – least of all by himself. Most of the time, he is given credit for having made the architecture of our time and other times vastly more interesting. He has probably

bibliothek in Boston, dem IDS-Komplex in Minneapolis und sogar in einigen seiner größeren Wohnhäuser führt ein zentraler Innenraum alles und alle zusammen; und wenn sich ihm die Chance bot, in größerem Maßstab zu planen, etwa bei den Außenräumen des PPG-Komplexes in Pittsburgh und dem Garten des MOMA in Manhattan, ließ er den städtischen Platz oder die Piazza wiedererstehen und gestaltete ihn schöner, als es vielen seiner gefeierten Zeitgenossen gelungen ist.

Schließlich, was noch erstaunlicher ist, hat Johnson einige beachtlich erfolgreiche «funktionale» Bauwerke geplant: Seine Hochhaus-Laborgebäude funktionieren besser und sehen häufig auch viel besser aus als manche weitaus berühmteren; seine Museen sind das Werk von einem, der begriffen hat, wie Kunst ausgestellt, belichtet und erlebt werden kann und sollte; seine Theater sind, wenn auch ein wenig zu prätentiös, von jemandem geplant, der weiß, was das Erlebnis einer Theateraufführung für die Zuschauer wie für die Schauspieler einprägsam macht; und seine öffentlichen Denkmäler sind, wenn sie auch dem Kitsch nahekommen, höchst einprägsam.

Johnson erfährt nicht oft Anerkennung als Funktionalist — am allerwenigsten von sich selbst. Meistens wird ihm Anerkennung dafür zuteil, daß er die Architektur unserer Zeit und anderer Zeiten sehr viel interessanter gemacht hat. Er hat vermutlich Diskussionen über die Architektur von dem Augenblick an angeregt, als er das erste moderne Gebäude sah, also vor über siebzig Jahren. In einer Ausstellung nach der anderen, in Vorträgen, Diskussionen und kritischen Aufsätzen hat Johnson Jahr um Jahr seine Kollegen angeregt zu denken, anstatt auf zweifelhaften Annahmen basierende Doktrinen zu akzeptieren. Und im Gegensatz zu vielen Theoretikern und Kritikern hat Philip Johnson gebaut, was er verkündete, und hat zu seinen Mißerfolgen ebenso gestanden wie zu seinen Erfolgen.

Wie der in der Einleitung zu diesem Buch erwähnte Philosoph hat Johnson fast alles in Frage gestellt, was andere ihm als geheiligtes Dogma oder als Doktrin präsentierten, und häufig angenommen, daß das Gegenteil richtig sei. Das Ergebnis war selbstredend nicht einheitlich überzeugend, aber einheitlich anregend. Es wäre schwierig, jemanden aus diesem Jahrhundert — ob Architekt oder Kritiker — zu benennen, der soviel getan hat, um die Debatte und den Dialog anzuregen, und der sich selbst und seinen Kollegen soviel über die Kunst beigebracht hat, der wir alle uns verschrieben haben. Und es ist schwer vorstellbar, wie langweilig der Verlauf der Architektur in den vergangenen fünfzig Jahren gewesen wäre, hätte es nicht Philip Johnson gegeben, der uns auf Trab gehalten hat.

stirred up debates in architecture from the moment he saw his first modern building, almost seventy years ago. In exhibition after exhibition, in lectures, debates, and critical essays, year after year, Johnson made his contemporaries think rather than accept doctrines based on dubious assumptions. And unlike most theorists and critics, Philip Johnson built what he preached, and stood by his failures as well as by his successes.

Like the famous philosopher quoted in the introduction to this book, Johnson questioned almost everything that others had presented to him as sacred dogma or doctrine, and often assumed that the very opposite was true. The result, needless to say, has not been uniformly convincing, but it has been uniformly challenging. It would be difficult to identify anyone, architect or critic in this century, who has done so much to generate debate and dialogue, and who has taught himself and his fellow architects so much about the art to which all of us are dedicated. And it is hard to realize how boring the course of architecture in the past fifty years would have been if there had not been a Philip Johnson to keep us on our toes.

Biographie

Biography

8. Juli 1906
Philip Johnson wird in Cleveland, Ohio, geboren.

1923–1930
Studium der Geschichte und Philosophie an der Harvard Universität, Cambridge, Massachusetts

1930–1934
Leiter der Architekturabteilung des Museum of Modern Art, New York

1940–1943
Architekturstudium an der Harvard Graduate School of Design

1942–1945
Architekturbüro in Cambridge

seit 1946
Architekturbüro in New York

1946–1954
Leiter der Architekturabteilung des Museum of Modern Art, New York

seit 1958
Vorstandsmitglied des Museum of Modern Art

1978
Goldmedaille des American Institute of Architects

1979
Pritzker-Preis

Philip Johnson ist Ehrendoktor von
Yale University
Pratt Institute
Ohio State University
University of Houston
University of Nebraska

8 July 1906
Philip Johnson is born in Cleveland, Ohio.

1923–1930
Studies of History and Philosophy at Harvard University, Cambridge (A.B.)

1930–1934
Director, Department of Architecture, The Museum of Modern Art, New York

1940–1943
Harvard Graduate School of Design, B.Arch.

1942–1945
Architectural practice in Cambridge

since 1946
Architectural practice in New York

1946–1954
Director, Department of Architecture, The Museum of Modern Art, New York

since 1958
Trustee, The Museum of Modern Art

1978
Gold Medal, The American Institute of Architects

1979
Pritzker Architecture Prize

Philip Johnson holds
Honorary Doctoral Degrees from
Yale University
Pratt Institute
Ohio State University
University of Houston
University of Nebraska

Werkverzeichnis/List of Built Work

Warburg Apartment
New York, New York
1934

Ash Street House
Cambridge, Massachusetts
1942

Barn, Townsend Farms
New London, Ohio (demolished)
1944

Mr. & Mrs. Richard E. Booth House
Bedford Village, New York (incomplete)
1946

Mr. & Mrs. Eugene Farney House
Sagaponack, New York
1947
Partner: Landis Gores

Philip Johnson House (Glass House)
New Canaan, Connecticut
1949

Mr. & Mrs. G.E. Paine, Jr. House
Wellsboro, New York
1949

Mr. & Mrs. Benjamin Wolf House
Newburgh, New York
1949

Mr. & Mrs. John de Menil House
Houston, Texas
1950

**Museum of Modern Art Annex
(Grace Rainey Rogers Annex)**
New York, New York (demolished)
1950

Mrs. John D. Rockefeller III Guest House
New York, New York
1950
Partner: Landis Gores

Mr. & Mrs. Henry Ford II House
Southampton, Long Island, New York
1951

Mr. & Mrs. Richard Hodgson House
New Canaan, Connecticut
1951
Partner: Landis Gores

Mr. & Mrs. George C. Oneto House
Irvington, New York
1951
Partner: Landis Gores

Philip Johnson Office
Museum of Modern Art
New York, New York (demolished)
1951

Mr. Burton Tremain, Jr. Barn, Renovation
Maryiden, Connecticut
1952

Schlumberger Administration Building
Ridgefield, Connecticut
1952

**The Aldrich Exhibition Gallery at
The Museum of Modern Art, R.I.S.D.**
Providence, RI
1952

Mrs. Alice Ball House
New Canaan, Connecticut
1953

Philip Johnson Guest House, Interior
New Canaan, Connecticut
1953

**The Abby Aldrich Rockefeller Sculpture Garden at
The Museum of Modern Art**
New York, New York
1953
Landscape Architect: James Fanning

Mr. & Mrs. Robert C. Wiley House
New Canaan, Connecticut
1953

Mr. & Mrs. Richard C. Davis House
Wayzata, Minnesota
1954

Mr. & Mrs. William Burden Apartment
New York, New York
1954

Joseph Hirschhorn House
Blind River, Ontario, Canada
1955

Meteor Crator Pavilion
Coconino County, Arizona
1955

Wiley Development Company House
New Canaan, Connecticut
1955

Mr. & Mrs. Eric Boissonnas House
New Canaan, Connecticut
1956

Kneses Tifereth Israel Synagogue
Port Chester, New York
1956

Mr. & Mrs. Robert C. Leonhardt House
Lloyd's Neck, Long Island, New York
1956

Dormitory, Seton Hill College
Greensburg, Pennsylvania
1957

**Auditorium and Classroom Buildings
University of St. Thomas**
Houston, Texas
1957

Nelson Rockefeller Art Gallery
Seal Harbor, Maine
1957

«American Room» UNESCO
Paris, France
1958

Asia House (Russell Sage Foundation)
New York, New York
1958–1960

Four Seasons Restaurant at Seagram Building
New York, New York
1959

Seagram's Executive Offices
Seagram Building, Floor 5
New York, New York
1959

Brasserie Restaurant
Seagram Building
New York, New York
1959

Munson-Williams-Proctor Institute
Utica, New York
1960

Research Nuclear Reactor
Rehovot, Israel
1960

Roofless Church
New Harmony, Indiana
1960

Dormitory, Sarah Lawrence College
Bronxville, New York
1960

Mr. Robert Tourre House
Vaucresson, France
1960

Amon Carter Museum of Western Art
Fort Worth, Texas
1961

Computing Center at Brown University
Providence, Rhode Island
1961

Pavilion at Pond
New Canaan, Connecticut
1962

Museum for Pre-Columbian Art
Dumbarton Oaks, Washington, DC
1963

Monastery Wing, St. Anselm's Abbey
Washington, DC
1963

**Sheldon Memorial Art Gallery at
University of Nebraska**
Lincoln, Nebraska
1963

Mr. & Mrs. Henry C. Beck House
Dallas, Texas
1964

Mr. & Mrs. Eric Boissonnas House II
Cap Bénat, France
1964

**Kline Geology Laboratory at
Yale University**
New Haven, Connecticut
1964
Partner: Richard Foster

**East Wing, Garden Wing, Remodeled
Sculpture Garden and Upper Terrace**
The Museum of Modern Art
New York, New York
1964
Landscape Architect: Zion & Breen

New York State Theater at Lincoln Center
New York, New York
1964
Partner: Richard Foster

Central Fountain and Central Plaza
Lincoln Center
New York, New York
1964

**New York State Pavilion
(Queens Theater in the Park)**
1964 World's Fair
New York, New York
1964
Partner: Richard Foster

Epidemiology and Public Health Building
Yale University
New Haven, Connecticut
1965

Mr. & Mrs. James Geier House
Indian Hills, Ohio
1965

Painting Gallery
New Canaan, Connecticut
1965

Kline Biology Tower
Yale University
New Haven, Connecticut
1965
Partner: Richard Foster

Kline Chemistry Laboratory
Yale University
New Haven, Connecticut
1965
Partner: Richard Foster

Henry Moses Institute at Montefiore Hospital
Bronx, New York
1965

Hendrix College Library
Conway, Arkansas
1965

Bielefeld Art Gallery
Bielefeld, Germany
1968

WRVA Radio Station
Richmond, Virginia
1968

**Mr. & Mrs. David Lloyd Kreeger House
(Kreeger Museum)**
Washington, DC
1968
Partner: Richard Foster

Sculpture Gallery
New Canaan, Connecticut
1970

John F. Kennedy Memorial
Dallas, Texas
1970

**Albert & Vera List Art Building at
Brown University**
Providence, Rhode Island
1971

Art Museum of South Texas
Corpus Christi, Texas
1969–1972
Partner: John Burgee

Burden Hall
Harvard University
Cambridge, Massachusetts
1969–1972
Partner: John Burgee

Neuberger Museum
State University of New York
Purchase, New York
1968–1972
Partner: John Burgee

Tisch Hall
New York University
New York, New York
1968–1972
Partner: Richard Foster

**Facades,
Andre and Bella Meyer
Hall of Physics**
New York University
New York, New York
1972
Partner: Richard Foster

Elmer Holmes Bobst Library
New York University
New York, New York
1967–1973
Partner: Richard Foster

Hagop Kevorkian Center for Near Eastern Studies
New York University
New York, New York
1970–1973
Partner: Richard Foster

IDS Center
Minneapolis, Minnesota
1968–1973
Partner: John Burgee

Boston Public Library Addition
Boston, Massachusetts
1966–1974
Partner: John Burgee

Niagara Falls Convention Center
Niagara Falls, New York
1974
Partner: John Burgee

Fort Worth Water Garden
Fort Worth, Texas
1970–1974
Partner: John Burgee

Morningside House
Bronx, New York
1971–1975
Partner: John Burgee

49th Street Subway Modernization
New York, New York
1975
Partner: John Burgee

Post Oak Central I
Houston, Texas
1974–1975
Partner: John Burgee

**Avery Fisher Hall Interior
at Lincoln Center**
New York, New York
1975–1976
Partner: John Burgee

Pennzoil Place
Houston, Texas
1972–1976
Partner: John Burgee

Century Center
South Bend, Indiana
1975–1976
Partner: John Burgee

General American Life Insurance Company
St. Louis, Missouri
1974–1976
Partner: John Burgee

Thanksgiving Square
Dallas, Texas
1971–1976
Partner: John Burgee

Fine Arts Center at Muhlenberg College
Allentown, Pennsylvania
1974–1977
Partner: John Burgee

Apartment Group
Isfahan, Iran
1978
Partner: John Burgee

80 Field Point Road
Greenwich, Connecticut
1976–1978
Partner: John Burgee

Tamanaco Office Building
Caracas, Venezuela
1978
Partner: John Burgee

Amon Carter Museum Addition
Fort Worth, Texas
1978
Partner: John Burgee

1001 Fifth Avenue Facade
New York, New York
1978
Partner: John Burgee

Post Oak Central II
Houston, Texas
1977–1979
Partner: John Burgee

Terrace Theater
Kennedy Center for the Performing Arts
Washington, DC
1977–1979
Partner: John Burgee

Marshall Field & Company Facade
Houston, Texas
1978–1979
Partner: John Burgee

Crystal Cathedral
Garden Grove, California
1977–1980
Partner: John Burgee

Library Study
New Canaan, Connecticut
1980

National Center for the Performing Arts
Bombay, India
1974–1980
Partner: John Burgee

Sugarland Office Park
Houston, Texas
1980–1981
Partner: John Burgee

Stage Set New York City Ballet
New York, New York
1981
Partner: John Burgee

Post Oak Central III
Houston, Texas
1982
Partner: John Burgee

Interior Renovation New York State Theater
New York, New York
1982
Partner: John Burgee

101 California Street
San Francisco, California
1980–1982
Partner: John Burgee

Peoria Civic Center Complex
Peoria, Illinois
1976–1982
Partner: John Burgee

Neiman-Marcus Department Store
San Francisco, California
1980–1982
Partner: John Burgee

Transco Tower and Park
Houston, Texas
1979–1983
Partner: John Burgee

The New Cleveland Playhouse
Cleveland, Ohio
1980–1983
Partner: John Burgee

United Bank of Colorado Tower and Plaza
Denver, Colorado
1979–1983
Partner: John Burgee

PPG Corporate Headquarters
Pittsburgh, Pennsylvania
1979–1984
Partner: John Burgee

Republic Bank Center (Nationsbank Center)
Houston, Texas
1981–1984
Partner: John Burgee

53rd At Third (Lipstick Building)
New York, New York
1983–1984
John Burgee Architects
With Philip Johnson

Johnson/Burgee Architects Offices
53rd At Third (Demolished)
New York, New York
1984
John Burgee Architects
With Philip Johnson

Dade County Cultural Center
Miami, Florida
1977–1984
Partner: John Burgee

AT&T Corporate Headquarters (Sony Building)
New York, New York
1979–1984
Partner: John Burgee

580 California Street
San Francisco, California
1983–1984
Partner: John Burgee

Ghost House
New Canaan, Connecticut
1984

33 Maiden Lane (Two Federal Reserve Plaza)
New York, New York
1982–1985
Partner: John Burgee

Lincoln Kirstein Tower
New Canaan, Connecticut
1985

500 Boylston Street
Boston, Massachusetts
1983–1985
John Burgee Architects
With Philip Johnson

School of Architecture
University of Houston
Houston, Texas
1983–1985
John Burgee Architects With Philip Johnson

The Crescent
Dallas, Texas
1982–1985
John Burgee Architects With Philip Johnson

Tycon Towers
Vienna, Virginia
1983–1985
John Burgee Architects With Philip Johnson

Clarke Memorial Fountain
South Bend, Indiana
1986
John Burgee Architects With Philip Johnson

190 South LaSalle Street
Chicago, Illinois
1985–1986
John Burgee Architects With Philip Johnson

One Atlantic Center (IBM Tower)
Atlanta, Georgia
1985–1987
John Burgee Architects With Philip Johnson

Momentum Place (Bank One Center)
Dallas, Texas
1985–1987
John Burgee Architects With Philip Johnson

One International Place at Fort Hill Square
Boston, Massachusetts
1983–1988
John Burgee Architects With Philip Johnson

Franklin Square
Washington, DC
1986–1989
John Burgee Architects With Philip Johnson

343 Sansome Street
San Francisco, California
1989–1990
John Burgee Architects,
Philip Johnson Consultant

Crystal Cathedral Bell Tower and Chapel
Garden Grove, California
1990

Detroit Center (Comerica Tower)
Detroit, Michigan
1989–1991
John Burgee Architects,
Philip Johnson Consultant

191 Peachtree Tower
Atlanta, Georgia
1987–1991
John Burgee Architects,
Philip Johnson Consultant

Canadian Broadcasting Center
Toronto, Canada
1987–1992
John Burgee Architects,
Philip Johnson Consultant

Two International Place at Fort Hill Square
Boston, Massachusetts
1988–1992
John Burgee Architects,
Philip Johnson Consultant

Ohio State University Science Library, Math Building and Geology Building (Brown Hall Annex)
Ohio State University
Columbus, Ohio
1987–1992
John Burgee Architects,
Philip Johnson Consultant

Museum of Broadcasting (Museum of Television and Radio)
New York, New York
1989–1992
John Burgee Architects,
Philip Johnson Consultant

Puerta de Europa
Madrid, Spain
1991–1995
John Burgee Architects,
Philip Johnson Consultant

Gate House
New Canaan, Connecticut
1995

Celebration Town Hall
Celebration, Florida
1995–1996
Partner: Alan Ritchie, David Fiore

Addition to Thanksgiving Square
Houston, Texas
1994–1996
Partner: Alan Ritchie, David Fiore

Millenia Walk
Singapore
1993–1996
John Burgee Architects,
Philip Johnson Consultant

Das Business Center at Checkpoint Charlie (Philip Johnson Haus)
Berlin, Germany
1995–1997
Partner: Alan Ritchie, David Fiore

**St. Basil Chapel
University of St. Thomas**
Houston, Texas
1996–1997
Partner: Alan Ritchie, David Fiore

Riverside South Housing
New York, New York
1996–1997
Partner: Alan Ritchie, David Fiore

Trump International Tower
New York, New York
1995–1997
Partner: Alan Ritchie, David Fiore

Apartment Building
Tremblay-en-France, France
1996–1997
Partner: Alan Ritchie, David Fiore

Sculpture «Turning Point»
Case Western University
1997
Cleveland, Ohio
Partner: Alan Ritchie, David Fiore

Bibliographie/Bibliography

**Aufsätze von Peter Blake über Philip Johnson/
Peter Blake Articles on Philip Johnson**

Magazine of Art, «Architectural Freedom and Order»,
October 1948, Philip Johnson and Peter Blake.
Art in America, «Outdoor Gallery: Addition to MOMA»,
April 1964.
New York Times Magazine, «Johnson and his Kunst-Bunker»,
1965.
New York Magazine, «Philip Johnson Knows too Much»,
May 15, 1978.
AIA Journal, «The Devil's Advocate and the Diplomat»,
June 1979.
Interior Design, «The Kreeger», June 1995.

**Ausgewählte Schriften über Philip Johnson/
Selected Publications on Philip Johnson**

John M. Jacobus Jr., «Philip Johnson», New York:
George Braziller, Inc., 1962.
Henry-Russell Hitchcock, «Philip Johnson Architecture
1949–1965», New York: Holt, Rinehart and Winston, 1966.
The Architectural Forum, «Philip Johnson», Preface by Philip
Johnson, Essays by Paul Goldberger and Philip Johnson,
Whitney Publications, Inc., January/February 1973.
IAUS Catalogue #9, «Philip Johnson: Processes, The Glass House,
1949, and the AT&T Corporate Headquarters», Preface by
Craig Owens, Introduction by Giorgio Ciucci. Essay by
Kenneth Frampton. New York: The Institute for Architecture
and Urban Studies, 1978.
«Architecture + Urbanism 1979 No. 6 – Philip Johnson»,
Tokyo, 1979.
Nory Miller, «Johnson/Burgee Architecture», New York:
Random House, 1979.
Progressive Architecture «Special Issue: Johnson and Burgee»,
Introduction by Susan Doubilet, Essays by Susan Doubilet,
Daralice D. Boles, John Morris Dixon, Pilar Viladas, Jim
Murphy, John Jacobus Jr., Reinhold Publishing, February 1984.
Carleton Knight III, «Philip Johnson/John Burgee Architecture
1979–1985», New York: Rizzoli, 1985.
Terence Riley «The International Style: Exhibition 15 and the
Museum of Modern Art», Foreword by Philip Johnson,
Preface by Bernard Tschumi, New York: Rizzoli, 1992.
David Whitney and Jeffrey Kipnis, «Philip Johnson,
The Glass House», New York: Pantheon Books, 1993.
Franz Schulze «Philip Johnson, Life and Work», New York:
Alfred A. Knopf, 1994.
Deutsch: «Philip Johnson, Leben und Werk», Heidelberg:
SpringerArchitektur, 1996.
Hilary Lewis and John O'Connor, «Philip Johnson,
The Architect in His Own Words», New York: Rizzoli, 1994.
Jeffrey Kipnis, «Philip Johnson, Recent Work», London:
Academy Editions No. 44, July 1996.

**Bücher von Philip Johnson/
Books by Philip Johnson**

Henry-Russell Hitchcock and Philip Johnson, «The International
Style: Architecture Since 1922», New York: W.W. Norton &
Co., 1932. New Foreword and Appendix: «The International
Style Twenty Years After» by Henry-Russell Hitchcock,
New York: W.W. Norton & Co. 1966.
Deutsch: «Der internationale Stil», Braunschweig/Wiesbaden:
Vieweg, 1985. (Bauwelt Fundamente).
Philip Johnson, «Machine Art», Foreword by Alfred H. Barr, Jr.,
New York: The Museum of Modern Art, 1934. Second edition
with new foreword by Philip Johnson, New York: The Museum
of Modern Art, 1995.
Philip Johnson, «Mies van der Rohe,» New York: The Museum of
Modern Art 1947, second revised edition, with added chapter
1953, third edition revised and enlarged, 1978.

Philip Johnson, «Philip Johnson Writings», Foreword by Vincent
Scully, Introduction by Peter Eisenman and Commentary by
Robert A.M. Stern, New York: Oxford University Press, 1979.
Deutsch: «Texte zur Architektur», Übers. Kyra Stromberg,
Nora von Mühlendahl-Krehl, Stuttgart: Deutsche Verlags-
anstalt, 1982.
Philip Johnson and Mark Wigley, «Deconstructivist Architecture»,
foreword by Stuart Wrede, New York: The Museum of
Modern Art, 1988.
Deutsch: «Dekonstruktivistische Architektur», Übers. Frank
Druffner, Stuttgart: Verlag Gerd Hatje, 1988.

Bildnachweis/Illustration credits

SpringerNewsArchitektur

Franz Schulze

Philip Johnson
Leben und Werk

1996. Etwa 450 Seiten.
Gebunden etwa DM 78,–, öS 550,–
ISBN 3-211-82768-4

„Es gibt keinen besseren Weg, das Auf und Ab der Architektur während der zweiten Hälfte des 20. Jahrhunderts zu verstehen, als Franz Schulzes Biographie über Philip Johnson zu lesen."

Witold Rybczynski

Dieses Buch ist die erste bedeutende und kritische Biographie über einen der berühmtesten Architekten und Architekturkritiker unserer Zeit. Franz Schulze dringt tief in Johnsons Leben ein, von seiner Kindheit, seiner Auseinandersetzung mit seiner Sexualität, dem Sympathisieren mit der Politik Huey Longs und Hitlers, zu seiner Entscheidung, im Alter von 34 Jahren Architekt zu werden, bis hin zu seiner gegenwärtigen Position als zentrale treibende Kraft in der Welt der Künste. Indem Schulze Johnsons Kuratorrolle am Museum of Modern Art für die bahnbrechenden Designausstellungen der 30er Jahre, seine oftmals kontroversiellen Gebäude – das Glass House, das AT&T Building, Pennzoil Place, die Crystal Cathedral und viele mehr – sowie seine Rolle als Kritiker und Lehrer durchleuchtet, entsteht eine lebendige Geschichte der modernen und postmodernen Architektur und architektonischer Ideen.

 SpringerWienNewYork

P.O.Box 89, A-1201 Wien • New York, NY 10010, 175 Fifth Avenue
Heidelberger Platz 3, D-14197 Berlin • Tokyo 113, 3-13, Hongo 3-chome, Bunkyo-ku

Große Architekten in der erfolgreichen Studiopaperback-Reihe:
The Work of the World's Great Architects:

Alvar Aalto
Karl Fleig
4. Auflage. 256 Seiten,
600 Abbildungen
ISBN 3-7643-5553-0
deutsch / französisch

Tadao Ando
Masao Furuyama
2. Auflage. 216 Seiten,
397 Abbildungen
ISBN 3-7643-5583-2
deutsch / englisch

**Architektur im
Widerspruch**
Bauen in den USA von
Mies van der Rohe bis
Andy Warhol
Heinrich Klotz und John
W. Cook
2. Auflage. 328 Seiten,
189 Abbildungen und
8 Architektenporträts.
ISBN 3-7643-5552-2

Mario Botta
Emilio Pizzi
2. Auflage. 256 Seiten,
666 Abbildungen
ISBN 3-7643-5570-0
deutsch / französisch

Filippo Brunelleschi
Attili Pizzigoni
208 Seiten, 240
Abbildungen
ISBN 3-7643-5571-9

**Johann Bernhard
Fischer von Erlach**
Hellmut Lorenz
176 Seiten, 172
Abbildungen
ISBN 3-7643-5575-1

Norman Foster
Aldo Benedetti
208 Seiten, 302
Abbildungen.
ISBN 3-7643-5569-7

Walter Gropius
Paolo Berdini
256 Seiten, 580
Abbildungen
ISBN 3-7643-5563-8

Herzog & de Meuron
Wilfried Wang
2. Auflage. 160 Seiten,
313 Abbildungen
ISBN 3-7643-5589-1
deutsch / englisch

Louis I. Kahn
Romaldo Giurgola,
Jaimini Mehta
4. Auflage. 216 Seiten,
423 Abbildungen
ISBN 3-7643-5556-5
deutsch / französisch

**Marc-Antoine Laugier
Das Manifest des
Klassizismus**
208 Seiten, 46
Abbildungen
ISBN 3-7643-5568-9

Le Corbusier
Willi Boesiger
7. Auflage 1994.
260 Seiten, 525
Abbildungen
ISBN 3-7643-5550-6
deutsch / französisch

Adolf Loos
Kurt Lustenberger
192 Seiten, 332
Abbildungen
Deutsche Ausgabe:
ISBN 3-7643-5586-7
Englische Ausgabe:
ISBN 3-7643-5587-5

Richard Meier
Silvio Cassarà
208 Seiten, 264
Abbildungen.
ISBN 3-7643-5350-3

Erich Mendelsohn
Bruno Zevi
208 Seiten, 421
Abbildungen
ISBN 3-7643-5562-X

**Ludwig Mies van der
Rohe**
Werner Blaser
5. Auflage. 204 Seiten,
126 Abbildungen
ISBN 3-7643-5551-4
deutsch / französisch

Richard Neutra
Manfred Sack
2. überarbeite Auflage.
192 Seiten, 291
Abbildungen
ISBN 3-7643-5588-3
deutsch / englisch

Jean Nouvel
Olivier Boissière
300 Seiten, 300
Abbildungen
ISBN 3-7643-5356-2
deutsch / englisch

J. J. P. Oud
Umberto Barbieri
200 Seiten, 340
Abbildungen
ISBN 3-7643-5567-0

Andrea Palladio
Die vier Bücher zur
Architektur
A. Beyer und U. Schütte
4., überarbeitete Auflage.
472 Seiten
ISBN 3-7643-5561-1

**Paolo Portoghesi
Ausklang der modernen
Architektur**
Von der Verödung zur
neuen Sensibilität.
240 Seiten, 223
Abbildungen
ISBN 3-7643-5559-X

Richard Rogers
Kenneth Powell
208 Seiten, 481
Abbildungen
ISBN 3-7643-5582-4
deutsch / englisch

Aldo Rossi
Gianni Braghieri
4., erweiterte Auflage.
288 Seiten, 290
Abbildungen
ISBN 3-7643-5560-3
deutsch / französisch

Carlo Scarpa
Ada Francesca Marcianò
2. Auflage. 208 Seiten,
400 Abbildungen
ISBN 3-7643-5564-6

Hans Scharoun
Christoph J. Bürkle
176 Seiten, 182
Abbildungen
Deutsche Ausgabe:
ISBN 3-7643-5580-8
Englische Ausgabe:
ISBN 3-7643-5581-6

Karl Friedrich Schinkel
Gian Paolo Semino
232 Seiten, 330
Abbildungen
ISBN 3-7643-5584-0

Gottfried Semper
Martin Fröhlich
176 Seiten, 192
Abbildungen
ISBN 3-7643-5572-7

José Luis Sert
Jaume Freixa
2. Auflage. 240 Seiten,
500 Abbildungen
ISBN 3-7643-5558-1
deutsch / französisch

Alvaro Siza
Peter Testa
208 Seiten, 300
Abbildungen
ISBN 3-7643-5598-0
deutsch / englisch

Mart Stam
Simone Rümmele
160 Seiten, 167
Abbildungen
ISBN 3-7643-5573-5

Louis Henry Sullivan
Hans Frei
176 Seiten, 208
Abbildungen
ISBN 3-7643-5574-3
deutsch / englisch

Kenzo Tange
Architektur und Städtebau
1946–1976
240 Seiten, 409
Abbildungen
ISBN 3-7643-5555-7
deutsch / französisch

Giuseppe Terragni
Bruno Zevi
208 Seiten, 490
Abbildungen
ISBN 3-7643-5566-2

Oswald Mathias Ungers
Martin Kieren
256 Seiten, 406
Abbildungen
ISBN 3-7643-5585-9
deutsch / englisch

**Robert Venturi – Denise
Scott Brown and
Associates**
Carolina Vaccaro,
Frederic Schwartz
208 Seiten, 431
Abbildungen
ISBN 3-7643-5576-X

Otto Wagner
Giancarlo Bernabei
2. Auflage. 208 Seiten,
330 Abbildungen
ISBN 3-7643-5565-4

Frank Lloyd Wright
Bruno Zevi
3. Auflage. 288 Seiten,
575 Abbildungen
ISBN 3-7643-5557-3
deutsch / französisch